W9-CLH-503

MICHAEL COLLINS
AND THE
MAKING OF THE IRISH STATE

MICHAEL COLLINS
AND THE
MAKING OF THE IRISH STATE

Edited by
GABRIEL DOHERTY
&
DERMOT KEOGH

MERCIER PRESS

MERCIER PRESS
PO Box 5, 5 French Church Street, Cork
16 Hume Street, Dublin 2

Trade enquiries to CMD DISTRIBUTION,
55a Spruce Avenue, Stillorgan Industrial Park, Blackrock, Dublin

© Dermot Keogh & Gabriel Doherty, 1998

ISBN 185635 211 0

10 9 8 7 6 5 4

DEDICATED TO MY BROTHER
SEÁN GERARD DOHERTY 1958–1998

This book is sold subject to the condition that it shall not, by way of trade or otherwise, be lent, resold, hired out or otherwise circulated without the publisher's prior consent in any form of binding or cover other than that in which it is published and without a similar condition being imposed on the subsequent purchaser.

Printed in Ireland by Colour Books Ltd.

CONTENTS

ACKNOWLEDGEMENTS

This volume is based on the proceedings of a conference, attended by over 500 people, held at University College Cork on 28 February and 1 March 1997. We had repeated requests from many people to send on copies of the papers and there was an unprecedented interest in the publication of the proceedings.

In response to the academic and general interest in the papers, we undertook to bring out a volume on Michael Collins and the making of the Irish State within a year of the conference. Each of the contributors was asked to revise his or her contribution for publication in a book which has been designed to explore the different aspects of the political life of Michael Collins. We decided, therefore, to expand the scope of the volume in order to cover the life of Michael Collins not covered in the papers.

We are very grateful to each of those who gave papers at the conference and who prepared them for publication so promptly. Our gratitude to Professors Joe Lee, Ronan Fanning, Tom Garvin and Eunan O'Halpin, Drs Deirdre McMahon, Martin Mansergh, John Regan and Diarmuid Ó Giolláin and Commandant Peter Young.

In addition, we sought to examine the west Cork background of Collins and were fortunate to secure a contribution from Fr Gearóid O'Sullivan, whose father, bearing the same name, was among Collins' closest friends. Apart from being the common west Cork link, O'Sullivan was his aide de camp and both men were to marry Kiernan sisters in a double wedding.

Margot Gearty, another contributor to this volume, also had a Kiernan connection, being the niece of Kitty, Collins' fiancée. Ms Gearty's essay, written with great sensitivity, sheds new light on the Kiernan family and on the first contacts between the Kiernan sisters, Michael Collins and Gearóid O'Sullivan.

We also decided to add essays on Collins and Northern Ireland. Dr Éamon Phoenix kindly obliged at short notice and contributed a strong chapter based on primary source research. Finding that no work had been published on the role of Michael Collins as Minister for Finance, we commissioned a piece from Dr Andrew McCarthy.

We are delighted that Mary Banotti MEP found the time to prepare the introduction to this volume during the middle of a very busy presidential campaign. We thank her for this and for her very gracious speech which opened the conference proceedings.

Thanks are due to Professor Denis Lucey, Peter Barry, TD, Gearóid O'Sullivan, Catriona Crowe and Jim McLoughlin for chairing the various conference sessions.

We would like to thank President Michael Mortell of UCC, Mr Gerry Reynolds of Radio Telefís Éireann, Bord Gáis, *The Examiner* and the UCC History Department for their generous offers of sponsorship for the conference.

RTÉ and Cork Campus Radio performed a very valuable service in recording the proceedings, and Aidan Stanley used this material to prepare three programmes which were broadcast on RTÉ radio in August 1997.

Ted and Alan Crosby from *The Examiner* gave great support and encouragement to the conference. A specially-commissioned 'Michael Collins' supplement was produced by the newspaper, under the expert supervision of Dan Buckley and Liam Moher. We also wish to acknowledge our thanks to Lilian Caverly for her help in securing illustrations for the book, and we thank *The Examiner* for permission to reproduce those photographs.

We would like to thank Commandant Peter Young, Director, Commandant Victor Lang, and the staff of the Military Archives, Cathal Brugha Barracks, for their extensive help in the preparation of this volume. We are very grateful for the generous access given to the extensive collection of unique photographs in their archives, a number of which they kindly allowed us to reproduce in this volume.

We are grateful to Charlotte Holland, Norma Buckley, Veronica Fraser and Deirdre O'Sullivan, secretaries in the Department of History, University College Cork, for their untiring efforts in assisting with both the conference and the preparation of this volume.

We thank the following postgraduate students of the Department of History, University College Cork, who volunteered their assistance for the duration of the conference: Bronagh Allison, Suzanne Brennan, Tracey Connolly, James Cronin, Pat Cullen, Robert Mac-Namara, Michelle O'Mahoney.

Thanks are due to all the staff of the Printing Office in UCC for their help in producing material for the conference.

We would also like to thank Lucette Murray for her help in publicising the conference.

We are grateful to Denis Bannon and the other staff of Áras na Mac Léinn for their help in staging the proceedings.

We would also like to thank Fr Gearóid O'Sullivan for the photograph of the wedding of Gearóid O'Sullivan and Maud Kiernan, 19 October 1922.

We would like to thank the staff of Mercier Press for producing this handsome volume in such a short time.

GABRIEL DOHERTY
PROFESSOR DERMOT KEOGH

FOREWORD

Gabriel Doherty and Dermot Keogh

Dev or Mick, the Big Fellow or the Long Fellow? It sometimes appears as if in the 1990s people are again being asked to choose sides between the two major protagonists of the Irish Civil War. But this is not 1922, the Civil War has been over for more than seventy years and there is no reason why students of history should be required to stand on the side of either Eamon de Valera or that of Michael Collins. It is a mark of the underdeveloped nature of the writing of the history of twentieth-century Ireland that contemporary debate tends to revolve around the personalities of De Valera and Michael Collins. Moreover, the problem is compounded because both men are often isolated from their historical context and their times in popular discussion.

This deficiency is not the fault of Neil Jordan's outstanding film in which the director and actors combine to portray the terrible events of the War of Independence and Civil War – events which have only recently been deemed suitable for historical study in Irish schools and universities. Popular and professional historians alike were refused access to personal papers and the official state archives until the 1970s and 1980s. The study of twentieth-century Ireland has really only become academically possible in the 1990s with the introduction of a thirty-year rule under which both the National Archives, Bishop Street, and the Military Archives, Cathal Brugha Barracks, Dublin, now splendidly operate. However, despite the introduction of the progressive thirty-year rule, there continues to remain great sensitivity about the release of certain Civil War records such as those contained in the files of the Military History Bureau. There is no justification for the continuation of this policy of restrictiveness. However, the essays by Commandant Peter Young and Dr John Regan in this collection demonstrate the possibilities of advancing the scholarly understanding of the Civil War based on the archives already in the public domain.

The more recent histories of other European countries well illustrate that areas of great sensitivity are often shielded by over-protective governments refusing to release files which might disturb 'public equilibrium'. Vichy France is a case in point. Just as

Jordan's film on Michael Collins has initiated a major debate on the personalities and on the interpretation of the 1916–1923 period in Ireland, so a few decades earlier *The Sorrow and the Pity*, directed by Marcel Ophuls, opened up a debate in French society on the taboo Vichy period. *Michael Collins* has, in a similar way, helped to develop a new sense of urgency about researching the years between 1916 and 1923. The essays in this volume respond to that challenge, being the most recent findings of historians who have been working in that area for many years.

The debate surrounding the Michael Collins film has shown how the 1919–1923 period remains relatively neglected and under-studied. Beyond Mick and Dev, what was known about other nationalist leaders like Arthur Griffith, Harry Boland and the other leading lights of the revolutionary generation? What was known, for example, about Harry Boland's political ideas and his political formation? The same question may be asked about scores of other leading revolutionaries of the time. Neglect, denial of access to archives and the slowness of historical scholarship, therefore, may explain the silences and the relative ignorance about most prominent members of that generation.

Michael Collins, at first sight, appears to be the exception. Biographies by Piaras Béaslaí, Frank O'Connor, Rex Taylor, Margery Forester, Leon Ó Bróin, Desmond Ryan and T. Ryle Dwyer amongst others point to his attraction as a subject for research. But the task of the historian is far from over. Dr Deirdre McMahon's essay in this volume warns against over-reliance upon the blind use of secondary texts. Yet there has been a tendency among writers on the subject of Michael Collins to accept without real question the provenance of certain quotations. It is important to subject all studies – but the earlier ones in particular – to a test for accuracy.

The Jordan film depicts Michael Collins using necessarily wide brush strokes. He was thirty-one years of age and full of unrealised promise when he was shot dead in an ambush in west Cork on 22 August 1922 by anti-Treaty Republicans, some of whom knew him personally. However successful Jordan's film artistically and aesthetically – and it has succeeded brilliantly at both levels – the historical depiction of Michael Collins focuses too much on the revolutionary 'man of action'. This is a somewhat one-dimensional portrayal of a figure who, during the period of time covered in the film, was a member of the Irish Republican Brotherhood, Minister for

Finance in the Dáil Éireann government and the main architect of the Dáil Éireann loan, a central figure in the leadership of the clandestine government after the departure of Eamon de Valera to the United States and, of course, a guerrilla leader. The essays in this volume have been chosen, therefore, to demonstrate the multi-faceted and complex character that was Michael Collins.

Fr Gearóid O'Sullivan, one of the contributors to this volume, is the son of Michael Collins' ADC and is also a nephew of Kitty Kiernan. Together with Margot Gearty, herself a niece of Kitty Kiernan, they have written uniquely personal memoirs of Michael Collins from the perspective of those who were closest to him during the revolutionary years. A genuine historical re-evaluation of Collins could not be undertaken without setting the analysis in this wider social and political context.

Dr Andrew McCarthy in his contribution, analyses the role of Collins as Minister for Finance, while Eunan O'Halpin traces his role in military intelligence. Dr Eamon Phoenix looks at his policy towards the north and there are two essays on the building of the Collins myth by the eminent folklorist Dr Diarmuid Ó Giolláin and by the editors of this volume.

It is professionally inadvisable to build up the historical role of Collins to the detriment of Eamon de Valera, and the essays by Professor Tom Garvin and the Head of Research in Fianna Fáil, Dr Martin Mansergh avoid such a simplistic approach. In its place they offer a more sophisticated, challenging and nuanced perspective, one which acknowledges the oft-neglected correspondence in attitudes between the two men as well as their better-known differences.

The thesis of the film presents a good working hypothesis. It may prove to be accurate or false by scholarship. But whatever the course of scholarly investigation, the results – as the essays by Professors Lee and Fanning show – will neither deify Collins nor demonise De Valera. This is a position with which we, as editors of this volume, wholeheartedly agree.

INTRODUCTION

Mary Banotti

I am extremely pleased and honoured to be invited to write the introduction to this impressive volume, to which many of the most distinguished historians in the country have contributed.

I approach this task wearing two hats. Firstly as an elected representative serving in the European Parliament, and secondly as a grandniece of Michael Collins. Both roles are inextricably linked in my own life because, above all, Michael Collins in his writings and with his vision of Ireland would have made a natural MEP. I have no doubt he would have thrown his hat into the ring the first chance he got which would have been in 1979.

In the first European parliament there were many elderly distinguished historical figures who had contributed in many ways to the creation of modern Europe. In the brief years Michael Collins flashed across the national scene he had a vision of Ireland which was characterised, not just by his passionate love of his own country but also by his very real and dynamic belief that our fate and our future lay not just within this island but also as part of a greater Europe. He saw us taking our place, not just in the dark shadow of our nearest neighbour, but also as an active contributor economically, politically and socially in a wider world. He showed enormous capacity for growth and development. As a fighting man, he knew when to choose peace.

Collins had a great and implicit faith in the Irish people and he urged them to unite and set about building a free and distinctive nation of which they could be proud. He perhaps more than anyone else of his time realised how great an opportunity was presented to this country by its freedom. He wrote:

> Ireland is one, perhaps the only, country in Europe which has now living hopes for a better civilisation. We have a great opportunity, much is within our grasp. Let us advance and use these liberties to make Ireland a shining light in a dark world. To reconstruct our ancient civilisation on modern lines, to avoid the errors, the miseries, the dangers into which other nations have fallen.

Notwithstanding the enormous strains and pressures under which he worked, his vision of Ireland's place in Europe was remarkably prophetic. In his book *The Path to Freedom* we see many references to the future role he saw for his country. He regarded the land as probably our greatest resource and wished to see fair distribution of it. He did believe in protecting our industries at the beginning to give them enough time to get off the ground without being smothered by dumping from more affluent outside producers, but at no stage did he ever believe in the kind of protectionism which unfortunately became the system in Ireland for the next fifty years. As he put it:

> We must offer our producers protection where necessary. Protection does not mean the exclusion of foreign competition. It means rendering the native manufacturer equal to meeting foreign competition. It does not mean that we shall pay a higher profit to any Irish manufacturer but that we shall not stand by and see him crushed by mere weight of foreign capital because his foreign competitor has larger resources at his disposal.

Intrinsic to that vision is the system operating within the European Union where we all agree to start with the same basic ground rules relating to safety, environmental protection and open markets.

He lamented, again prophetically, that while the seas around Ireland were teeming with fish we still continued to import such produce from England at that time. The depressed state of the Irish fishing industry of his time dismayed him and I would say that he would be equally dismayed at the situation as it stands now. The need to modernise our transport and communications systems was also a concern to him but the tragedy was he had so little time to devote his mind to these issues. The modernisation in very recent years of our transport and communications systems has been the single most valuable advance we have made in terms of infrastructure. He even recognised the importance of media and was amongst the first to recognise the political and social value of the film industry and of photography.

The concept of marketing goods, a practice then only in its infancy, had also occurred to him, as evidenced by his observation that 'it will be important to create efficient machinery for the economic marketing of Irish goods' and, foreseeing perhaps the development of financial services in Dublin, he remarked:

> a first step in this direction is the establishment of a clearing house in

Dublin or the most convenient centre. It would form a link between a network of channels throughout Ireland through which goods could be transmitted, connecting with another network, reaching out to all markets abroad. It would examine and take delivery of goods going out and coming in and dealing with the financial business on both sides.

I would confidently state there were few leaders in any country whose vision was as clear and prophetic as was that of Michael Collins.

Let me briefly refer to the other aspect of Michael Collins which is close to my heart. I was born more than twenty years after Michael Collins died. As a small child, without knowing anything about history, I experienced attitudes, feelings and impressions from the people I loved around me, most particularly my grandparents, my grandfather having been his eldest brother and my grandmother Nancy O'Brien, whose memories were a very rich source of material for Tim Pat Coogan's book, having worked for him in the post office.

I was never taught to hate or resent but I instinctively felt there was some great sorrow surrounding our family. Probably that is why in 1996–7 the effect of the film *Michael Collins* was such a positive and joyous one for our family. Undoubtedly Collins has been air-brushed out of the national psyche in the past seventy-five years. This wasn't totally the case – every so often something would happen that would give me a glimpse of what he had meant to the people of his time. In Cork I remember visiting a very old pensioner and, while chatting to him about other things, some mention came up about Michael Collins and I told him of my relationship with him. He got up slowly out of his armchair and to my utter amazement he knelt down and blessed himself in front of me. I was completely overcome.

I do not remember being told specifically in words but I certainly understood from my grandmother that I should be cautious about talking about our family and this relationship. Perhaps she feared I would evoke a reaction which I could not understand or cope with until I was older.

The advent of the film has changed all that. I grew up with a rich lore of family history and virtually total silence from outside the family. Certainly there was no mention of him in the history books. There was never a mention of his name in the discussion of national life, except on the occasion of a visit to Béal na mBláth in August or to Berkeley Road for the annual commemorative Mass. All of that changed in 1996–7. The experience that made me most happy came one Sunday morning as I stood browsing in a book-shop. A little girl of about ten came in with her mother looking at the books, and she leaned across in front of me, saying to her moth-er: 'Oh Mum, look, here is a book about Michael Collins, can we buy it?' I was so thrilled because certainly up to then I do not think there were many little ten year old girls who had ever heard of him and would have been as excited as she was at buying a book about him and hopefully reading it.

So the film has been a great catalyst. Let us hope that the dis-cussions it has precipitated will lead not to a settling of old scores but to a reconciliation that allows all of us, particularly here in the south, to confront the still existing griefs and anguishes that the Civil War and those years evoked in our country. A great know-ledge of our history will hopefully help to heal the old wounds. Each of the contributors in this fine volume will add to our knowl-edge and give a greater understanding of those vital years in which the state was founded.

THE CHALLENGE OF A COLLINS BIOGRAPHY[1]

J. J. Lee

It cannot be credibly claimed that Michael Collins has been neglected by historians and biographers. If anything, the contrary is the case. For one whose public career was compressed into a few short years, and who died at the age of thirty-one, he has attracted intense biographical attention by Irish standards. More words have probably been written about him than about Eamon de Valera, whose public career spanned sixty years. Far more work has been devoted to him than to Arthur Griffith, founder of the original Sinn Féin, and leader of the Treaty delegation. Of the remaining four members of the Sinn Féin cabinet that split over the Treaty in December 1921, only a handful of biographies have been, at most, devoted to Cathal Brugha, Austin Stack and Robert Barton, and it is only very recently that any biography at all has engaged with W. T. Cosgrave, who would succeed Collins in 1922 to become effectively Prime Minister for ten years. Even the most celebrated 1916 leaders, Patrick Pearse and James Connolly, have attracted far fewer biographers than Collins, with Thomas MacDonagh, Seán MacDermott, and Tom Clarke attracting fewer again.

Of others active in the War of Independence and Civil War, Constance Markiewicz is out on her own, with four biographies. Richard Mulcahy, Kevin O'Higgins, Eoin MacNeill, Erskine Childers and Liam Mellows have to make do with one or two. Personalities as prominent as Desmond Fitzgerald, Ernest Blythe, Fionán Lynch, Paddy Hogan, Joe McGrath, and Eamon Duggan, still await any biographer at all. Looking somewhat further ahead, few of even the leading ministers in the governments of the Free State and the Republic have attracted a single biography, despite the long records of public service of men like Seán MacEntee, Frank Aiken, Paddy McGilligan, Gerry Boland, P. J. Ruttledge, Seán T. O'Kelly, John Marcus O'Sullivan or even John A. Costello, twice Taoiseach, for whom we still need biographers.

On the face of it, then, Collins is relatively well served, at least if the number of words written about him be the criterion. And in addition there is now the Neil Jordan film to bring his name before a much wider audience. Nevertheless, it is easy enough to understand the feeling that we are in many respects still scratching the surface.

One reason is that it is only recently that some essential sources have begun to become available. Apart from important archival sources remaining closed, there was naturally a great sensitivity among survivors concerning the Civil War. As that generation remained active in politics for more than forty years, neither their papers, nor much of their information, would begin becoming available, for the most part, until quite recently. And there was, particularly in the case of Collins, a reluctance among some of his enemies to confront their possible responsibility for his death, and a reluctance among some of his friends to probe too closely in case their hero turned out to be all too human, and a reluctance among some of his other colleagues to encourage exploration in case their connection with him might be exposed as one more of convenience than conviction.

Nor was the number of potential labourers in this particular vineyard especially great. It wasn't until the 1960s that the numbers of staff in Irish history departments, or the number of research students, began to increase to any significant extent. Even when the body count did begin to increase, researchers found precious few resources at their disposal. Given the small size of history departments in universities, and given the almost total lack of support for postgraduate research, one could hardly expect the systematic exploration of the raw material to be nearly as comprehensive as might be wished. It would, I suspect, be safe to claim that the investment in Neil Jordan's film surpasses the total investment in historical research in the Irish state since independence.

Research might however have proceeded faster had not the onset of the Northern Ireland crisis from 1968–9 cast its malign shadow over historical perceptions as well as over current events. As almost anything one could write on Collins might be used or abused for the propaganda purposes of the present, some historians who might otherwise have ventured into this area may have chosen to avoid it rather than have their work twisted to their purposes by current belligerents.

It is nevertheless hard to avoid the impression that historians and biographers, despite the objective obstacles to be overcome, could have advanced the study of Collins much further if they had shown the degree of commitment and of imagination that Tim Pat Coogan did in tracking down sources, not least oral ones, for his best-selling biography. There can be differing views about Coogan's interpretation of much of his material, but finding the material in the first place made an important contribution to the study of Collins.

Academic historians were long inhibited not only by problems beyond their control, but by problems of their own making. Foremost among these was their suspicion of contemporary history in general, and oral sources in particular, to say nothing of their incompetence in the relevant research techniques. It is no accident that it was T. Desmond Williams, the champion of contemporary history amongst Irish historians, who initiated interviews with De Valera on the Civil War in 1958.

If archival sources long remained closed, it cannot be claimed that published sources were adequately scrutinised. It can be said of the study of Collins, as of modern Irish history in general, that vast tracts of the newspaper press remain virtually *terra incognito* to the historian. The press did not, and often still does not, enjoy the status of the archival source in the minds of many historians. But for the study of contemporary opinion and perception, as well as for much basic information, it remains absolutely essential.

All this helps explain why so much remains to be explored about Collins, despite the number of words lavished on him. It must, however, be conceded that even if all the desired sources, and resources, were available, Collins would still prove an exceptionally elusive subject – almost as elusive for the biographer as for the British. The discovery of more source material is unlikely to actually solve some of the central problems confronting his biographers. It may even add to them. For Collins was a protean personality, who had a knack of making himself all things to all men, and of leaving people with the view of him that he wanted them to have.

One legacy of Collins is that there are many legacies of Collins. Different groups, sometimes conflicting groups, were convinced that they were his only true heirs. One of the ironies of the events surrounding the Army Mutiny of 1924, for instance, was that both mutineers and their suppressers, and then the suppressers of their suppressers, all believed they were acting in the spirit of Collins. They could all – Liam Tobin, Joe McGrath, Dick Mulcahy, Kevin O'Higgins – persuade themselves they were behaving as he would have wished them to behave. And in a sense they were all right. For they all had legitimate ownership of a part of his memory. But none of them had full ownership. It was precisely because Collins combined in himself a cluster of personality types and behaviour patterns, from the man of action to the contemplative, from the soldier to the politician, from the bureaucrat to the self-publicist, from the impulsive to the calculating, from the charmer to the tough, from the sensitive to the ruthless, from the conspirator to the statesman, that he was so formidable a personality.

If this combination of qualities makes it difficult for biographers to capture the totality, it makes it virtually impossible for film makers. The genre – or at least the market for the genre – simply does not permit it. With that qualification, it is only fair to add that Neil Jordan's film is an impressive one in many ways. Judged by the standards of Hollywood's treatment of historical topics more generally, it cleaves with remarkable fidelity to the spirit of the historical record as far as Collins himself is concerned, however impressionistic some of the detail may be, and however unsatisfactory its portrayal of De Valera. It might easily have succumbed to the temptation to weave the story line around sex, with titillating treatment of his relations with Lady Lavery, etc., to satisfy the mass voyeuristic market. Few film makers would have had either the integrity or the courage to resist the temptation. Neil Jordan had. For that alone he deserves enormous respect.

It is virtually inevitable, however, that in the film genre the complex personality of Collins has to be over-simplified, with the action man coming to dominate the screen. It is certainly not wrong to stress this. It was central to his personality, to the hold that he exerted over so many people, and to his legend. It is not wrong. But it is incomplete.[2]

Nevertheless, the film probably comes strikingly close to the image Collins wanted to project of himself. He liked to portray himself as the bluff, straight-speaking soldier, uncontaminated by the sordid manoeuvres of mere politics. He may, like several IRA men, have genuinely cherished this self-image. But he would also have been alert to its political potential for his standing among many active IRA activists, who regarded politics as a synonym for compromise, and compromise as a synonym for corruption, who identified politics with the discredited Home Rule Party, with the seduction of Irish representatives in Westminster, and who cherished a self-image of immunity from these decadent blandishments precisely because they were fighters and not politicians. The more Collins could project himself as the simple soldier, the more he might appeal to that mentality. Ironically, at a later stage, it was the politician par excellence, De Valera, who somehow conjured up among Fianna Fáil loyalists, the image of the sea-green incorruptible who, although in politics, was somehow not of it.

To imagine Collins simply as a soldier, somehow indifferent to, if not disdainful of, the arts of politics, is simply to fail to understand him.[3] He would have been nowhere as formidable a personality, nor would he have wielded anything like the authority, if he were not an energetic and eager player of the political game. It may be that he himself became a prisoner of his own image, so that at the end he behaved more like the character of his public relations image – and he was a large part of his own public relations – than the cool calculator of the odds that in practice he so often had been. Nevertheless, the man of action image can capture only one part, however important a part, of a highly complex personality.

Precisely because Collins combined so many different, and sometimes conflicting, characteristics in his personality, because he meant so many different things to so many different people, there has to be ultimately a leap of the imagination from the source material, however rich, to our understanding of him. Even if we had every word that Collins wrote or spoke, in every context, we might still differ on precisely what weight to attach to any of them. Interpretation must always be compatible with the evidence. But as with so many of the really challenging men and women in history, the evidence in his case is often compatible with alternative interpretations. And where alternative formulations are equally plausible in the light of the evidence, the historian must be guided by judgement in determining the most historically valid one. And judgement, however rooted in evidence, always involves a subjective dimension.

It is difficult for those who have never known decision-making in war to think themselves into the minds of those operating in wartime – any wartime, but especially into the minds of those fighting against overwhelming odds, for whom any miscalculation could mean disaster for oneself, for one's comrades, and for one's cause. Hindsight is always a curse for the historian, but it is a particular curse when dealing with events in a pressure cooker situation, where circumstances can change with unpredictable rapidity, when cause and consequence are jumbled so closely together, when decisions have to be taken at high speed for high stakes. How effectively students of Collins prove able to transport themselves into the mind of someone in the eye of the storm, operating under the type of pressure none of them is likely to have ever experienced in their own lives, will at least partly determine their response to the evidence.

Collins will therefore continue to give rise to sharp differences of opinion however much he is studied, even among genuine seekers after historical truth. There are, however, certain areas of general agreement among his biographers. Few dispute his exceptional energy, exceptional physical courage, exceptional moral courage, exceptional administrative ability, and exceptional intellectual ability, all meshed into a larger than life personality.

But sharp differences exist concerning the quality of his political judgement, above all during the Treaty negotiations and the post-Treaty period. Should he have gone to London at all, or like Cathal Brugha and Austin Stack, refused the poisoned chalice – or at least refused unless De Valera supped from it as well? Was he first out-manoeuvred by De Valera in Dublin, and then by Lloyd George in London? Was he a novice in the hands of these allegedly more astute operators? Was he right to sign the Treaty? Did he subsequently, as Chairman of the Provisional Government, 'try to do too much' to avoid the Civil War, in contrast to De Valera's 'too little', in the lapidary formulation of Desmond Williams?

These are all legitimate questions, which can elicit legitimate differences of opinion. Before suggesting answers to some of them, my main purpose here is to stress that no serious discussion can be conducted on issues of this type unless we specify at all times our assumptions about alternatives – about what exactly we think would have happened, if only what did happen hadn't happened. That will not resolve the differences. But it should focus them. Once discussants clarify their assumptions, they can then disagree on the basis of clearly articulated assumptions about alternatives, rather than on the basis of often inadequately specified, not to say internally contradictory, assumptions. That is the only way the quality of the debate can be sustained on a proper historical plane, and rescued from the predatory purposes of the propagandists.

Once we adopt this approach, it becomes immediately clear

how our judgements about the performance of Collins, and by definition, of De Valera, derive from assumptions about alternatives. If only De Valera had gone to London, if only Collins hadn't signed the Treaty, if only De Valera hadn't opposed it, if only he hadn't withdrawn from the Dáil, if only Collins had attacked the Four Courts immediately Rory O'Connor occupied it, if only he had delayed the attack further, if only he hadn't attacked it at all, if only he had attacked Northern Ireland, if only he had withheld all support from the IRA in the north, if only he hadn't deluded himself that he could cod Churchill with a 'Republican' Constitution, if only he had defied Churchill's insistence that the Constitution must stick to the letter of the Treaty, if only he hadn't sought compromise in the Pact election with De Valera, if only he hadn't denounced the Pact, if only, indeed, he had taken a different route from Macroom to Cork on 22 August, and if only, in the end, he had chosen to drive through the ambush at Beál na mBláth, instead of continuing to fight, if only he had lived for – how long – and with what assumed consequences. Even this cursory list, which could be easily extended, makes it clear how littered with 'if onlys' our judgements are bound to be. That is why it is incumbent on practitioners of 'if only' history – and the history of Collins has to be suffused with 'if only' – to specify exactly where we think our 'if onlys' would have led.

Having exhorted others to adopt this approach, let me now briefly attempt it myself, by taking some examples, in the hope of illuminating something of both its potential and – no doubt – its pitfalls. The first example concerns the Treaty negotiations. It is ironic that the basic assumptions made by Irish critics of the behaviour of both De Valera and Collins during the Treaty negotiations don't really refer, in the first instance, to De Valera or Collins themselves. They all hinge on assumptions about British behaviour. They are based on the premise that the British would have yielded terms acceptable to Sinn Féin if either De Valera, as Sinn Féin's presumed best negotiator, had gone to London, or if only the signatories had done what the critics assume De Valera would have done – called Lloyd George's alleged bluff in imposing a deadline, under threat of war, in December 1921. According to this script, the British would then have conceded Sinn Féin demands without a resumption of war. How plausible are these assumptions?

The two main bones of contention in the Treaty negotiations were partition and the oath. How compelling is the proposition that

De Valera could have extracted better terms on these twin major issues of territory and status?

Why is it assumed that De Valera would have achieved what Collins didn't, or that Collins could have achieved what De Valera would have, if only he refused to sign under duress? We will have to work our way through the possibilities, but that is what scrutinising our own assumptions means.

Consider, in the first instance, partition. It was for long believed that partition was a key issue, if not indeed the key issue, on which the Treaty split occurred, and on which the Civil War was fought. Most of the anti-Treaty survivors said so, most of the media continues to say so, and therefore it was, and often still is, assumed that that must have been the case. It was the late Mrs Maureen Wall who first drew attention to the fact that the record simply didn't bear this out. Working her way systematically through the Treaty debate, she established how relatively little complaint there was about partition compared with complaint about the oath. That did not mean that partition was deemed unimportant. It did mean that the 'solution' to the partition problem, the proposal of a Boundary Commission in Article 12 of the Treaty, was deemed a satisfactory negotiating achievement, given that it was widely assumed that the consequences of the Boundary Commission would be the transfer of the Irish nationalist areas of Northern Ireland to the Free State, resulting in the economic collapse of Northern Ireland, which it was then assumed would be obliged to seek unification with the Free State. The issue at stake here is not the validity of these assumptions – events would soon expose their naiveté – but the fact that the assumptions were widely shared by both sides.

It is indeed striking how the issue of the north was evaded in the Treaty debate, even when it appeared to be a logical target for critics. A classic case was Constance Markiewicz's passionate contribution, reeking with disdain for the Anglo-Irish, with all the enthusiasm of the convert from her own class. She denounced the Anglo-Irish from a 'left wing' point of view, depicting them as capitalist exploiters, predators on a poor peasantry. Given the ferocity of her onslaught on the capitalist ascendancy, one would have assumed as a matter of course that she would have launched an attack on Northern Ireland industrialists as well as landlords as the final bastion of reaction, capitalist hyenas blinding the eyes of their wretched workers to where their true interests lay in a united Ireland. Not a bit of it. She didn't breath a word about the north from start to finish, however many other topics, some singularly improbable, she managed to work into her speech. Nor did some of the most powerful anti-Treaty speeches, even by such committed critics as Liam Mellows and Harry Boland, as much as once refer to partition.

This hasn't prevented later charges that the Treaty created partition, or 'gave away' Northern Ireland. Much media history continues to insist that it was the Treaty that partitioned Ireland. Genuine historians have long since recognised that the Treaty did no such thing. It couldn't. Northern Ireland had already been created by the Government of Ireland Act of December 1920. Elections were held in May 1921, and the northern parliament opened on 14 June. The opening was the set occasion for the king's speech urging conciliation, the hand of friendship, etc. – a safe ploy now that Northern Ireland had been carved into existence. It was in response to this plea that the Truce emerged on 9 July. The Treaty did not create Northern Ireland. On the contrary, the creation of Northern Ireland was a prerequisite for the Treaty. The Treaty could not 'give away' the north, because it didn't have it to give away in the first place.

It is nevertheless wrong to claim that partition did not feature prominently in the negotiations. It did.[5] But it was almost entirely shadow-boxing. If Sinn Féin continued to delude itself that partition was still an open question, as if somehow Northern Ireland did not already exist, that was its problem. Negotiations might have been serious if a Northern Ireland had to be still created. But Britain had taken that trick, lock, stock and barrel. As long as she was determined to hold Northern Ireland, and to keep the border she had imposed, there was little Sinn Féin could do about it. Of course, if Britain had chosen to mobilise her full potential power against the IRA, she need not have withdrawn from the south either. In practice, she did not do so, at least partly because of the skill with which Sinn Féin conducted the propaganda war, not only at home, but in America, in the Dominions and even in Britain itself, where the revulsion of a sufficient number of influential people at the atrocities committed in their name helped prevent the government from deploying the full potential military force at its disposal. But the British will to fight in Northern Ireland was very much stronger, apart entirely from the will of the Ulster unionists to protect themselves and to dominate as many Irish nationalists as militarily possible.

Was it really conceivable that the British army, not least the officer class, whose connections with Ulster unionists, already strong in 1914, had been further reinforced by the bonds of the First World War, was going to stand idly by if there was any danger that their kith and kin would be driven into an independent Ireland, to be left, as they saw it, to the beastly designs not even of a John Redmond, whose aspirations to a united Home Rule Ireland had been successfully thwarted, but of an Eamon de Valera or a Michael Collins? And even if the British army were to remain spectators, were unionists themselves deemed to be so supine that they were willing to wait to be handed over to the leaders of what many of them regarded as a 'slave revolt'?[6] Were they really expected to surrender so easily to the lesser breed? Were the Ulster Volunteers to meekly lay down on the Lagan the weapons they had wielded so valiantly on the Somme? Was it for this so many of their comrades had fought and fell? Anybody who could believe this had, in my view, taken flight from reality. However repulsive Irish nationalists found some of the tenets of Ulster unionism, surely they had to acknowledge the fighting qualities of the Ulster unionist, affirmed in blood on many a field, at home and abroad. Were they both so mean and so myopic as to deny the fighting qualities of a frontier breed and a ruling race?

If the British army had withdrawn from the north, and if the IRA had launched an all-out assault, it is possible that it might have wrested the border areas with substantial nationalist majorities from the unionist grip. Assuming, however, that the unionist forces would have been well supplied with weapons, it is inconceivable that an IRA assault would have been militarily successful against the heartland of unionist Ulster, the north-east. The likeliest outcome would have been a new line of partition, conforming more closely to the actual distribution of ideological loyalties among the population, possibly after horrendous losses and savageries on both sides. What the longer-term consequences would have been is beyond any realistic assumptions of 'virtual history'.

Was there some recognition, however reluctant, of this during the Treaty debate? Was it because of this that the number of allusions to partition was so small, despite the anti-Treaty search for any argument with which to discredit the signatories? On the face of it, the anti-Treaty reluctance to attack on the partition issue required self-denial of truly heroic order. For it needed no clairvoyant to anticipate the outcome of the Boundary Commission. Nor is this to rely on hindsight, as Seán MacEntee's contribution correctly anticipated the consequences, as did Arthur Balfour, Austen Chamberlain and others on the British side. If other anti-Treatyites chose to ignore this, it was not because they had answers. Is it implausible to assume that, at least subconsciously, they saw no other way out? Whether that was the case or not, one is obliged to ask, what could De Valera have achieved on partition in the Treaty negotiations that the delegates did not?

The British were not prepared to make any concessions on the existence of Northern Ireland in principle, or on any change in the line of the actual border at that time. The furthest they would go, in even keeping the issue open, was to offer a Boundary Commission as duly contained in Article 12 of the Treaty. De Valera might have threatened continued conflict. But continued conflict to achieve what? The British knew that they, and the unionists, held the military whip hand in the north. How De Valera's negotiating skills would have changed the British view, or the unionist view, has never been explained. He could have threatened to resume the war. But if the IRA hadn't been able to prevent the imposition of partition in the first place, what were its chances of destroying the border now that it had been imposed, especially when Britain could trumpet that she was offering a Boundary Commission? Were they to be cowered by De Valera, the politician, when they were prepared to resist Collins, the gunman?

There is a view that the Irish negotiators were out-manoeuvred, out-witted, out-psyched, by more formidable and more experienced negotiators on the British side. The British were certainly more experienced. But what would more experience have achieved? The Irish delegates did, after all, achieve more than previous Irish representatives, including the vastly more experienced John Redmond between 1912 and 1918. If Sinn Féin were out-witted on the north, it was not in December 1921, but already in December 1920, when they had proved powerless to prevent the imposition of the Government of Ireland Act. And that wasn't as much a question of being out-witted as of being out-gunned. The bottom line that is so easily forgotten in the welter of discussion about the diplomacy of the Treaty negotiations is that Britain carried far the bigger gun. Until 5 December it was kept more or less discreetly hidden. Then Lloyd George pulled it out, laid it on the table, and threatened to use it.

29

Allowing for the greater experience of the British negotiators –what would this experience have got them if they were negotiating from the Sinn Féin position? Would they have achieved more than the Irish delegates achieved against them, once they no longer carried the bigger gun?

De Valera's views on the north in the winter of 1921 seem to have been very similar to those of Collins. He had courageously argued for county option in the secret sessions of Dáil Éireann in August 1921. In practice, that would presumably have meant, or so Sinn Féin assumed, that Fermanagh and Tyrone would have opted for the Free State, and four counties would have remained within 'Northern Ireland'. Collins too seems to have been thinking mainly in terms of the wishes of the inhabitants, at least as recorded in his most sustained intervention on the north during the Treaty negotiations, on 14 October 1921:

> There would have been an alternative to your Boundary Commission. Local Option. You did not stand aside in 1913. There is no analogy in the Dominions on this particular case but there are some in the Treaty of Versailles. This is a case which can be settled by Irishmen. By force we could beat them perhaps, but perhaps not. I do not think that we could beat them morally. If you kill all of us, every man and every male child, the difficulty will still be there. So with Ulster. That is why we do not want to coerce them but we cannot allow solid blocks who were against partition in the north of Antrim, through a part of Derry, and a part of Armagh to Strangford Lough. If we are not going to coerce the north-east corner, the north-east corner must not be allowed to coerce.[7]

This is not identical with the 'county option' concept of De Valera. But it does accept, in principle, the right of unionists, where they actually constitute the local majorities, to self-determination. What is striking is that, like De Valera, he accepts that unionists have a moral right in this regard. What they don't have is the right to deprive Irish nationalists of that same right. One may of course surmise that at the back of both their minds this would have made not just Northern Ireland, but any conceivable Northern Ireland, functionally inoperable. Perhaps. But that still does not detract from the manner in which Collins put a moral case for a unionist right to self-determination. De Valera explicitly confronted the issue in his interview with the *Evening Standard* in 1938. Asked what he would do if he had the power at his disposal, he responded bluntly that he would feel absolutely entitled to bring the Irish nationalist areas of Northern Ireland under Dublin jurisdiction. He then went on to ask himself whether he would have a moral right to incorporate the unionist areas as well. His frank answer was that he didn't know. It was of course a hypothetical question at the time. But it does confirm that he was at least aware of a moral dilemma. In this, as in so much else, Collins and De Valera, for all their differences in style, had much in common.

Collins would support the IRA in Northern Ireland at various times after the Treaty. What was his ultimate objective in these cases? Kevin O'Shiel, his choice to head up the North-East Boundary Bureau, claimed that Collins never believed the Boundary Commission could achieve enduring conciliation.[8] But then nobody can say with confidence exactly what Collins really believed. The IRA operated mainly in Irish nationalist areas, and from Collins' point of view, as expressed in October 1921, had just as much moral right to do so as the UVF had in unionist areas. What he hoped to achieve in practice by his support for the IRA in 1922 is unclear. On the face of it, it was provoked by unionist assaults on nationalists. And his thinking may have been primarily defensive. But it can be argued that, at least at times, it was intended to destroy partition entirely, 'to prevent them from carrying on', as one cabinet document put it,[9] and to compel the unionists to come in to a united Ireland in just the same way as they had compelled Irish nationalists to come into their state.

A further uncertainty in assessing the northern policy of Collins concerns not what he said in October 1921, nor even what he said or did in 1922, but what he would have done with more power. Had he commanded the equivalent of British military superiority in Northern Ireland, would he have coerced even the areas of unionist majority, and forced them into a united Ireland? Did he share British and unionist thinking about territory? His intervention of 14 October 1921 suggests not. But would he have adhered to it? Those who don't have the power are spared decisions that might show them up very differently if they had the power. We know what the British/unionists did with their superior command of violence. We don't know what Collins would have done if he had disposed of comparable violence.

As he didn't, awareness of moral dilemmas on the north was an academic issue in 1921. As the IRA did not have the power to incorporate the Irish nationalist areas occupied by British/unionist forces, much less the unionist areas, it remains distinctly unclear what breaking off the Treaty negotiations on the partition issue might have achieved.

But might it have achieved something for Sinn Féin on the other main issue of contention, and the prime issue for the vast majority of the contributors to the Treaty debate, the oath? The Irish delegates signed the Treaty under the threat of renewed war. Collins denied that this threat had influenced his decision to sign. But this beggars belief. His main supporters, like Richard Mulcahy, took the line that a resumption of the war would be disastrous for the IRA. Collins himself felt that the IRA was under extreme pressure.[10] If he didn't feel under the pressure of an immediate threat, there would have been no need to have signed the Treaty without referring it back to Dublin. A sense of the apocalyptic pervaded the discussions among the delegates on 5 December 1921 on their return to London from Dublin, in the face of Lloyd George's threat. It smacks of the type of schoolboy braggadocio to which Collins was occasionally capable of descending to claim that his signature, after hours of agonising, was unrelated to his assessment of the alternatives – among which Lloyd George's threat must surely have loomed largest of all. Otherwise, why the agony?

Difficult though I find it to believe that a refusal to sign could have made much difference on the north, because partition already existed, it may be argued that it could have made a difference on the oath. For the oath did not yet exist, at least in the context in which it was now to be introduced. Could a refusal to sign have won greater concessions on the oath issue, at least to the extent of De Valera's Document Number Two? Could the British have been induced to drop their insistence on the oath, which was the proximate cause of the Treaty split, if only the delegates had refused to sign? Was it on this issue that De Valera's negotiating skills would have made a crucial difference? What were the likely scenarios?

If the British were bluffing, then presumably Sinn Féin could have won De Valera's demands on the oath. These still fell short of the pure Republican position, as represented by Rory O'Connor and Liam Mellows. These might still have resisted, whatever the Dáil vote. But there would be a widespread assumption that if De Valera had supported a Treaty containing his External Association scheme, then the anti-Treaty forces would have secured much less public support. There might still have been *a* Civil War, but there would hardly have been *the* Civil War.

If the British were not bluffing, then all De Valera's vaunted negotiating skills would have made no difference. The British would then presumably have resumed war, true to their threat. What happened then would depend on what resources they were prepared to commit, and whether they chose to continue the fight as a limited war, or went all out for total victory. In the latter case they would, to put it conservatively, have stretched the IRA to the very limit of their capacity for resistance.

Could they have been persuaded by De Valera? What arguments could he have mobilised that the delegates had not already used? They had, after all, deployed all his arguments already. The question revolves far more around the British will to fight than around De Valera's negotiating skills. If they were determined to fight, no diplomacy could have dissuaded them. How important then was the oath to them? No one can ever be sure, of course, but my belief is that the balance of probabilities was that they were not bluffing. The oath symbolised the fundamental issue of status. Even if Lloyd George himself had been willing to concede this issue, it seems highly doubtful that the Tories would have permitted him to do so. His Irish critics have tended to exaggerate Lloyd George's authority – apparently as mesmerised by his reputation for negotiating skills as they claim the delegates were mesmerised by his bewitching performance. So mesmerised are the critics that they rarely pay adequate attention to the fact that Lloyd George was the leader of the minority Liberal group in a coalition government, in which the majority, the Conservative and Unionist party, actually had enough support to rule on its own. The Conservatives didn't need Lloyd George. Indeed, within ten months, in October 1922, they dismissed him on a Turkish issue far less close to their hearts than Irish issues, and installed Bonar Law, that staunch unionist, as Prime Minister. Lloyd George had far less room for manoeuvre than his Irish critics allow. In fact, one of the most remarkable features about the Treaty was that it was essentially a Tory government that conceded Dominion Status to Ireland, those same Tories who a few years earlier had bitterly rejected, under Bonar Law's leadership, much more modest concessions on Home Rule.

Whether it would have been wiser for De Valera to have gone to London from the outset, or at some stage subsequently, can be debated interminably. On my assumptions, which may of course be wrong, the strong balance of probabilities is that even he could not have secured better terms than the delegates. What those who take a different view must make clear is precisely what were the better terms they feel De Valera could have achieved. It is pointless claiming that better terms were available, unless we can specify what they were.

Whatever our judgement on the Treaty, several key issues arise concerning the role of Collins in subsequent developments. So long a shadow does Collins cast, that it is easy to forget that, at the moment of signing, he was still only third in command in the Sinn Féin political hierarchy. From that moment on he becomes the single most important figure. Within six weeks he had supplanted both De Valera, the then President of the Republic, and Griffith, his leader on the Treaty delegation, as the effective Prime Minister of the provisional state.

It can be argued that Griffith played a more crucial role than Collins in the actual negotiations themselves, and in leading the delegation towards acceptance of the Treaty. From the moment of signature, however, Collins becomes more important for carrying the Treaty. Widely respected though Griffith was, he had few personal votes to deliver among the waverers. It was Collins' personal influence that swung many of the undecided to support the Treaty. It was partly because he himself was so reluctant a signatory that many who voted for the Treaty could bring themselves to support it, in the conviction that as his heart was in the right place they were not reneging on their Republican ideals, but merely regrouping for a final thrust in more favourable circumstances. Even then, four votes would have changed the outcome. But for Collins, those votes would almost certainly not have been there.

Despite Collins' crucial rôle in securing the majority vote for the Treaty, the immediate beneficiary of De Valera's demotion appeared to be Griffith, voted by a majority of only two, 60–58, to succeed De Valera as President of the Dáil on 10 January 1922. At that stage it still seemed to be assumed on the anti-Treaty side that Griffith would also become Chairman of the Provisional Government, charged under the Treaty with the actual implementation of the agreed terms. But the promise that De Valera extracted from Griffith at the end of the Dáil debate, that he would uphold the Republic until it was formally disestablished, seems to have made it impossible for Griffith to assume formal membership of the Provisional Government, much less its Chairmanship.[11] Although Griffith frequently attended meetings, his role remained far more circumscribed than had he assumed the Chair. If this reading be correct, it was thus quite abruptly that the way became clear for Collins, in these obscure and confused circumstances, to become Chairman of the Provisional Government on 14 January.[12] As it was with this government that real decision-making authority lay, Collins had leaped not only De Valera, but Griffith, in the decision-making hierarchy. As he came very quickly to dominate his cabinet, his demonic energy, his unique position straddling the political-military divide, and his public repute enabling him stand head and shoulders above even the most formidable of his colleagues, this shift in the power hierarchy which appears to have happened almost casually, in deference to the mystique of 'the Republic', had momentous consequences.

A Provisional Government chaired by Griffith would in all likelihood have taken a more positive attitude towards implementation of the Treaty, and made fewer efforts to effect reconciliation with the anti-Treaty forces. Irreconcilable tensions could have arisen very quickly between Collins and Griffith on that score. Tensions did of course arise, given Griffith's unhappiness over Collins' penchant for seeking conciliation, instead of confrontation, with the dissident IRA elements, and in particular over Collins' handling of the Pact with De Valera on the eve of the general election. Had Collins and Griffith both survived much longer, it is highly likely they would have found themselves on opposite sides on a whole series of issues, perhaps culminating in a major split, with incalculable consequences.

Collins, the pre-Treaty conspirator, was accustomed to squaring circles. He carried something of the same style over into the operation of the Provisional Government, a style all the more tempting in that it seemed only too appropriate to the confusion and complexity of the imbroglio confronting him. He sought desperately to avoid, or at least postpone, civil war, partly because of a genuine revulsion against the prospect, partly because he himself was torn in different directions, with his heart going one way and his head another, and partly because he feared the anti-Treaty IRA would gain the military upper hand if war broke out immediately – again with incalculable implications for the British response. Given that the majority of active service IRA units appear to have opposed the Treaty, he badly needed time to raise and equip a state army. But how could he have persuaded himself that he might manage to run a constitution so contrary to the terms of the Treaty past the vigilant eye of Winston Churchill, when only a few months before the British had threatened war over the oath? Did he really think he could carry the internal contradictions of conspiracy onto the more open stage of state-craft? Nevertheless, it is easy to overlook his role in building up the civic infrastructure of the new state, given the looming cloud of civil war. However confined the constitution found itself by the terms of the Treaty, the constitution still repays analysis as a document in its own right, providing the best clue we have to the internal organisation of the new state as envisaged by Collins at that stage, however rushed the circumstances of its composition.

Many of his hopes floundered in the spring and summer of 1922. What was the real quality of his thinking in the frenetic circumstances of these months? How far did the rhetoric of the *Path to Freedom* translate into the reality of his specific decisions on state-making? If he failed in his constitutional manoeuvring, was the delay by the anti-Treaty IRA in pressing home their initial military superiority after the Treaty influenced by an assumption that Collins would find a way out, and by a reluctance to go to war against him?[13] How important was his role in the general election of June 1922? Griffith fumed against the Pact – but how much did the pro-Treaty side depend on Collins, a formidable election campaigner, to deliver the vote?[14] How many were there who disliked the Treaty, but would not vote against Collins? The media of the time, of course, records public opinion as heavily in favour of the Treaty. But then the media itself was heavily in favour. Would the majority have been so large but for public confidence in Collins? Does the sharp increase in the anti-Treaty vote in the August 1923 general election, which must surely rank as one of the most unexpected election gains in Irish history, given all the horrors of the Civil War, reflect to any extent the absence of the Collins factor? Would it have made a significant difference to the size of the government vote at that election, or at least at whatever the first election after the Civil War would have been – for of course nothing would have been exactly the same had Collins lived?

Even the achievements ascribed to Parnell, if only he had attained the biblical span of three score and ten (to 1916 as it so happens) fade into insignificance compared with the burden of expectation borne by the dead Collins. But there can be few whose future performance is as unpredictable, for at least two reasons.

Firstly, Collins was still developing rapidly at the time of his death. Who could have predicted his performance in the final twelve months from his performance in the previous twelve months? It would be equal folly to pronounce too dogmatically on what would have come in the following twelve months, much less beyond. What he would have developed into, when or how he would have levelled out, we cannot know.

Secondly, we cannot hold everything else constant, because the very fact of his presence would have changed the parameters of the possible. Could he have brought the Civil War to a rapid conclusion, without the executions, thus presumably softening the legacy of bitterness, and leaving party politics more fluid? How would he have related to De Valera? Would he have allowed Cumann na nGaedheal cede the social centre and left to Fianna Fáil – if Fianna Fáil had come into existence? Or would he have founded something like Fianna Fáil himself to allow him escape from his more socially conservative colleagues? Which, indeed, of his multiple legacies would Collins himself have chosen? Or would he have sought to continue to balance them all? Almost any answer is plausible, depending on one's assumptions.

The verdict on the living Collins can be almost as uncertain as on the dead Collins. There can be as many legitimate differences of opinion on whether Griffith or Collins was the more 'correct' in their reading of the situation in 1922 as there can be on whether they or De Valera were the more 'correct' on the Treaty negotiations. As with all assertions about those negotiations, what is necessary for progress in the study of the post-Treaty Collins is the explicit avowal of our assumptions about likely alternatives. Historical judgement on his performance in this period is nearly as much in danger of succumbing to our own silent assumptions, inevitably coloured by our contemporary concerns, as they are on the Treaty itself. Unless historians and biographers spell out explicitly the assumptions underlying every judgement they make, claims and counter-claims will continue indefinitely at cross purposes. It is not for me to anticipate the verdicts of the participants, but this book will mark a significant step forward if it contributes to the clarification of the multiple assumptions underlying our evaluation of Collins.[15]

MICHAEL COLLINS
THE GRANARD CONNECTION

Margot Gearty

J. Curwin remarked, on his arrival in Granard in 1818,

> Granard is a neat town, consisting of one handsome street about a
> mile long, at the head of which stands the castle, built on a singular
> hill rising to a considerable height: As the surrounding country is per-
> fectly flat, the hill has the appearance of a work of art.

In 1860, on this considerable height and under the shadow of the
Moat of Granard, St Mary's Roman Catholic Church was built in
neo-gothic style – the octagonal spire was added later. Thus the first
glimpse of Granard as one approaches from any route is a dramatic and imposing one. So this is the first view that a young Corkman
would have while being driven to Granard by motor-car in 1917 to
stay at a small hotel there.

It is also the view that, much earlier, my grandfather Peter
Kiernan would have had as he walked to Granard in the early 1870s
to seek his fortune. Peter's family home was five miles west of Granard in the townland of Aughagreagh, where his family had worked
a small farm for many generations. His brother Larry would continue to farm there and his childrens' children up to the present day.

Peter took a job working in a shop in Granard, learned his trade
and saved for his future. Within ten years he was ready to fulfil his
dream of owning his own place. But meanwhile, and most significantly, he had met the woman who would be his wife, his friend
and support for the rest of their lives together.

Peter Kiernan and Bridget Dawson were married on 4 October
1886 in the old church of Mullahoran, County Cavan. Peter was
thirty years old and Bridget twenty-five. She came from a farming
background in Cloncovid, five miles north of Granard. Her family
was ambitious, realising the value of education. An uncle was a
priest in the diocese of Ardagh and Clonmacnoise and Bridget kept
house for him for a period. At least one of her brothers attended St
Mel's College in Longford, later doing well for himself in Ontario,
Canada.

Business flourished for Peter and Bridget in their new premises 'The Corner House', Granard, their motto being 'from a needle to an anchor'. Friends and neighbours from their respective home areas loyally patronised the shop which became known for its hospitality and warmth and a kettle always on the boil. Bridget, the Cavan woman, was shrewd and diplomatic while Peter was popular, respected and had a flair for business. A photograph from the Lawrence collection (late 1890s) shows a thriving and lively premises with fine living quarters above. Soon they purchased a further small shop in Market Street.

Having lost their first baby girl at birth in December, 1887 Bridget gave birth the following year to twin girls Lily and Rose. After them came Christine, Lawrence Dawson, Catherine, Helen and Maud in quick succession. The family remembered nothing but happiness from the years that followed. They were part of a lively, busy menage, comfortably off with a solid base and loving parents. Twenty years later Kitty (Catherine) would write to her 'very dear Micheál':

> I'd love to feel you wanted me always beside you just the way Daddy and Mother used to be.

Family folklore has it that after a busy day in the shop, the children in bed, and the money counted, Peter would take Bridget into 'the snug' where they'd have a nightcap together.

By 1899, Peter was an elected member of Longford County Council and attended the first meeting that year. Later he was appointed to the Board of the Mental Hospital in Mullingar.

On the night of 31 March 1901 he must have felt a happy and fulfilled man as he recorded on his census form that seventeen people resided in his home – his wife and seven children, six shop assistants and two domestic servants. All could read and write and all were Roman Catholic.

In 1903 William Mullen, member of the Church of Ireland and proprietor of the Greville Arms Hotel, died. When the hotel came on the market Peter and Bridget set about buying it. I understand this transaction had to be done through a third party as a Catholic might not have been an acceptable buyer. Later they bought a further property next door to the hotel and established their hardware store there. They retained their corner house as grocery, bar and provisions outlet.

With business thriving, the top priority for Bridget and Peter now became the education of their children. In 1906 they enrolled their only son Larry as a boarder in St Mel's College. Chrys, Kitty, Helen and Maud boarded at the Loreto Convent in Bray, County Wicklow. The twins remained at home – I suspect because of health reasons. Peter himself was not now in good health, though a family photograph taken about this time shows a fine bearded man, carefully dressed and immensely proud of his family.

However, there was great cause for anxiety. In 1907 nineteen year old Rose was sent off to a sanatorium in Davos, Switzerland in the desperate hope of a cure for her tuberculosis. It was not to be – she died there in a strange land far way from her loving family. Meanwhile her twin sister Lily, too ill for treatment, died at home in Granard on 27 November 1907. Exactly a year later, their mother Bridget died suddenly at the foot of the stairs, her life cut short at only forty-five years.

The young girls in Bray were called to the parlour and informed by the mother superior that they must return home immediately as their mother had died. 'But it can't be so,' said Chrys the eldest, 'it was our father who was ill'. Only two months later, on 29 January 1909, their father was also dead. Larry returned from St Mel's, just seventeen years old, to be head of the house and to run the, by now, extensive business. Chrys, his older sister by a year, stayed home to help him while the younger girls returned to Loreto. It would be difficult to overestimate the devastating effects this succession of deaths had on these five teenagers. The positive thing to emerge from the double tragedy was that they drew closer together, and remained so for the rest of their lives.

An uncle by marriage, Andrew Cusack, a draper in Granard, was appointed guardian to the children. He was a supporter of Sinn Féin, with strong views on everything including education. After the summer holidays of 1910, having removed Kitty, Helen and Maud from Loreto, he sent them with his own daughter Minch to a new experimental school for girls at Cullenswood House, Ranelagh, County Dublin. The school was St Ita's, its Director Pádraig H. Pearse BA, Barrister-at-Law.

The prospectus of the school stated:

The primary aim of St Ita's will be to foster the elements of character. It will endeavour to ground its pupils in sound moral and religious principles, to train them in practical Christianity and to awaken in them a spirit of patriotism and a sense of duty to their country.

Despite these lofty ideals life at St Ita's was quite unconventional and stimulating. The four Granard girls adapted quickly to the spacious homely house in beautiful surroundings and with a view of the Dublin mountains. Kitty was appointed school captain and her cousin Minch Cusack became school secretary and editor of the *Annals*. This journal gives a day-by-day account of the school's activities. There were visits to the Municipal Art Gallery in Harcourt Street, to the Botanic Gardens and the Abbey Theatre. They exchanged regular visits with the students of St Enda's (Pearse's school for boys). With them they had debates and discussions, had joint lectures from visiting personages, held ceilidhs and made friends.

Sadly, St Ita's closed its doors after only two years and with it ended the formal education of the Kiernan girls. After some brief business training, they returned home to help Chrys and Larry run the business. They settled down well to life in Granard, using many of the imaginative and creative skills developed at St Ita's. While each worked hard in their own department of the shop or hotel, they led a keen social life and I understand went for long walks in the country. They got a little musical ensemble together and entertained their friends in the drawing-room of the hotel. They were extremely fashion conscious and were encouraged by their artistic and bohemian cousin Paul Cusack to develop their own style. He and his brothers also urged them to have political opinions and, sure enough, by 1917 when the McGuinness by-election campaign was raging in South Longford, some of 'the girls' were out electioneering. I have been told that their presence 'en bloc' at a rally would lend not only glamour but a strong and solid support to proceedings.

'Vote early, vote often' was the catchphrase of this election and I believe Kitty and Maud encouraged others to do just that. An old gentleman here in Granard tells me he remembers them coming to borrow his sick father's voting card so they could do some personation in favour of McGuinness. Joe McGuinness, who had been in prison for his part in the 1916 Rising, had been nominated to oppose the Irish Party's representative – a slogan in the campaign being 'put him in to get him out'.

It was to campaign for McGuinness that the dashing young Michael Collins came to Longford for the first time. At the suggestion of McGuinness' niece – the young and political Dr Brigid Lyons

– he was taken to stay at the Greville Arms Hotel, Granard. Frank O'Connor writes in *The Big Fellow* of this visit: 'Here in Longford, he fell in love. Here in Longford he found a second home, and after this episode Longford was linked in his mind with Cork'.

No wonder Mick Collins responded with interest to the energy emanating from this household of young people. On the one hand they were hard-working, serious and I believe had a strong spiritual sense. On the other hand they were fun-loving, quick-witted and had a keen sense of humour. It is said that at first it was Helen who caught Collins' eye, but as she was bespoken for he turned his attention to Kitty – even though his friend Harry Boland had the same idea.

However, an event was to occur that would cast a shadow on the Kiernans for long days to come. On Sunday 31 October 1920, at about 9.30 p.m., while the girls were entertaining in the drawing-room with music and singing, a young district inspector was shot dead in the bar downstairs. He was Philip Kellagher, a native of Macroom and a past pupil of Castleknock College, who had become quite friendly with the family during his short time in Granard. The *Longford Leader* of 6 November reports: 'He was unarmed at the time of the terrible tragedy and was in the company of Messrs L. D. Kiernan, Paul Cusack, B. Macken and Seán Cawley at the time, when two masked men entered the bar and fired point blank at the officer, four bullets taking effect'. Larry and Kitty were taken to Longford Barracks under arrest but released almost immediately (Kitty later told Collins in a letter that 'the military were very kind to me').

By Monday, businesses were closed and the town deserted, awaiting the reprisals that would surely follow. The *Longford Leader* reports:

> At 11.30 on Wednesday night 11 lorry loadfuls of uniformed men entered the town. At 12 o'clock the visitors commenced firing rifle bullets into the houses on the Main Street, apparently as a signal for the destruction that followed. At 12.30 they commenced the destruction of Mr. L. D. Kiernan's Corner House, grocery and bar and after the third attempt with petrol and bombs the houses were fired. The hardware establishment of Mr. Kiernan's was next fired and Mr. Kiernan's Greville Arms Hotel with the Market House, a splendid block of buildings estimated to cost £70,000, were totally destroyed.

Nearly all the major buildings in the town suffered the same fate.

The family had fled at only the last moment on Wednesday evening to Omard House, in Killnaleck, County Cavan, the home of old friends Nicholas and Maria Sheridan, a couple famed for their open house hospitality. This became their home for some time. However, by the following week, the *Longford Leader* could report that 'one small little shop, used as a leather store was saved from the wreckage and here the Kiernan family took refuge and endeavoured to start their business again'.

In Kitty's third letter to Collins of 20 January 1921 she writes rather primly thanking him for his concern and stating 'we are carrying on business but have made no definite plans until we have peace'. However, the rebuilding of the hotel and shop commenced soon and progressed throughout 1921. This year also saw the marriage of Chrys to the bookish and cultured Tom Magee from Belfast while Helen married solicitor Paul McGovern with whom she visited Collins (now engaged on the Treaty negotiations in London) while en route to their honeymoon in Paris. By 1922, Kitty and Maud were planning a double wedding in the October of that year to the two Corkmen Michael Collins and Gearóid O'Sullivan. Meanwhile, Larry was announcing with huge adverts in the local papers the official re-opening of the hotel. He had also announced his engagement to my mother Peggy Sheridan. Everything seemed to be falling into place for the family.

Collins was by now visiting Granard at every opportunity and writing daily to Kitty while in London or Dublin. For her part, she always seemed more concerned with Collins' health and safety than in the momentous affairs with which he was involved. In her very last letter she grieves for Griffith and the loss which Collins must have felt at his death. Someone has warned her that if he goes to the funeral he'll be shot, 'but God is very good to you, and we must both do Lough Derg sometime in thanksgiving' she wrote.

But it was not to be. The awesome tragedy of Collins death at Béal na mBláth on 22 August 1922 was the final grief for Kitty, her devastation total. Instead of the planned double wedding – Maud married Gearóid in October – Kitty sat by her sister dressed in black from head to foot. My parents married in January 1923 but Kitty does not appear in any of the photos. She lived with them in Granard for a few months, sitting in the drawing-room responding to the thousands of letters she received from all over Ireland and abroad. When she left to go to stay with Maud and take up a small government position, she seldom returned. The pain of her memories was too great. She later married a friend and colleague of Collins, Major-General Felix Cronin, and had two fine sons.

I was born into the Greville Arms in 1933 the youngest of four children of Larry and Peggy. While having a rich and vibrant childhood we were touched by the spirit of the past. As we ate our meals in the coffee room, the eyes of Michael Collins and Arthur Griffith looked upon us from the handsome framed portraits on the walls. We children had black-bordered mortuary cards of Collins in our prayer books and the two volumes of Piaras Béaslaí – with a dedication to my father – were eagerly read during measles and mumps. Old friends from 'the movement' – now perhaps government ministers or people in high office – called regularly and spoke of 'the girls' in hushed tones. 'The girls' indeed came themselves with their children, bringing excitement and glamour as ever. In 1940, Helen came back to Granard to die, elegant and lovely to the end. Six months later Maud died of the same ailment. Kitty lived only a few more years and was buried near the grave of Michael Collins at Glasnevin. We watched sadly as our parents silently grieved for 'the girls' but in December 1948, a few days before Christmas, my father Larry died suddenly and with him the little empire that had been Kiernan Stores virtually came to an end. The depression of the 1950s took its toll and the next generation followed other paths. The hotel changed hands in the early 1960s.

Granard is quite a thriving town again and happily the Greville Arms Hotel has been recently restored by a young local couple. They are conscious of the historic links and have a Kitty Kiernan restaurant and a Michael Collins lounge.

I am the last of the family to live in Granard. I still take my visitors to climb the Moat and remember how Collins wrote to Kitty from 15 Cadogan Square Gardens, London on his birthday, 16 October 1921:

How I wish I were there now – on the Moat, early morning. Do you remember? I looked across the Inny to Derryvaragh over Kinale and Sheelin to Mount Nugent and turning westward saw Carinhill where the beacons were lighted to announce to the men of Longford that the French had landed at Killala ...

GEARÓID O'SULLIVAN
FRIEND AND ALLY

Gearóid O'Sullivan

One of Collins' closest comrades during the Anglo-Irish struggle was a fellow west Cork man, Gearóid O'Sullivan, who was, incidentally, just a few months younger than him. To correctly assess the part that Gearóid O'Sullivan played, not alone in the 1916 Rising but in the movement that led to it and in the resultant freedom that has come our way since, is not easy. To do so one would need to collect a great deal of information not easily available at present.

Throughout his life, Gearóid O'Sullivan was passionate in the promotion of the Irish language he loved and the ideals that inspired him. It is, however, for his connection with the Volunteer movement and his services in the Anglo-Irish struggle, that he was best known.

Born in January, 1891, Gearóid O'Sullivan was the fourth son of Michael and Margaret O'Sullivan, Coolnagurrane, Skibbereen. His father, who was a native of Lough Ine, and his mother (nee McCarthy) who was born at Coolnagurrane, were members of well-known west Cork farming families. Gearóid received his primary education at the local national school, where, under Johnny Hayes, who was head teacher at that time, he showed signs of intellectual brilliance at an early age and was elected monitor. He subsequently attended Mr Daniel Duggan's Intermediate and University School in Skibbereen. Both these schools were situated in the building where the De La Salle Brothers now teach.

Two Skibbereen men, James Duggan and Peadar O'Hourihane, both of whom were later to have a long association with the *Southern Star* were to influence Gearóid in his formative years. His interest in national affairs was probably due in some way to the effect on him of the family friendship of James Duggan of High Street, who brought him into the Gaelic League. James Duggan, who was a close friend of Michael Collins, was a pioneer of the Sinn Féin movement in the Skibbereen area, and was later to become Managing Director of the *Southern Star* from 1937 to 1942.

Peadar O'Hourihane, of Lightford, Skibbereen was a prominent Gaelic League activist all his life and was one of the early organisers for the Munster area. Peadar was Editor and Director of the *Star* during very difficult times in 1917–8 and continued his association with the paper right up to 1961. Peadar and Gearóid were to share many common experiences during the Anglo-Irish struggle and, although they held divergent views on the Treaty, maintained a life-long friendship.

Gearóid's long association with Dublin started in September 1909 when he entered St Patrick's Training College, Drumcondra to prepare for the teaching profession. Although he was still under nineteen years of age, he had already done the second arts examination of the Royal University of Ireland, and it was soon apparent to everybody at the college that he was one of the most able students to enter that year. During his two year course he was always in or about the head of the list in all examinations, being especially strong in mathematical subjects and Irish. Though a keen follower of the college teams, especially hurling, he was never himself a great exponent of games – his interest being rather in the language movement and other national activities.

Having passed from the Training College in the First Division in the summer of 1911, Gearóid shortly afterwards took up a teaching appointment at Kildorrery in north Cork. Here he was kept without his salary for nine months because sufficient pupils would not attend the school. However, as a result of the case being tried in court, the Reverend Manager found himself compelled to pay the salary, and a very important principle was thus established regarding the rights of teachers.

Gearóid transferred his activities back to Dublin after Easter 1912, when he joined the staff of St Peter's National School, Phibsboro. Immediately on going to Dublin he joined the Keatinge branch of the Gaelic League and very soon became a member of its committee. It was here that his association with Michael Collins began. On his return from London in January 1916, Collins joined the Keatinge branch of the Gaelic League where he associated with the men who, apart from becoming leaders in the struggle that lay ahead, were to become his closest allies and, some, in time, his bitterest enemies. These included Gearóid O'Sullivan, Richard Mulcahy, Cathal Brugha and Rory O'Connor.

Here Gearóid's enormous capacity for work was to manifest itself. Several evenings in the week he taught classes of enthusiastic members of the branch at a time when, in addition to his daily work of teaching at St Peter's, he had started to study for his BA degree in the National University. And this, we should mention, was voluntary teaching, for in those days Gaelic League branches were unable to pay their teachers, and indeed, these most enthusiastic of the language revivalists probably never thought of looking for payment. Early and late he worked in every field of national endeavour – the Keatinge branch of the Gaelic League, the Volunteers where he served, the Fáinne of which he was a founding member, and the Aisteoirí, a society for the revival of Gaelic plays.

In the autumn of 1913 Gearóid got his BA degree with honours in the Celtic Studies group, and in the following year he was awarded the Higher Diploma in Education, again with honours, and in 1915 he obtained his MA in Educational Science.

Peadar O'Hourihane, who was at that time teaching in Coláiste Cairbre in Glandore, later recounted how in August 1915 Gearóid, while a member of staff therein, taught for a few hours each day, gave an hour or two to studying in order to face up to the test of winning his MA degree (which he did with honours a few months later), and when evening came he mounted his bicycle and headed off over some of the rugged roads of Cairbre to interview Volunteer officers or attend a Volunteer drill and parade, returning late at night or early the following morning. And these were his holidays.

Gearóid was present at the inaugural meeting of the Irish Volunteers which was formed by the Professor of Early Irish History in UCD, Eoin MacNeill, at a meeting in the Rotunda, Parnell Square Dublin in November 1913. The Irish Volunteers were formed with the intention of defending Home Rule should force be used against it, and though still without an indigenous government, Irish nationalists now had an army. Gearóid became a member from the beginning. When the companies were subsequently formed he became a member of F Company, 1st Battalion, and remained a member of that company until he was chosen by Seán MacDiarmada as his Aide-de-Camp a week before the Rising. His activities as a Volunteer were again manifold – he assisted in getting out *Irish Freedom*, the organ of the Irish Republican Brotherhood (of which he became a member in 1914) and, after suppression of the paper, he helped in the distribution of other organs of extreme national opinion which were issued under various names.

From 1914 on secret plans for a Rising began. The date fixed was for Easter Sunday, 23 April 1916. As the day for the Rising approached a series of misfortunes and misunderstandings were to doom it to failure, even before it started. Three days before the appointed date MacNeill, Chief-of-Staff of the Volunteers, who until then was unaware of the plan, learned of the developments and promptly cancelled the orders for manoeuvres on Easter Sunday. Subsequently, on being informed of the Casement arms expedition expected to arrive from Germany on the eve of the Rising, he changed his mind, taking the view that the die had been irrevocably cast. On Easter Saturday, MacNeill learned of the failure of the arms landing and of Casement's capture. The news seemed to him a disastrous blow to the prospects of the Rising and he at once reverted to his former position and issued countermanding orders. The majority of the leaders of the Volunteers, however, were determined that a Rising must take place despite all difficulties and decided on the following day, Easter Monday. The Rising had little prospect of success in the strictly military sense. The object was, however, in the view of the leaders, to assert Ireland's claim to independence and to show that men were prepared to die for it.

At midday on Easter Monday, 24 April, a party of Citizen Army men and Volunteers, including Gearóid O'Sullivan, marched from Liberty Hall and occupied the General Post Office in O'Connell Street. They were led by five of the men who signed the Proclamation of the Republic, Pádraig Pearse, Tom Clarke, James Connolly, Seán MacDiarmada and Joseph Plunkett. This was to be a glorious day for the boy from Coolnagurrane, who, at the behest of his commander Pádraig Pearse, raised the tricolour over the GPO between 1 and 2pm on that historic Easter Monday.

Gearóid fought beside Michael Collins during the ensuing week. He took part in the evacuation of the GPO and in the attempt to storm the factory of Messrs Williams and Woods during which the Volunteers sustained some of their heaviest casualties of the week. Following the unconditional surrender by the Volunteers on Saturday afternoon, 29 April, they were rounded up and taken to the green area in front of the Rotunda Hospital in Parnell Place. Here, huddled together, they were kept until the following night. Many of them were ill-treated, including Gearóid, who, when asked his name, replied in Irish and was struck by a British soldier. Gearóid was shackled to Seán T. O'Kelly as the prisoners were marched through the city to Richmond gaol on Sunday night. Here he was to meet up again with his friend from Skibbereen, Peadar O'Hourihane, who had been arrested in Cork.

Every morning six prisoners were told to attend to the sanitary arrangements. These were the usual camp model and were situated in the barrack yard, behind a canvas awning. The conveniences for the British soldiers were the same and, though separate, were alongside those the prisoners used. It was the duty of the inmates to clean out their own latrines and this was done by the fatigue party appointed for the day.

On the fifth morning it was the turn of a party led by Gearóid O'Sullivan. When they had done the job, they received an order to clean the latrines used by the British soldiers. Gearóid at once refused. He said he was prepared to take his turn in attending to the requirements of his comrades, but that nothing would induce him to do so for the British soldiers. The sergeant of the guard hurried off to report the matter to his superior officer. The major arrived immediately in a towering rage. Gearóid repeated his refusal. Saying he would give him two minutes to obey, the major walked back five paces and, drawing his revolver, he took his watch in his other hand. This scene took place in the barrack yard, and from the windows the prisoners could see the major's lips moving, and the resolute expression and unflinching attitude of Gearóid.

When the two minutes were up Major Orr repeated his challenge, but already he knew he was beaten, and calling some of his men to arrest them, he ordered Gearóid and the five men with him to be taken to solitary confinement, preparatory to being court-martialled for refusing to obey a military order.

The trial was held the next day. The military authorities decided that it was not the duty of the prisoners to clean the latrines of the soldiers and Gearóid and the other men were released from solitary confinement. By this courageous act Gearóid had displayed his scorn and contempt for the trappings of his jailers and won the respect and friendship of his fellow prisoners.

From Richmond gaol Gearóid was deported to Wandsworth prison and subsequently transferred to Frongoch with many of the other Irish prisoners where he was interned until the general amnesty of 21 December 1916. On his release, Gearóid, in the company of Michael Collins, arrived back in Dublin on Christmas Eve.

Gearóid returned to teaching in 1917 and took up the position of Professor of Languages at St Mary's College, Knockbeg, County Carlow. Here he paid great attention to developments throughout the country and was actively involved in providing a safe haven and a hiding place for some Volunteers who sought refuge at the college. Kevin O'Higgins was amongst those who used this facility and later acknowledged the part played there by Gearóid O'Sullivan. P. J. Doyle was Rector of the college at this time and he also took many risks in accommodating and aiding Volunteers. Michael Collins was an occasional visitor to St Mary's and on one occasion, when he arranged for the escape of a Volunteer, Pádraig Fleming, it was to Knockbeg he took him for shelter.

In the summer of 1918 he was again arrested for a speech made at Skibbereen and imprisoned in Cork gaol for four months. Yet another term of imprisonment was served by him in the summer of 1919. Following his release he went to west Cork to organise the local Volunteers. As a result of work undertaken by himself and Dick McKee, the first training camp for Volunteers was established at Glandore. A round-up of the camp was made by the British and Gearóid was among those taken prisoner. He was sentenced to six month's imprisonment and was only released after a hunger strike in Mountjoy gaol.

Prior to February 1920 Michael Collins had fulfilled the functions of Adjutant-General, but in that month Gearóid was appointed to the office, and he was to hold the position for the remainder of the Anglo-Irish War and until 1924. Other members of the O'Sullivan family were also prominently identified with the fight for independence. His brothers Tadhg, Paddy, Donal and Eoin were all active. As a direct result of such activity the family home at Coolnagurrane was burned down in 1920 by members of the Essex Regiments.

In 1921 Gearóid was elected to the Dáil for Carlow-Kilkenny alongside W. T. Cosgrave (he was to be re-elected as a Treaty candidate in the Pact election of June 1922). He supported the Treaty during the Dáil debates and voted in favour of its ratification in the key vote on 7 January 1921. From then until June the country seemed to drift into Civil War. Gearóid was among those who strove tirelessly to avoid such a development. He tried desperately to hold together her former comrades whose paths were then parting. When these efforts failed it became his unpleasant duty to enforce the people's will.

The Civil War, which broke out in late June 1922 and which lasted until May 1923, was a most traumatic and harrowing time for him. Once again night merged with days of endless toil and worry; death crossed his path anew; he saw old friends and comrades, now locked in conflict, fall around him. His own family divided on the Treaty issue and, as was the case in many families, brother was set against brother. The shooting of Michael Collins at Béal na mBláth on 22 August 1922 had a particularly profound effect on Gearóid. Through the tensions and stress of the previous six years the two west Cork men had developed an unbreakable bond.

Happier days were to follow and they brought many compensations, including the healing of old wounds and the renewal of old friendships. Gearóid married Maud Kiernan on 19 October 1922. Maud was a member of the renowned Kiernan family of Granard, County Longford and was closely associated with the national movement. She had first met Gearóid when Michael Collins and he had stayed there during the South Longford by-election of 1917 (the house was to be destroyed by the Black and Tans in 1920). Maud's sister, Kitty, had been engaged to Michael Collins and the two sisters had planned a double wedding. Collins had however been killed and an air of sadness must have hung over the wedding party that day as Kitty, still in mourning and dressed in black, acted as a bridesmaid.

Gearóid O'Sullivan retired from the army in March 1924 following the crisis of the same month. He had been studying law and after a brilliant course at the King's Inn he was called to the bar. He was asked to stand for the by-election caused by the assassination of Kevin O'Higgins, and was elected with a huge vote. He held the seat until his defeat in the 1937 general election. From 1932 until 1940 he practised law on the western circuit, and was subsequently appointed as a commissioner for the special purposes of the Income Tax Acts.

Gearóid O'Sullivan died on Good Friday 1948 and was buried on Easter Monday. His coffin, draped in the same tricolour which had covered the coffin of Michael Collins, paused at the GPO thirty-two years to the day after he had raised the national standard over the building at the beginning of the 1916 Rising.

MICHAEL COLLINS
MINISTER FOR FINANCE 1919–22

Andrew McCarthy

That any man has greatness thrust upon him is a myth; in truth fate merely presents the opportunity while ambition and ability determine the performance. So it was with Michael Collins, the unlikely Finance Minister who proved himself an administrator *par excellence*. When the First Dáil appointed Collins to Finance, in succession to Eoin MacNeill, a more appropriate appointee could hardly have been visualised. For despite his relative anonymity and comparatively young age – at twenty-nine he was the youngest in a cabinet whose average age was forty-four years – he discharged his duties with considerable ease, incomparable efficiency and definite purpose during the Anglo-Irish and Civil Wars. Collins retained the Finance portfolio until July 1922, and from that January simultaneously held it in the Provisional Government and the Dáil ministry. His greatest achievement in finance was undoubtedly the successful organisation of the first National Loan. Yet, amongst his cabinet colleagues, Collins was *facile princeps*, demonstrating an administrative flair that was both meticulous and perspicacious.

Although his résumé hardly suggested cabinet material Collins had already acquired useful experience in a variety of administrative fields. Aged fifteen he passed the post office examination for the position of boy clerk and in July 1906 joined his older sister Johanna in West Kensington, London, remaining there until 1916. Despite taking Customs and Excise preparatory classes in Kings College, Collins crossed to Moorgate in April 1910, joining the stockbrokers, Horne & Company, as a clerk in charge of messengers. Shortly after the outbreak of the Great War he moved to Whitehall as a Labour Exchange clerk, but left in April 1915 to join the London office of the Guaranty Trust Company of New York. He remained there until his return to Ireland on 15 January 1916, when he then secured a position in Dublin as 'Financial Advisor to Count Plunkett', a self-styled misnomer as he was in fact a three-days-a-week clerk tending to the family property accounts. His £1 weekly income there was supplemented with temporary employment in the accountancy firm Craig, Gardner & Company, for whom he worked from 23 February until the Rising. After internment Collins returned to Dublin and on 19 February 1917 he became Secretary of the National Aid Office. It was, however, his clandestine work, in Frongoch and in the reorganisation of the Irish Republican Brotherhood from 1917, that propelled him into Finance.[1]

When, on 2 April 1919, Alex MacCabe proposed, and Harry Boland seconded, Collins' nomination as Minister for Finance,[2] it was clearly for a covert operation. The appointment made him second in importance only to the Príomh Aire, Eamon de Valera, and, in Collins' eyes, ensured 'the hanging that was only probable had we remained members of the Dáil'.[3] The same day the Defence Minister, Cathal Brugha, moved that Standing Order no. 14 be suspended in favour of defined powers for Collins. But the Dáil accepted Ernest Blythe's amendment that 'Standing Order no. 14 be suspended until November 1st, 1919, and the Secretary of Finance is hereby authorised without specific reference to the Dáil, to apply monies to such specific objects as the ministry (when not reduced below five in number) shall unanimously approve.' Two days later Brugha moved that the Ministry be authorised 'to issue Republican Bonds to the value of £250,000 in sums of £1 to £1,000.' This proposal was, however, superseded when, on 10 April, De Valera delivered the Ministry's declaration of policy and outlined Collins' vital role in the administration. He told the Dáil that:

> It is obvious that the work of our government cannot be carried on without funds. The Minister for Finance is accordingly preparing a prospectus, which will be shortly published, for the issue of a loan of one million sterling – £500,000 to be offered to the public for immediate subscription, £250,000 at home and £250,000 abroad, in bonds of such amounts as to meet the needs of the small subscriber.[4]

This was an unprecedented undertaking for a political party in Ireland. Most observers, even Arthur Griffith, were sceptical as to the prospects of success. In the past the Irish Parliamentary Party had raised £10,000 which, according to Stephen Gwynn, was a 'big achievement'. But there was potential if the cause was sufficiently emotive for the people to embrace. The Irish had, for example, contributed £250,000 in 1918 to the Anti-Conscription Fund. In America the 'Friends of Irish Freedom' had raised $1m by February 1919. However, Sinn Féin had little success in acquiring much of these funds. Only $10,000 was received from America. About £17,000 passed to the Sinn Féin Self Determination Fund from the defunct Anti-Conscription Fund when in March 1919 the custodians, the Mansion House Committee, began disbursement.[5]

Collins was, however, confident that the target would be met. De Valera, along with Harry Boland, took responsibility for the American fund-raising, and Collins immediately set about arrangements for the Loan. He established the finance office at No. 6 Harcourt Street, working closely with fellow Corkonians Gearóid O'Sullivan ('George'), Diarmuid O'Hegarty, the Secretary to the Ministry, and his trusty office manager, Joe O'Reilly. On 9 May Collins treated the Dáil to a wide-ranging deprecation of the financial injustices of the union. Drawing on the report of the Childers' Commission of 1896 and some unclear arithmetic, he told a suitably indignant Dáil that Ireland was overtaxed by £290m between the abolition of the Irish exchequer in 1817 and 1893; by £50m between 1894 and 1913; and by £50m during the Great War. In addition, he accused the British of draining the country of £1,000m in capital, destroying industries and banishing millions of the population.[6]

That summer Collins established a Finance Committee of the Dáil, whose purpose was to establish the machinery to issue the Loan and collect subscriptions. However, as the Loan was being issued, there were some disagreement with De Valera as to when interest would be paid. De Valera noted with alarm that on the American issue the date from which interest was payable would be from the day on which the certificate was fully paid. He proposed payment from the date of recognition and evacuation, and took measures to ensure that would be the case for foreign issues. However, Collins, having consulted Griffith, reiterated his intention to pay from the date of payment, and recommended against differences in the American terms which would result in unfavourable Irish terms.[7] In early October Collins issued the following guidelines to organisers:

> The mode of procedure in starting work, and developing the necessary organisation, has been in the first instance to call a conference of the prominent supporters of the constituency. As already explained, this conference should not be confined to those who are active members of the Sinn Féin clubs, but an endeavour should be made to secure the services of supporters who may not, up to the present, have taken an active part. It is of the utmost importance that this particular point should not be overlooked. In places where most satisfactory

results have been obtained, a good deal of money has been forthcoming from people who have not hitherto subscribed to Sinn Féin at all.[8]

Constituencies were divided into six categories: letters were sent to deputies who were available; the Cómhairle Ceanntair undertook the work on behalf of deputies imprisoned; in constituencies where the Sinn Féin candidate had withdrawn at the 1918 election that person acted as an elected deputy. There was no rule for defeated candidates, but if large support existed they acted as in the latter case. Within this general framework Collins intended that:

> once preliminary meetings are notified the work must go ahead rapidly. It will be essential to get on with a rush. The Finance Committee will issue for distribution several leaflets explaining the intention of the Loan, the need for the money, etc. A big advertising campaign will be indulged in, and it is hoped to secure the assistance of *all* the Irish Ireland organisations in the undertaking. It is, however, not feasible to go with the main public advertising until we have a sufficient number of copies of the prospectus delivered to meet our requirements. Deputies will understand that the print of the prospectus was a large and extremely difficult undertaking. The Finance Committee decided to get 250,000 copies, and it is hoped to secure delivery of these during the next three weeks. When these have been delivered the general advertising will be started at once. The *type* of advertising will of course largely depend on the actions of the British censorship towards our notices. It is to be expected that the interference will be considerable, hence the great need for increased individual effort on the part of all members of An Dáil.[9]

Also, the Finance Committee asked all Sinn Féin cumainn to explore possible trading arrangements with any existing bank, and establish the amount available for the establishment of a co-operative bank.[10] In addition, four constituency organisers were appointed: E. Flemming for Leinster, E. Donnelly for Ulster, P. Ryan for Connaught and P. C. O'Mahony for Munster. They were empowered to appoint sub-organisers if it was deemed necessary.[11] And it was necessary. Some time after October 1919 Collins had to take over the work of the Finance Committee himself. The four provincial organisers were paid directly by Finance at a total cost of £30 per week, as were the forty-three (rising to a maximum of forty-seven) sub-organisers, whose total cost was £172 weekly.[12] It was exasperating for Collins to see such disorganised activity, and occasionally he vented his anger. On 19 April 1920, for example, Collins wrote to

Boland that 'this enterprise will certainly break my heart if any thing ever will. I never imagined there was so much cowardice, dishonesty, hedging, insincerity and meanness in the world, as my experience in connection with this work has revealed.'[13]

Nevertheless, the work did get on with a rush. Advertisements told the public that:

> The proceeds of the loan will be used for propagating the Irish case all over the world; for establishing in foreign countries Consular Services to promote Irish Trade and Commerce; for developing and encouraging Irish Sea Fisheries; for developing and encouraging the re-afforestation of the country; for developing and encouraging Irish industrial effort; for establishing a National Civil Service; for establishing National Arbitration Courts; for the establishment of a Land Mortgage Bank, with a view to re-occupancy of untenanted lands, and generally for national purposes.[14]

Similar advertisements were placed in the *Cork Examiner* and twenty-two separatist and provincial weeklies. They were duly suppressed. This proved the greatest advertisement of all for the Loan. Still, Collins had risked his anonymity by appearing briefly in a film promoting the Loan, made for £600 by the Irish Film Company and given cinema screenings across the country by 'forceful young men'.[15]

Apart from newspaper suppression the further difficulties encountered in organising the Loan were enormous. The Dáil was suppressed on 11 September 1919 and the following day 6 Harcourt Street was raided, along with searches throughout the country. Collins bluffed his way out of the office and escaped through the skylight to the roof of the Ivanhoe Hotel. However, the Assistant Secretary of Sinn Féin, Pádraig O'Keefe and Ernest Blythe were arrested. The raid prompted Collins to secure another premises and, with the Ministry's sanction, Batt O'Connor, a builder, purchased 76 Harcourt Street in his own name. O'Connor built a secret closet into the walls which secured important documents for the staff. In addition, he provided an escape route for Collins through the skylight which, by arrangement with the 'Boots' in the Standard Hotel two doors away, provided an effective exit.[16] It was, however, necessary for Collins to occupy a number of premises to avoid detection by the authorities. Recent estimates suggest that Sinn Féin used eighty-five different addresses in Dublin to conduct government business, and the Finance Department operated, at various times, out of ten different premises.[17] Under different guises, Collins worked from 21 and 22 Henry Street (after Harcourt Street, the principal office until its discovery just before the Truce), and from 29 Mary Street and 3 St Andrew Street.

It was also necessary to devise guises to protect the Loan bank accounts. Thus funds were lodged in individuals' names, such as George Nesbitt, Mrs MacGarry, Patrick Corrigan and Richard Tynan, whose shop at 5 Wexford Street was used as a clearing house for money and literature. Outside of Dublin there were further difficulties, not just with collection but also the transmission of funds to head office. In some cases bank managers co-operated, allowing Loan deposits in their banks which were forwarded as drafts to Dublin branches and collected by Collins' agents. Failing this, monies were secretly brought to Dublin by trusted couriers.[18] In Dublin, for example, Seán McGrath (known as *Bainc ar Suibhall*) carried the wages to employees scattered about the city. Again, Dáithí Ó Donnchadha carried thousands of pounds on him about the city and escaped detection.[19] In fact he was so indispensable that Collins wanted-ed to raise his salary to £500 (on a par with a cabinet minister) since he bore 'much responsibility'.[20]

The difficulties of organising the Loan on the ground were equally enormous. Possession of Loan literature, ranging from leaflets to lists of subscribers, could result in imprisonment, as Alex MacCabe discovered having advocated the Loan in public. On 2 October 1919 Terence MacSwiney reported from the Mid Cork constituency that the 'police are causing us much trouble'. The same day, from Macroom, he reported a 'narrow shave yesterday – armed police held me up & searched bag – got nothing'. Later, on 21 October, he told Collins that they needed 5,000 more copies of the prospectus for house to house canvassing. They relied on volunteers for distribution and chose a particular night for the simultaneous distribution throughout the whole constituency.[21]

The British authorities in Ireland began concerted efforts to counter-act Sinn Féin and undermine the Loan in the spring of 1920. From 23 February Dublin was placed under curfew and nationwide raids began. More particularly, Alan Bell, RM, was appointed to investigate the hidden bank accounts of the Loan. Bell had successfully tracked down Land League accounts earlier and his ongoing investigations led to summonses served on Munster and Leinster and Hibernian Bank officials to attend hearings commencing at

Dublin Castle from 8 March 1920. Collins also took action. On 26 March Bell was taken from a crowded tram in Dublin and shot by members of the 'Squad'. This action proved decisive. In late June Collins reported to the Dáil that the bank accounts were 'perfectly safe as the non-success of the bank inquiry will assure you all'. In total they had lost only £100 in interest on account of the inquiry, but they 'need not regret that now'.[22] However that October Richard Mulcahy was not so fortunate. He was captured with incriminating papers by the head of British intelligence in Ireland, Ormonde Winter. Mark Sturgis, an Assistant Under Secretary in Dublin Castle, recorded in his diary that 'O … had been pinching M. C.'s "war chest" from the Munster and Leinster Bank – quite illegally I expect – brought in about £4,000. £15,000 more to come.'[23] This prediction was in fact accurate as the audited accounts indicate that £18,732 was seized in the second half of 1920.[24]

In the event, the Loan was an outstanding success, though contributions came in slowly at first. By 31 October 1919 the sum of £10,160 had been received at head office in 76 Harcourt Street. However, by the end of April 1920, an additional £144,598 had been received, and this was followed by a major rush in May which, by 24 June, netted another £126,816, thus exceeding the target by June 1920.[25] Collins then moved that the Loan be closed on 17 July to ensure order for future issues, and while a further Loan of over £5m was mooted in August 1921, it fell foul of the Treaty split.[26] The final total when the Loan closed was in excess of £370,000 on the Irish issue, and upwards of £500,000 when American funds sent to Ireland were included (the regional contributions can be seen in cumulative form in the table across). The most striking feature of the Loan remains the phenomenal success in Munster, which contributed almost as much as all other provinces combined. In Munster itself the strongest support was in Limerick, where in excess of £50,000 was forwarded to head office. Apart from these funds Collins also built up a gold reserve which totalled £25,000, part of which was buried in a child's coffin beneath Batt O'Connor's house, and part of which fell into republican hands after the Treaty.

First National Loan: Regional Contributions, June–September 1920

Region	June 1920 £	August 1920 £	September 1920 £
Connaught	41,767	54,755	57,797
Munster	120,005	165,897	171,177
Leinster	76,171	85,822	87,444
Ulster	32,731	39,673	41,297
Britain and France	10,388	11,457	11,647
Cumann na mBan	710		801
Totals	*281,772*	*357,604*	*370,163*

Sources: NAI DE 2/7, Finance Reports, June 1920, August 1920, September 1920.

The Self Determination Fund did not enjoy such success. Then again, it was by nature a different fund; contributions were straightforward donations which, unlike the Loan, did not involve obligations of repayment – however unlikely repayment by an Irish Republic appeared in 1919. By 31 October 1919 the Fund had accumulated £42,054, though this total included £22,607 received from America. Thereafter donations slackened. The cumulative total by 24 June 1920 had risen to £55,770, and this figure only rose by £3 in Collins' report for August.[27]

As Finance secretary, Collins financed the business of government not the actual war effort, which was Brugha's responsibility. With limited funds he organised an administration accordingly. Expenditure from the Loan and Self Determination Fund by October 1919 was just over £30,000. By the end of June 1920, a further £67,000 had been spent. However, his estimated requirement for thirteen departments and contingencies for the following half-year was in excess of £262,000.[28] The requirements for the first half of 1921 were originally estimated at £185,900, but when expenditure of £261,500 was voted Collins queried the status of the American funds. De Valera felt Collins was 'not taking too rosy a view of affairs in America', which was little consolation as the government faced a deficit of £14,000 for that half-year.[29] Financial affairs were less troublesome after the Truce, and in August 1921 Collins moved an estimate of £144,000 for the second half of the year. Collins Duties

Apart from Finance, Collins also held three other important military positions: Adjutant-General, Director of Intelligence and Director of Organisation. He conducted his military duties from offices in Bachelors Walk and Cullenswood House, Ranelagh, while his covert Brotherhood operations were directed through verbal instructions from secret locations, usually 'Joint no. 3' (Vaughan's Hotel). Because Collins was extremely well organised and efficient, he was unwilling to allow social activities impinge on his work. In January 1920, for example, as the head of the London office, Art O'Brien, was visiting Dublin, Collins advised him that 'I am so busy at present that a few hours away from my work on an ordinary day means a serious upset to me.' If O'Brien came over, Collins would prefer to see him on Sunday rather than Monday.[30] His work in Finance extended to sorting out difficulties between Gavan Duffy and Seán T. O'Kelly in Paris, and sending a typist to London to work for Art O'Brien. The actual value of a typist could not be underestimated in Collins' mind. After all, much of his intelligence was gathered from such sources, like Ned Broy in New Brunswick Street. Thus personnel decisions could not be left to chance.

Collins' high standards of efficiency were not always matched by his colleagues and occasionally led to confrontation. He famously chastised Austin Stack with the rebuke: 'Your department, Austin, is nothing but a bloody joke'.[31] Collins also clashed with Darrell Figgis over the progress of the National Commission on the Resources and Industries of Ireland. The problem for Collins was the poor return on investment in terms of reports. He wanted immediate results and threatened 'to do in one year what the commission was going to take five years to do'.[32] Figgis appears to have repaid the criticism in early 1922 by suggesting that since the Provisional Government was administrative, it was unnecessary to have a Finance Minister.[33] In December 1920 Collins, anticipating requests for further funding, warned Griffith that the Dáil 'will make an awful "rumpus" if we give them this further amount – at any rate until more results are shown'. Even after responsibility for the commission was transferred to the Director of Trade and Commerce, Ernest Blythe, the problems persisted. In May 1921 the Dáil ordered the commission to report that October, but the deadline extended into 1922 when eight reports were published. More serious, however, were the differences with Brugha which culminated in the acrimonious exchange during the Treaty debate. As Defence Minister, Brugha was Collins' superior in military operations, and he resented the manner in which supplies were appropriated by Collins for the IRB.[34] Relations deteriorated during De Valera's absence, especially when Collins briefly replaced Griffith as Acting President of the Dáil. Then, during De Valera's first Dáil attendance after his return, Brugha openly reproached Collins over the presentation of the Defence accounts.[35] That March Brugha questioned irregularities in the accounts relating to efforts to import arms from Glasgow.[36] In all events, Brugha suspected that Collins was diverting supplies from the Defence budget and other funding to IRB-controlled operations.

Such were Collins' divided loyalties that, at the same time, he sought improved financial procedures. From 18 June 1919 he began to field Dáil questions on all financial matters, even those relating to the salaries and costs of the Ministry or specific departments. It was indicative, too, of his standing amongst deputies that most of these questions were addressed to him.[37] At the same time he worked in tandem with Griffith towards the establishment of an Income Tax Department, even though major problems were foreseen. They acknowledged that very few Sinn Féin supporters were liable for income tax, while efforts to deny the British revenues from customs and excise, through a boycott of goods, would impact on Irish trade.[38] Nevertheless, on 29 June 1920 Collins moved that a 'Department for the collection of income tax be instituted', and persons paying to that body who would otherwise pay to the British be exempted from losses.[39] Thus, in his report to the Dáil that August, he stated that the proposal would go ahead, though the position in relation to another proposal, auctioneers' licenses, was not yet clarified.[40] That October the Ministry approved the measure and recommended that income tax be levied at the rate of 60% of the British assessment up to £500, and at 75% above £500.[41] On 8 March 1921, however, the Ministry conceded that income tax was 'impossible to collect in present circumstances. Possible to instruct income taxpayers not to pay and hold for Republican government.'[42]

Collins was more successful in imposing stricter financial procedures on Ministry and Dáil business. In August 1919 he secured the appointment of an auditor of the Loan accounts, Donal O'Connor, and thereafter fully audited half-yearly statements appeared with the Finance reports.[43] On 27 February 1920 Collins put the resolution that 'the passing of money payments be the first business taken up at ministry meetings (such payments arising only out of previous decisions)'.[44] Again, mindful of the time constraints on Dáil meetings, he asked deputies from June 1920 to consult with him after reading the written reports rather than occupy the meetings with routine questions.[45] Also in June 1920 Collins sought, and secured, the appointment of an Accountant General to the Finance Ministry who would have 'charge of all accounts' except Defence.[46] In his report to the Dáil Collins proposed

> to make each department of the Dáil self-contained in so far as accounts are concerned. All payments on behalf of a particular department being made by that department in a form and manner prescribed by the accountant general. The accounts of the department to be audited monthly by him, and the books and vouchers kept as laid down by him on a general scheme. The value of this would be uniformity and constant check. The report ... would show exactly the financial position of all departments, the outgoings and receipts, the amount being spent, and the return if any; by a general co-ordination all books and accounts expenses would be saved and, by paying a first class man, all expenditure will be regularised and placed upon a business basis. The accountant general would institute a scheme under which an order in writing by the persons responsible in each department would be supplied for any goods received, and would also ensure regular payment of bills due, which I regret to say is not the case at present in some departments.[47]

George McGrath, who had worked with Collins in Craig's, was duly appointed, and he later became Comptroller and Auditor General of the Free State.

Collins' preoccupation with financial procedures continued into 1921. That January he urged De Valera to adopt measures quite similar to the later practice of the Vote on Account. At the end of each month he wanted an estimate sent from each Department to Finance stating the amount required to carry on the following month. It would be accompanied by a statement of expenditure for the previous month, and an indication of the balance, if any existed. Departmental receipts would not be spent by individual departments but credited to the account of the trustees – in effect, an attempt to establish a Consolidated Fund for the government.[48] That August, however, Collins rejected proposals to establish an Estimates Committee. He argued that since all figures were based on the previous half-year, and checked by Finance, such a committee would not have an adequate knowledge of the workings of various departments to operate feasibly.[49] This was, in fact, a remarkably astute observation as these were the precise reasons why the existing Estimates Committee at Westminster was failing in practice.[50] Again, after the Truce, Collins was worried about deputies' associations with various nebulous financial schemes. He secured Dáil approval for the appointment of a Registrar/Supervisor of Societies, arguing that 'we are starting now what is a new order in Ireland and one of the first duties of the National Government is to secure that thrifty people shall not be deprived of their savings by any kind of scheme, or any kind of society, or group of individuals'. De Valera shared this concern and requested that deputies should not involve their names with investment schemes. Collins' personal distaste with developments registered with his private comment that 'I never did allow my name to forward for any such and never intend to'.[51]

Yet, for all of this professionalism, there was a brief period during the Treaty negotiations when Irish inexperience of public finance was exposed. It was one thing for Collins to deprecate the financial injustices of the Union before the Dáil, it was a more difficult task to sit down with the British and disentangle the complexities of Anglo-Irish financial relations. Thus, in October 1921, the inexperienced Irish delegation faced a formidable team of British politicians and Treasury officials. To balance the sides, Patrick McGilligan, Private Secretary to the Local Government Minister, Kevin O' Higgins, suggested they approach Joseph Brennan, a former classmate in Clongowes who was then prominent in the castle's financial administration. It bears testimony to Collins' persuasive powers that having met for a couple of hours around 21 October, Brennan agreed to assist the delegation. Working secretly by night, he personally typed 8 full memoranda and 2 statements, all untraceable to him, which saved the Irish delegation from accepting unnecessary liabilities and facilitated deferral of major settlements.[52] Brennan, a future Department Secretary at Finance and Governor of the Central Bank, worked closely with Collins in an official capacity the following year when he was called upon to establish the Irish Exchequer.

Brennan's interpretation of the Treaty suggested that the Free State would 'enjoy the fullest financial autonomy. It will have power to establish and maintain its own exchequer, to impose and collect its own taxes of whatsoever description, and to appropriate its own revenue and regulate its own currency.'[53] This freedom was not immediately available as Collins entered an entirely new phase as Minister for Finance after the formation of the Provisional Government on 16 January 1922. He dominated proceedings, as the cabinet minutes simply record that 'Mr Collins indicated that he would take charge of the finance arrangements and that Mr Cosgrave would be associated with him.'[54] The new government immediately issued a proclamation stating that there would be no alteration of the status quo without its approval. But Collins became less involved in the day to day running of Finance and increasingly preoccupied with questions of general policy. His official duties dictated that he should oversee the transfer of administrative powers to the Free State, and this involved co-ordination of activities with the Treasury (Ireland), the Northern Ireland parliament and the British government.

However, the British believed that both Collins and Griffith displayed 'remarkable misunderstanding' of the powers of the Provisional Government. According to Sir Robert Horne, the British Chancellor of the Exchequer, they were under the impression that the Provisional Government could engage in spending not authorised by the British cabinet. In fact, the Comptroller and Auditor General could not provide funds for any purposes other than those provided for in the votes.[55] Nevertheless, on 1 April Collins and Churchill agreed that the transfer of functions of most departments should take place, excepting six which were held over either for administrative reasons, out of deference to Belfast's interests or to provide constitutional safeguards for Britain.[56]

At the same time Collins restricted the work of the Treasury (Ireland) under the direction of A. P. Waterfield through the proclamation of 16 January, effectively bringing to a halt all the machinery at the heart of the administrative transition under the Government of Ireland Act, 1920. Communications with Collins were only re-activated after the appointment of William O'Brien, formerly Inspector of Taxes, as Secretary of the Finance Ministry, an appointment not officially acknowledged by Collins until 7 February.[57] These communications notwithstanding, the Provisional Government's position hardened against co-operation with the decision, three days after O'Brien's appointment, that in relation to allocations of staffs for Northern Ireland 'no facilities are to be given'.[58] In May, Collins placed an embargo on all communications with Treasury (Ireland) unless they were cleared by his department. He had in fact moved to a reserved position which shortly became clear to the British. Constitutionally, Collins came to view Northern Ireland as a parliament subordinate to the United Kingdom, and potentially to the

Free State, and as such it was unnecessary to include Northern Ireland in negotiations which were essentially between two superior parliaments. This line of administrative obstruction took the place of a military attack on the north that Collins was no longer in a position to launch. That same month he advised the cabinet that

> it is most desirable for general administrative purposes that you should get the advice of good experts on the exact powers and limitations of the Northern Parliament in the British act of 1920. These should be studied carefully and your experts should prepare for you whatever statements are necessary explaining and simplifying these powers and limitations.[59]

Furthermore, they should guard against the north extending its powers and prepare plans in every way to make it impossible for the north to carry on. There was, however, limited success in these plans; only agriculture and education proved obstructionist.

It was in May, too, that Collins realised the financial implications of independence. The sum of £50m in taxation attributable to the whole of Ireland in 1919–20 was no longer realisable. A rough budget estimate in May 1922 anticipated a deficit of about £10m. Expenditure stood at £30m, while revenue was unlikely to raise more than £20m. A treasury official on Loan, T. K. Bewley, warned William O'Brien that there was 'no surplus on which to draw', and 'every new penny of expenditure is an addition to a loss.'[60] There was no recourse to further tax increases either as the Free State was bound by the Transfer of Functions Agreements to remain within the fixed spending guidelines of the 1922 British Finance Act. In the circumstances, Collins had little scope to manoeuvre. In mid-May, he asked each Minister to prepare a summary of the work of their departments with an outline of the policy to be adopted after the elections, including reforms, economies extensions and improvements. In addition, Collins deemed it 'essential' that each department became 'Irish', and Ministers were to make alterations accordingly.[61] Time was, however, running against Collins, and the distraction of the political situation meant he devoted less time to finance and more to military duties.

There was an ironic element to Collins' ill-fated final trip to Cork, for he was now the hunted-turned-hunter, forced at times to employ against his former comrades the same methods the British had used against the Loan. Republicans required money and, more importantly, information as to where and how existing funds were controlled. It was then ominous, but hardly surprising, that Collins' private office was raided and important documents taken a week after the signing of the Treaty. He was certain it was not the work of the British and wryly asked the Dáil: 'Is there any member here who accepts responsibility for that raid?'[62] More alarming for the Provisional Government, however, were reports from John Devoy in March 1922 to the effect that De Valera had withdrawn $250,000 from American banks the previous January – most likely, as Collins surmised, under power of attorney.[63] Later, in July, the Provisional Government faced a particularly disturbing but by no means unique situation in Cork where republicans appeared to manipulate certain banks, bank accounts and government officials to their advantage. The government proceeded to regularise the situation and even after Collins left the cabinet to become Commander-in-Chief on 12 July, he remained interested in the bank controversy in Cork.

His successor in Finance, William T. Cosgrave, corresponded regularly with Collins on the Cork situation. On 17 July Collins arranged that Cosgrave would lead cabinet discussions on the possibility of closing the Cork banks. The following day, the cabinet considered Bank of Ireland reports concerning the situation in the south. On 24 July Cosgrave met the governor of the Bank of Ireland, who conceded that Cork bank closures were inevitable and warned that a sum of £80,000 silver bullion in the Provincial Bank of Ireland in Cork was in danger. Further cabinet discussions aimed at closing the banks were inconclusive, and on 27 July the government agreed to defer closures but asked all the banks to withdraw facilities for negotiable instruments in Cork.[64] The real thrust of the cabinet's intent is, however, clear from Diarmuid O'Hegarty's (Secretary to the Provisional Government) request to the Irish Banks' Standing Committee on 5 August. Pointing out that stolen money was hidden in existing or fictitious account names, O'Hegarty sought the committee's assistance in recovering it, recommending inquiries be undertaken by 'Officers of mature discretion who might be relied upon to regard all information obtained as strictly confidential.'[65]

Collins pursued the issue directly in Cork and, on the day before his death, he received two telegrams at the Imperial Hotel from H. A. Pelly, the Manager of the Hibernian Bank. Pelly advised Collins to inspect all Bank of Ireland paid vouchers on the Customs Account in connection with the anti-Treatyites, and all paid cheques signed by S. MacSweeny. He also advised inspection of the Provincial Bank records and Land Bank records of all paid cheques drawn by parties 'whose names were furnished to Mr Brennan'. Furthermore, Pelly confided that £10,000 had been lodged in the Munster and Leinster Bank by the Land Bank, in their own name, and withdrawn a few days later. As the deposit consisted of a cheque for £10,000 drawn by S. MacSweeny in the Bank of Ireland Pelly contended that 'some explanation should be forthcoming as to what was done eventually with the proceeds of this deposit.' This was particularly questionable since Pelly could not see how the Land Bank could have issued two drafts for £5,000 in the first instance.[66] Collins received the information with uncharacteristic puzzlement. Questions lay in his mind also about the safety of payments from the local breweries, Beamish and Murphy's, as well as the County Council. In the end circumstances dictated that he would never resolve these issues.

In overall terms, Collins' performance in Finance was outstanding by any criteria. The successful organisation of the Loan in the face of the authorities' specific counter-measures established Collins as a force to be reckoned with. His unrivalled reports to the Dáil were accurate, concise and bore the imprimatur of a professional, which was remarkable given the circumstances of their production. His innovative nature and concern for procedures established useful guidelines for future administrations. Collins' personal organisation skills were exceptional, allowing him to hold four major positions simultaneously, prompting him to impose order and clarity on a world of disorder and confusion. If his unexpected death robbed the state of its most capable administrator, it also denies the historian the opportunity to compare him with his successors in Finance. For the circumstances of his tenure were unique as he presided over a department in a constant state of transition from uncertain, even humble, origins to the most powerful bureaucracy in the Free State. And all the while Collins was denied the power to raise revenue, that most basic power of his successors, as he strove to organise an administration. Yet, even if Collins was unlikely to have remained in Finance had circumstances been different, his record there marks him out as arguably Ireland's most distinguished Finance Minister.

Collins and Intelligence
1919-1923
FROM BROTHERHOOD TO BUREAUCRACY

Eunan O'Halpin

Michael Collins' unique contribution as Director of Intelligence in establishing and controlling the republican intelligence effort during the War of Independence quickly became part of popular memory. The guile, the impudence and the ruthlessness of the 'Big Fellow' in orchestrating the secret war against the crown in Dublin made him a living legend within the IRA as well as amongst the wider nationalist community. Yet, as often happens with covert activities where written records are scant and where the key figures lived a clandestine life, the nature and the achievements of that effort have frequently been misinterpreted or distorted. It is a measure of Collins' own grasp of intelligence and wider military realities that throughout his time as Director of Intelligence, Chairman of the Provisional Government and Commander-in-Chief of the National Army he appears never to have subscribed to the mythology which already attached to his name and achievements.[1]

This essay examines some of the difficulties which arose in the sphere of intelligence organisation and operations in the years immediately before and after the Truce. Up to the time of his death Collins exercised a crucial influence on intelligence matters. When he turned most of his attentions to wider political, administrative and military affairs, intelligence was initially run by his closest lieutenants. Despite their reverence for him, a combination of circumstances ensured that, from being the cornerstone of the war against the British, within months of the Truce intelligence organisation and work was wreathed in confusion which was not finally dispelled until the spring of 1923, while the coterie of Collins men became a millstone around the neck of the new state after his death. The explanation lies largely in the difficulties inherent in transforming what was essentially a brotherhood held together by personal loyalty to Collins into one subordinate element in a conventional national army. In that it reflects the wider problems of transition which Tom Garvin has described, as the structure and ethos of the 'Public Band' was gradually supplanted by the altogether more formal organisational apparatus of a new democratic state.[2]

THE CHARACTERISTICS WHICH MARK COLLINS out as a remarkably successful Director of Intelligence during the War of Independence include his evident appreciation of the importance of the collection and assessment of information as primary elements of intelligence operations which should precede action; his partial penetration of his adversary's own intelligence system; the efficiency and ruthlessness with which action based on good intelligence was taken; and his success in preserving the security and efficiency of his own organisation both in Dublin and in Britain despite the pressures it operated under because of the constant threat of raids, arrests and the capture of documents.

These achievements have been extensively documented. They include the securing of well placed informants within the DMP, the RIC, and most government departments in Dublin; the development of extensive arms purchasing and smuggling organisations in Britain and the United States; the penetration of the postal, telephone and telegraph systems from 1917 onwards, which enabled a high degree of covert access to government communications; the accurate delineation of the government's own police and military intelligence systems; and, not least, the maintenance of a very high degree of security in respect not only of his own activities but of his many informants, despite the various seizures of IRA documents which took place in 1920 and 1921.[3]

Collins' achievements are all the more remarkable for the fact that intelligence was only one of the hats which he wore, since for most of his time as director he was simultaneously also a very active Minister for Finance, President of the IRB, and *de facto* arms' supplier in chief because of his control of gun-running. Furthermore, while notionally subordinate to the Chief-of-Staff Richard Mulcahy, whose efforts to bring some central direction and coherence to IRA activities in the field have only been clearly described in recent years, it is well known that he frequently involved himself in the active direction of operations in various parts of the country, and most of the fighting men undoubtedly regarded him as their military leader. In the words of one officer Collins 'in pre-Truce days was … the Commander-in-Chief and the man. He was everything … Anybody knows that.'[4]

Most of the activities over which Collins exercised sole and uncontested control as Director of Intelligence during the War of Independence appear to come under four broad headings: field or military intelligence, counter-intelligence, assassinations and arms' procurement. All four were necessarily clandestine, and all four depended on disciplined and trustworthy groups of people capable of following orders and keeping their mouths shut. Strictly speaking, however, only military intelligence and counter-intelligence should be termed intelligence functions. Arms' procurement was a separate operation involving purchasing and smuggling networks abroad and in Irish ports, while the difference between intelligence proper and assassination was marked at an organisational level in 1919 with the creation of the 'Squad' as a unit of gunmen independent of the IRA headquarters' intelligence organisation but under Collins' direct control.[5]

Turning to the two functions which unarguably came within the remit of the intelligence organisation, that is military intelligence and counter-intelligence, it appears that, in the circumstances of 1919–21, the IRA headquarters' intelligence organisation could not contribute a great deal directly to the operational conduct of the war outside Dublin or to the evolution of strategy at headquarters level. The War of Independence was fought as a series of isolated local engagements, each planned and conducted with reference almost exclusively to local conditions. Operational intelligence, for example on police strength or on troop movements, was the responsibility of the local units who would use it. The quality of a local unit's information, where 'success or failure depended largely on the vision and energy of the responsible local officers' and on the willingness of the local population to play their part, was a reliable litmus test of its general efficiency. To quote Florence O'Donoghue, Collins 'would have been largely powerless outside Dublin, were it not for the work done in the local brigades.'[6] The 'regular and reasonably speedy exchange of information between the three Cork brigades and between each of them and the Director of Intelligence', which O'Donoghue recalled and for which he was largely responsible, was not matched in many other parts of the country.[7] Some areas remained inert despite the best efforts of Collins and of Mulcahy to galvanise them into action through the despatch of men such as Ernie O'Malley to knock local units into some sort of shape. Others with more active units were simply not in the habit of re-

porting general intelligence to Dublin, reserving their communications to headquarters for the more pressing business of pleading for
weapons and ammunition. Furthermore, it is clear that Collins' position as President of the IRB, and his commanding personality, were
of more significance than his formal intelligence responsibilities in
shaping his relations with officers in the field.

The influence which headquarters played in counter-intelligence operations was a quite different matter. Counter-intelligence,
that is the conduct of operations to detect and to thwart or manip-
ulate the activities of the enemy's intelligence organisation, was unequivocally the realm of intelligence activity in which Collins' headquarters organisation excelled.[8] In Todd Andrews' words, 'for the
first time in the history of separatism we Irish had a better intelligence service than the British … this was Michael Collins' great
achievement and it is one for which every Irishman should honour
his memory.'[9] It is no exaggeration to say that it was the decisive
element in the War of Independence. It compensated for the IRA's
material and numerical weaknesses; it usually protected the political
and military leadership of the independence movement from capture; and it enabled key elements of the underground Dáil administration, most importantly the Department of Local Government,
to function to surprising effect.[10]

The British seem never to have penetrated Collins' inner circle
of assistants and protectors in Dublin, perhaps because, for all his
ruthlessness towards enemy agents and informers, the security of
his system was based primarily not on fear but on trust. It has, however, recently been argued that Collins was at best a dupe of the
shadowy Andy Cope, the Joint Assistant Under Secretary appointed to Dublin Castle in May 1920 with a brief to open covert lines of
communication with the independence movement, and that Cope's
influence resulted in an unnecessary truce and a betrayal of the Republic in 1921. This claim is fantastic but, like all the best conspiracy
theories, it possesses its own internal logic, is invulnerable to contrary evidence, and should be left to its promoters to contemplate
and to refine.[11]

Collins' extraordinary administrative capacity enabled him not
only to retain control of diverse strands of the independence campaign, but to infuse each element with an activist spirit. Inevitably,
however, despite his own clear-headedness there were some blur-
ring of the lines between the different functions and operations

which he oversaw. An example is the assassination of the elderly magistrate Alan Bell, who was taken off a tram and shot dead in broad daylight in Ballsbridge in March 1920. Bell, a former RIC inspector, was involved in inquiries about separatist finance, which threatened to undo much of Collins' hard work as Dáil Minister for Finance in raising and hoarding the first public Loan. As his notebook and other documents show, however, Bell was also making enquiries into Volunteer organisation and operations in Dublin (including the failed assassination attempt on Lord French) for Basil Thomson's Directorate of Intelligence at Scotland Yard. Such enquiries posed a direct threat to the Volunteers' operational effectiveness; on 15 February he wrote that he had 'just got in touch with a party in a prominent position in the Dublin dockyard and am in hopes that some useful information may be obtained as I believe that it is a happy hunting ground for S[inn] F[éin]', and elsewhere he recorded other promising leads. In that sense, he was shot on each of two counts, although it is doubtful that his killers appreciated the subtlety of their dual mandate.[12]

Bloody Sunday is undoubtedly the single act of clandestine warfare with which Collins' organisation is associated. The operation to kill suspected British agents was, however, arguably more significant for its ramifications as a calculated political act, and for the atrocities which it provoked, than it was as the blow which marked the 'defeat of the police and the nullification of their intelligence service.'[13] There is a good deal of evidence to suggest that the coup slowed but did not reverse the cumulative build up of British military pressure on the independence movement. That was a consequence of the use of ever more draconian coercive measures under the Restoration of Order in Ireland Act and the introduction of martial law in the southern counties, as well as the gradual systematisation of the British intelligence effort after June 1920, not only through the influx of agents but by the centralisation and efficient collation of information. A few weeks after Bloody Sunday Mark Sturgis, a British official newly arrived in Dublin Castle, wrote that the head of the British combined intelligence services in Ireland, the colourful Brigadier Ormonde de l'Epée Winter or 'O' as he styled himself, would 'I'm sure ... regard peace now as a tragedy.' Sturgis, a shrewd observer of castle life, commented that the assassinations appeared to have dispelled the 'amateurish attitude' of intelligence officers of the type described by Florence O'Donoghue as those 'courageous men' travelling about in civilian clothes with a 'boy scout mentality' whom the Cork brigades encountered and dealt with, rather than to have cowed them into inactivity.[14] In his spirited though patently unreliable memoirs Winter also argued that intelligence gradually improved in the months between Bloody Sunday and the Truce, largely because 'the Irish had an irresistible habit of keeping documents' which were liable to be uncovered in raids.[15] Such seizures of documents not only revealed an uncomfortable amount about IRA organisation and operations, but also greatly hampered the work of Dáil Ministries.

Winter may be dismissed as a Micawberish figure, but there is other evidence to suggest that, despite personal rivalries and continuing inefficiencies, what might be termed the continuing bureaucratisation of intelligence slowly bore fruit after November 1920. The ability to detain indefinitely meant that the authorities could worry about problems of identification and arraignment long after people were swept up simply on suspicion. Some well informed military men on the Irish side, including the experienced intelligence operator Florence O'Donoghue, afterwards commented that cumulatively the British intelligence effort had strengthened rather than faltered in the year leading up to the Truce, and speculated that had Winter 'got sufficient support and facilities ... [he] would have made it very awkward for Irish intelligence and the whole organisation, military & civil.'[16] There may have been somewhat less emphasis placed on the collection of information by agents in the field after Bloody Sunday, particularly in Dublin, but that was only one highly risky and somewhat theatrical way of acquiring intelligence. The accumulation of material through the impersonal analysis, collation, cross-referencing and analysis of reports, photographs and captured documents undoubtedly yielded quite significant results in Dublin, despite Collins' spies in the castle.[17] As the capital remained, to quote the conclusions of a secret viceregal committee on intelligence in December 1919, 'the storm centre and mainspring ... [of] an organised conspiracy of murder, outrage and intimidation', increased British successes there bore heavily on the leadership of the independence movement.[18]

It is of course necessary not to over stress the argument about increased British intelligence effectiveness, as O'Donoghue's appraisal of a captured British weekly summary of events in the south in the spring of 1921 demonstrates.[19] On the other hand, the very large number of people killed as informers in County Cork between 1920 and 1923 – over 200 by one recent estimate – scarcely bespeaks either rock solid support for the IRA even in the rebel county, or IRA confidence that no one would betray them. The reality there was that the local IRA was impelled to or chose to resort to terror on a wide scale in order to discourage the passing of information to the British (and after the Treaty to Provisional Government forces), to settle local scores and to exact revenge on people considered pro-British in retaliation for the sufferings of northern nationalists – over seventy of those shot by the IRA as 'spies' were Protestants.[20]

A final aspect of Collins' approach to what might be termed preventative intelligence before the Treaty requires brief discussion. It has often been argued that, during the arduous Treaty negotiations in the autumn of 1921, he allowed himself to be distracted from his duty by the fleshpots and flattery on offer in London. It has also been claimed that one of the two secretaries of the Irish delegation, his protégé John Chartres, was a British spy. Two points need to be made here. Firstly, however raucous the parties, heavy the drinking or lewd the behaviour of members of the Irish delegation, there is no worthwhile evidence to indicate that any of them were in any way compromised by anything which they did during their sojourn in Hans Place. Secondly, on the basis of the quality of evidence adduced against Chartres – being English by birth, having served the British government in an information capacity during the war – any conspiracy theorist worth his salt could work up at least as good a case against Childers, another Englishman and one-time imperialist who had been decorated for gallantry early in the war and who had afterwards worked in naval intelligence.[21]

COLLINS' RECORD IN INTELLIGENCE MATTERS indicates that, in clandestine activities as in other areas of administration, he was a remarkably able man. As in other areas, however, after the Truce even his closest intelligence associates were unable to maintain the standards which he had set. The discipline and success which had characterised most of the intelligence and other covert operations directed by Collins during the War of Independence did not endure in the new circumstances of state formation.

When the Truce came into operation Collins' immediate concern appears to have been that the British might seek to steal a march by reorganising their intelligence services in Ireland in preparation for a resumption of hostilities, and the maintenance of vigilance against the British in the twenty-six counties remained his first intelligence priority until the Treaty was signed and ratified by the Dáil. His second priority was intelligence on political and military affairs in Northern Ireland, where nationalists were already suffering under the new Stormont regime and where there appeared to be possibilities for eventual action. It seems unlikely at this stage that he consciously set his people the task of monitoring political feeling within the independence movement, although he presumably kept his ear to the ground both through his intelligence network and through the IRB. Shortly after the Truce Collins established the plainclothes unit which soon became known as Oriel House, and subsequently was officially styled the Criminal Investigation Department or CID. Its initial functions were to provide protection for key figures in the independence movement, to monitor the covert intelligence activities of British military and civilian agencies, and to tackle armed crime in Dublin. Its activities subsequently expanded to include intelligence work against opponents of the Treaty and, notoriously, the suppression of the IRA in Dublin during the Civil War.

Oriel House was staffed largely by poachers turned gamekeepers, men who had worked in headquarters intelligence or in the 'Squad' during the War of Independence, together with a handful of DMP detectives who had taken pains to steer clear of any involvement in the investigation of political affairs during the War of Independence, or who had acted as informants for Collins and had so survived. It was run by officers personally loyal to Collins, although it adopted the form of a civilian detective bureau rather than a military organisation, its staff holding police ranks such as 'Detective Officer'. Confusingly, however, as an off-shoot of the pre-Truce IRA intelligence organisation, Oriel House also had links with the Intelligence Directorate of the National Army which Collins had begun to organise in January 1922.[12] In the new army, intelligence was also dominated by former members of the 'Squad' and others who, under Collins' direction, had 'carried out the most objectionable side of the pre-Truce operations', that is the killing of officials, intelligence officers, informers and collaborators. Experts in clandestine assassination, men of action who had lived on the edge since 1919, once hostilities were suspended they posed a serious problem for their chief. A colleague later commented that 'the very nature of their work' before the Truce 'had left them anything but normal ... if such a disease as shellshock existed in the IRA ... the first place to look for it would be amongst these men.'[23] They expected recognition for the risks they had run and the job they had done, and they assumed that this would come through senior postings in army intelligence. But as a group they were doers, not organisers or analysts, and they were unsuitable for the somewhat bureaucratic environment of a strictly military intelligence headquarters. This may explain why, under the Deputy Director of Intelligence Liam Tobin, a number were assigned to the more active milieu of Oriel House. But there the main job to be done was a police one, the investigation and suppression of the armed crime which had mushroomed in the lax conditions created by the Truce and the withdrawal to barracks of the British police and military forces. According to one army officer Tobin, who retained his army intelligence position despite his transfer to what appeared to be a civilian organisation, was initially given a vague brief to develop a national detective bureau: 'somebody mentioned Scotland Yard, and at the same time pointed to Oriel House, and beyond that I do not think any further instruction was given'. Although 'a genuine attempt was made to organise a kind of Scotland Yard ... there was no time to consider details and consequently interest was lost'.[24]

On the other hand David Neligan, a veteran of the DMP, Oriel House and military intelligence, and subsequently head of the Garda Special Branch from 1925 to 1933, stated in 1924 that from the start Tobin's group in Oriel House formed a separate 'military section ... to do with military intelligence', and said that they 'had not much to do in peace time'. Most of the active work fell to 'the CID section' who dealt with 'bank robbers, etc. They were armed police and were very necessary because the DMP were unarmed and the Republican Police were inefficient.'[25] The suspicion arises that Tobin's old intelligence hands were sent to Oriel House at least partly to keep them out of harm's way while the National Army was being formed.[26]

The Treaty split created a new situation and new dangers within the IRA. Who would be loyal to the new Provisional Government and who would be loyal to the Republic? What would those pledged to oppose the Treaty do? Where were dissidents gathering, where did they store their weapons, what War of Independence safe houses were they continuing to use? These were points on which an efficient domestic intelligence service with clear lines of responsibility might have cast some light. However in intelligence, as in everything else in post-Treaty Ireland, the organisation of a reliable service was bedevilled by politics, by inefficiency and by the unsuitability of some of those involved. Because of his success during the War of Independence, Collins placed a premium on good intelligence, and his principal lieutenants and most of his pre-Truce workers remained loyal to him. But, as rapidly became clear in the new army and in Oriel House, his former lieutenants had great difficulty adapting to the largely administrative work of building up an efficient state intelligence machine, either civil or military. One crucial result was that the Provisional Government was left surprisingly ill-informed about republican strength and intentions both before and after the occupation of the Four Courts.[27]

It was only when Collins, in the chaotic first weeks of the Civil War, turned his mind to the overall intelligence problem that the Provisional Government's intelligence efforts began to receive the direction required. On 8 August he complained that, contrary to a government decision, Oriel House was 'still nominally' an adjunct of the Army Intelligence Department. He ordered 'the removal of the military intelligence officers from it' and its transfer to civil control, evidently with the intention of making a functional distinction between political and military intelligence work.[28] This, however, did not dispose of the problem posed by his own people, whose work prior to the Truce had been mainly in the realms of counter-intelligence and of assassination rather than of straightforward military intelligence, and who were showing signs of unhappiness at their treatment. Yet action to improve army intelligence was sorely needed. This was stressed in a circular to all commands which outlined the duties of command intelligence officers, and observed that:

> intelligence has not for some time past been given the attention, thought and energy that is vitally necessary … there was never a time when a thoroughly efficient intelligence service was more vitally essential.

A week later Joe McGrath, the newly appointed Director of Intelligence, told Collins that the army's 'intelligence service is only being re-organised. So far no reports have been received from the commands'. The biggest difficulty was to 'get the officers to interest themselves in intelligence', presently 'looked upon with something like contempt. I find that both officers and men prefer to be more actively engaged than doing intelligence work'. An efficient service would, he believed, require 'the willing co-operation of the various staffs at GHQ and the ... commands'. Ironically, Ernie O'Malley had almost identical criticisms to make of the anti-Treaty IRA's approach to intelligence at that time. He complained to Liam Lynch that 'it was extremely difficult to get a good man in charge' as 'there is too much of the touting idea about intelligence ... and higher intelligence has been neglected.'[29]

The documentary indications are that within the newly formed National Army intelligence operations both before and during the Civil War, while largely in the hands of Collins' War of Independence lieutenants, were conducted mainly without reference to the lessons learned in the campaign against the British or to the mistakes which the British had made. It was said of those transferred back from Oriel House to army intelligence that 'whenever there was anything exciting or dangerous on ... these men were to be found in the thick of it'.[30] In contrast to the wait and watch approach adopted against the British between 1919 and 1921, army intelligence in Dublin became infected with a raiding mentality once the Civil War broke out. In other parts of the country intelligence appears to have operated largely as an adjunct to local commanders, with headquarters in Dublin frequently left in the dark about events. Dan Bryan later claimed that in the capital information 'simply poured in and was sent ... for action without any selection.' Instead of building up a coherent picture of their opponents' activities, organisation and intentions, time and again good information was vitiated by precipitate army action; 'as soon as any interesting bit of information came in' the officer running affairs in the Dublin area 'got the whole staff out and sent them out to raid about it.' This 'broke up entirely the investigative and collective [sic] side of the action.'[31] Bryan complained that the Civil War was almost over by the time that army intelligence headquarters began the systematic collation and analysis of the thousands of IRA documents seized, and he was particularly critical of what he termed the mishandling of local successes such as the discovery in early August of the IRA's plans to blow the main bridges around Dublin (a matter which seems to have come to light through an apparently minor tip-off from the wife of the manager of the Maypole Dairy in George's Street about the suspicious behaviour of a young employee). Bryan maintained that had the intelligence acquired through investigation of the tip-off been properly exploited, almost the entire Dublin IRA could have been captured and their support organisation destroyed.[32]

Despite his other pre-occupations as Commander-in-Chief, Collins continued to press for action to improve intelligence in the months before his death. His conception of how army intelligence should be organised and what it should do owed at least as much to his clandestine experience during the War of Independence as to conventional military thought. His instructions show that, whatever the nominal civil/military division of responsibility between Oriel House and the army, the army organisation he wanted would be concerned with political as well as with purely military intelligence, both inside and outside the state, and would also deal with counter-intelligence against British and northern unionist intelligence activities. It would be highly centralised and secure, with its own 'fully developed' communications system and codes. By these means the command intelligence officers would keep in constant independent touch with intelligence headquarters, and would not simply be the creatures of the command GOCs. As ever with Collins such plans were linked to the need for action. A fortnight before his death he told McGrath, then the Acting Director of Intelligence, to establish an 'intelligence system' in Northern Ireland, 'on the basis of one command for the entire area', gave orders to collect information on anti-Treatyites through well disposed Irish people in Britain, and said that telephone tapping should be organised with post office help, together with postal interception. He had in mind a range of suspect organisations and activities: 'We could start off with ... the prominent politicians, well-known Anti[-Treatyite]s, Bolshevics [sic]. Cumman [sic] Na mBan, I[rish] W[omen] W[orkers Union] etc.' A terse note to McGrath displays the familiar impatience and itch to set matters on the right track: 'are we receiving definite reports from Commandant Thornton ... When he does come to town I am anxious to see him' as it 'appears to me that he is not confining himself to the intelligence system in the command ... He must be instructed strictly in his own duties.'[33] Collins evidently realised that the penchant for action displayed by his former lieutenant Frank Thornton, along with other members of the pre-Truce intelligence organisation, was an impediment to effective intelligence work in the changed circumstances of open warfare, where the Provisional Government in Dublin was seeking to impose its authority throughout the country and therefore needed to be able to direct military and security operations effectively from the centre.

Despite his belligerent personality, one of the keys to Collins' astonishing success during the War of Independence had been precisely his ability to stay out of trouble time and again by walking the other way – he had appreciated that he was far more useful as an orchestrator of violence than as a gun-slinging foot soldier. It is ironic that at Béal na mBláth it was his evident unwillingness to be chased out of his own district by his own people, together with his physical courage and his relative lack of experience under fire, which led to his unnecessary death at the hands of men who still revered him. 'Stop! Jump out and we'll fight them' are scarcely the words of someone who had undergone the spiritual transformation from man of action to administrator which he recognised as necessary in his subordinates for the effective conduct both of intelligence work and of wider military operations in a new state.[34]

THE ORDERS WHICH COLLINS GAVE to improve intelligence in the last weeks of his life lend weight to the hypothesis that, had he lived, many of the army's intelligence difficulties during the Civil War would have been addressed and overcome. We can only speculate that firm direction and example from him, together with his continuing patronage and protection, might have wrought a change in the approach and outlook of his former associates. Instead, many of them became embittered with the new army and with their increasingly marginal place in it. This discontent was to culminate in the Army Mutiny of March 1924. Taking their lead from Liam Tobin they were particularly resentful of developments within intelligence headquarters, which by the end of the Civil War had finally been organised along rational administrative lines appropriate for a national agency, with a 'Director's Office', a 'Command Branch', a 'Secret Service Branch', a 'Finance Branch', a 'Cyphers Branch' and a 'Records Branch'. In July 1923 one disgruntled Tobinite complained to the Chief-of-Staff that, from being the hub of the struggle against British rule, intelligence had become largely 'a machine for putting together a number of files regarding a number of names'.[35] What better way to describe the necessary transition from underground brotherhood to national bureaucracy?

MICHAEL COLLINS

A MILITARY LEADER

PETER YOUNG

The investigation of Michael Collins as a military leader is an extremely difficult subject. While the many studies over the years have discussed Collins as an intelligence leader or as a politician or, for example, dealt with the circumstances of his death, his role as a military leader in its purest sense has never really been highlighted due to the intermingling of his various and, at times, conflicting roles. However Neil Jordan's film has now given his role as a military leader a standing that may need to be questioned.

A second major difficulty to be faced is that original source documentation originating from Collins in his purely military function is very scarce. With such exceptions as his papers as Director of Organisation or Emmet Dalton's Liaison Files in the Military Archives and what survives in such collections as Dick Mulcahy's, military documentation, particularly from the beginning of 1922 to his death in August, is incomplete due to the lack of a properly constituted, centralised reporting system, a system strongly advocated by Collins early in 1922.

A current definition of military leadership can be stated as 'the process of influencing and directing others to accomplish the mission by providing purpose, direction and motivation. Allied with leadership are the interrelated principles of command, the legal authority vested in an individual, and management, the process of co-ordinating and employing the resources of an organisation to achieve the desired aim.[1]

If one applies this definition to Collins and his work, it would appear at first glance to fit perfectly. Yes, he did influence and direct others and he did provide purpose, direction and motivation. However there are some observations that warrant discussion. For example, was he a military leader in the true sense or was it his personality and obvious charisma that created an illusion of military leadership?

On 1 February 1922 the first barracks was formally handed over by the British army to the fledgling forces of the Provisional Government. As this small unit, numbering forty-six men in all, marched past Collins on the steps of the City Hall on their way to Beggars Bush Barracks, it was an emotional moment. These men, led by Paddy O'Daly, were drawn from the Active Service Units of the Dublin Brigade. Consequently he knew them all personally and was later to depend greatly on them in the difficult days ahead. Yet of those forty-six, seven were later to fight for the anti-Treaty side, a development that was typical of the period.[2]

However his other responsibilities were to take precedence over military affairs for some months and it was left to others to shape the reconstituted army, though not without his influence and advice. The difficulties caused by the split in the IRA into pro- and anti-Treaty factions are well known and there is no need to underline them. However the foundations of the new army were not laid at this time but in the years beforehand. After 1916 the internment of so many, particularly in Frongoch, 'a Sinn Féin University' as it was described by Tim Healy in the House of Commons,[3] was a vital factor in the prosecution of the War of Independence, and indeed of the Civil War, that were to follow.

The internees were drawn from every county, with Dublin predominating. The continuous transfer of the leaders from camp to camp only succeeded in blooding another wave of potential leaders. Personalities such as 'Ginger' O'Connell, Terence MacSwiney, Michael Brennan, Tom MacCurtain and Dick Mulcahy, to mention just a few, came to prominence at this time. Friendships were created that were to have an enduring effect and the skeleton of an organisation was to evolve that was to form the foundation of the Irish Republican Army.

The IRB was also re-organised, Collins being one of those instrumental in this regard. After the internees were released, Collins' appointment as organiser of the Volunteer Dependants Fund, then to membership of the Volunteer Provisional Executive and also the IRB Supreme Council, combined with his obvious organisational skills and attention to detail, pushed him rapidly to the forefront of affairs. He began to epitomise the hard-working, decisive personality that was badly required at this critical stage.

Along with Dick Mulcahy, the Chief-of-Staff, Collins, as Director of Organisation, set up units around the country, insisted on weapons and tactical training, the procurement of weapons and proper administration. He compiled lists of officers and equipment from the affiliation forms he insisted upon being returned to him and slowly and methodically drew up a detailed picture of what was available. He insisted on uniformity in procedure and reporting and also tried to build up a logistical system without which operations could not succeed. In conjunction with this work, he was to lay the foundations of a communications network that was to have a major effect on his future intelligence operations.

So, prior to the War of Independence, the foundations of a military organisation had been established, largely through his influence and direction. As Professor O'Halpin has dealt with his intelligence operations, I only want to refer to two aspects. Firstly one of the main principles of warfare is 'know your enemy'. It is not an exaggeration to say that this was probably Collins' greatest contribution to this period. He knew where the strengths and weaknesses lay and acted accordingly. He also knew the strengths and weaknesses of his own side, another vital aspect of his leadership. His contacts with the local commanders were not peripheral. He knew them personally, from his work after 1916 and especially through the IRB.

Guerrilla warfare, by its very nature, is localised. Consequently local initiative is essential and so it proved with a complete imbalance of effectiveness from area to area. The role of GHQ, embodied in Mulcahy and Collins, came under severe criticism at times particularly from the active divisions but it, and they, were in an impossible position due to the nature of the war.

The antipathy of some of the local commanders to GHQ was later to have repercussions in the Civil War. The War of Independence was not a nationwide affair. With the exception of Munster and Dublin, the war tended to be sporadic in nature. Notwithstanding these observations, over 65,000 British troops, including Auxiliaries and Black and Tans, were required to keep order.

The main leadership problem facing Collins during the War of Independence was that while he did influence and direct others to accomplish the mission, he had not got the level of military command to do so. It was rather his charismatic nature and his reputation for decisiveness that led people to seek him out for assistance and advice. This, of course, led to difficulties with those who were by-passed. For example, the antagonism between the civil and military sides, as evidenced by the relationship between Collins and Brugha, did little to foster an atmosphere of unity. The role of the IRB further divided the civil and military sides and even within the military there were divisions as to its function, particularly among non-members. When asked to join the IRB, Roger McCorley in Belfast refused to do so as it totally weakened the principles of military leadership.[4] Many felt that Collins was interfering in areas that were their responsibility. His impatience, particularly with those he felt were slow to act, created enmities that were to endure. These leadership issues were not resolved by the Truce in July 1921, but merely held in abeyance.

As I have already said, GHQ had become unpopular in many areas during the War of Independence. Even their attempts to establish divisions – a perfectly logical military development – while eventually agreed to, led to much criticism, though much of this grew out of frustration with the limitations imposed by guerrilla warfare. Mulcahy, as Chief-of-Staff, bore the brunt of this criticism but it was aimed at Collins as well. Following the Truce GHQ attempted to exert more control over the various units. As it looked to many at this time, the period of guerrilla warfare was going to end and it was essential that a professional army was developed. This attempt resulted in some areas in only further alienating some of the local commanders. Liam Lynch, OC First Southern Division wrote to the Chief-of-Staff on 4 January 1922: 'Officers and men here realise that the Government, GHQ Staff and the Army in the rest of Ireland outside the Southern Divisions and the Dublin Brigade have outrageously let them down.'[5] Even in areas that had been relatively inactive resentment over criticism by GHQ also grew. There were also problems at local level. Personal animosities and jealousies were to play an important role in the reaction to the forthcoming Treaty.

Following the signing of the Treaty the military problems became exceptionally difficult. The speedy withdrawal of the British meant that many of the barracks were taken over by those who were later to fight on the anti-Treaty side. Large areas of the country were now held by such forces. It was obvious that a loyal army was essential if the Provisional Government was to survive but of course this could not be announced publicly as it would destroy the attempts being made to keep the army united.

The appointment of Eoin O'Duffy as Chief-of-Staff in November 1921, while somewhat bizarre as to method of selection, was welcomed by Collins. O'Duffy's organisational and administrative skills, to the surprise of many, laid a foundation that was to survive even through the Civil War. In his interview with me in 1981 Major Roger McCorley, then of the Belfast Brigade, had great praise for O'Duffy's work in this regard.[6] Later opinions formed by others and later actions by O'Duffy tend to overlook his vital contribution at this time.

The influence exerted by any leader can be seen in the selection of subordinates. Because of his involvement in the IRB and through his work on the Volunteer Executive, allied with his appointment as Director of Organisation, Collins was well placed to appoint his own people in vital positions. However it would be fair to say, from a command perspective, that Mulcahy, and probably to a lesser extent O'Duffy, would have had an important say in the selection of such people as Michael Brennan, John Prout, 'Ginger' O'Connell and Emmet Dalton, if only for the reason that Mulcahy and O'Duffy were in critical army appointments from the beginning of the War of Independence and were also involved full-time, as opposed to Collins who had to divide his time between political, financial and military duties. The fact that three of these four had foreign training, two in the American army and one in the British army, only served to underline the inexperience of what was available.

The selection of officers such as these was crucial in ensuring that the army was sufficiently well organised as to be able to successfully prosecute the Civil War when called upon to do so. However, in the months leading to the attack on the Four Courts, how much influence did Collins really exert? He was involved in post-Treaty negotiations with the British administration; as Chairman of the Provisional Government he was dealing with the day-to-day problems of running the government; and of course he was proceeding with secret operations in Northern Ireland. Even with his legendary attention to detail, and his obvious interest in the army, it was obviously beyond his capabilities to be as involved as much as he would have liked.

If one accepts Napoleon's cry of 'give me a lucky general anytime', there is no doubt that, from a military point of view, the Provisional Government was very lucky. For example, the reluctance of former comrades-in-arms to fight each other, especially underlined in Limerick in March, provided much-needed breathing space. Collins' previous relationships with many of those who now opposed him was an important factor in this aspect, particularly those in the IRB. His northern policy neutralised the northern divisions and confused those opposing him in the south. On the anti-Treaty side the lack of any concerted military policy dissipated their initial position of strength. Rory O'Connor's comments about a military dictatorship and efforts by the anti-Treaty forces to raise funds were public relations disasters. The decision by the British not to attack the Four Courts following Wilson's assassination was of vital importance to the Provisional Government because, had such an attack taken place, it would have put them in an impossible situation. Finally the kidnapping of 'Ginger' O'Connell was extremely fortunate in its timing.

Collins was also lucky in the calibre of the senior officers working for him at this time. He was particularly lucky in having Mulcahy on his side, a man who has never been given the prominence due to him. He was also very dependent on men like MacEoin and Brennan who did not let him down.

A proper military assessment of the decision to open fire on the Four Courts is difficult in the absence of contemporary documentation. While the political leaders regarded it as a necessity, the military commanders must have been in a quandary. Their forces were small, ill-trained, ill-equipped and not always reliable. Against that, they knew that their opponents were similarly disadvantaged. The hope that the anti-Treaty forces might draw back from open warfare, fostered by the government's decision to release Liam Lynch, was dashed at an early stage. The occupation and control of the capital city was essential and militarily possible, and it looks, from this remove, as if this was the primary objective of the attack. Once the position in Dublin was consolidated, attention could be paid to the rest of the country.

An interesting perspective on the days following the attack on the Four Courts and the attitudes of the opposing sides is provided by a hitherto unpublished account by a Mr J. F. Homan, a senior member of the St John's Ambulance Brigade, who took it on himself to try and arrange a ceasefire following the surrender of the Four Courts garrison. On Saturday 1 July he met Collins, who said:

> Tell these men that neither I, nor any member of the government, nor any officer in the army (and I learned the feeling of every officer in Dublin on my rounds yesterday) not one of us wishes to hurt a single one of them in any way that can be avoided. They, and their leaders, are at liberty to march out and go to their homes unmolested if only they will – I do not use the word surrender – if only they will deposit

their weapons in the National Armoury, there to remain until and unless in the whirl of politics these men become a majority in the country in which case they will have control of them.[7]

He then sought out Fr Albert who brought him to Robert Barton who told him:

> If we were to make peace today on the terms proposed by Mr Collins, the vast majority of the men would simply disregard us, select other leaders and continue the fight. The only proposal that Michael Collins could make that we would consider looking at, would be to come over and stand by our side and let us both fight England.

Not satisfied with this reaction, Homan sought out De Valera the following day and put Collins' proposal to him. They discussed the matter for one and a half hours and Homan recorded the main points of the discussion as follows:

> Mr de Valera described the difficulties created for him by the Treaty, his efforts to reconcile the opposing parties in the Dáil, the reasons for the two pacts and his disappointment at their results, the setting up of the Army Executive without his wishing it, his anxiety and his wishes for peace and for unity, his warning (which he declared his opponents were very wrong in describing as a threat) that the acceptance of the Treaty might involve the country in civil war, the unsatisfactory character of the proposed Constitution and his despair of amending it while his opponents had a majority which they were prepared to make subservient to English ministers, and finally his utter inability to prevent the present outbreak which he declared was begun by the Government in obedience to English ministers ... However he was anxious for an immediate peace. Coming at last to Mr Collins' terms, he described them as a distinct advance on what Mr Collins had said to the archbishop, when His Grace took to the government the proposal that the insurgents be allowed to march out with their arms in their hands. Mr Collins' answer, he said, was 'let them lay down their arms and then we will talk to them.' After much discussion, in the midst of which Mr de Valera left me for a while to consult the Brigadier [Traynor?], he told me he would be prepared to recommend to the insurgents, and was confident he could get them to agree, to go home, each man carrying his weapon with him.

The following day, Monday 3 July, Homan again met Collins. Collins considered De Valera's proposal to retain the arms unreasonable. Among his considerations in this regard were the following:

> the uselessness of trying to reason with the insurgents, the crimes that many of them had committed, the anarchy they had set out to achieve, the feeling on the part of the law-abiding population of Ireland, as well as the conviction of the friends of Ireland throughout the world, that if the government of Ireland failed to assert itself now it could never be trusted to do so, the danger of strengthening that feeling resulting in (a) the complete loss of world opinion, (b) the destruction of all hope of bringing in Ulster and (c) the return of the British. And all for what? To gratify the alleged sentimental desire of some desperadoes to retain in their hands the weapons which would enable them to hold up the government of the country any time they liked, and indulge in bloodshed, raids and anarchy.

Finally he said that permission for the fighting men to retain their weapons was not defensible.

A persistent man, Homan again sought out De Valera at the Hammam Hotel. De Valera was elsewhere and he eventually met Cathal Brugha. Homan describes the meeting:

> I was brief, he even briefer. 'Lay down our arms?' said he, 'never. We are out to achieve our object or to die. There is no use negotiating with Mr Collins. What exactly did Mr de Valera propose?' I told him. 'He could not carry the fighting men with him in that,' said Mr Brugha, 'the most they would agree to would be to leave this place with their arms and go and join our men fighting elsewhere. And, for my part, I would oppose even that. You are wasting your time. We are here to fight to the death.'

Homan then drew up a memorandum covering the points made by both sides in consultation with James Douglas and on Wednesday went again to the Hammam Hotel to find De Valera. He describes the attempt as follows:

> I made my way to the Hammam. It was ablaze and no one replied to my knocking at the door in the lane. Heavy firing was proceeding from government troops in Cathedral Street and from their two machine guns at Cahill's and from the insurgents' machine gun further up the lane. This gun, I afterwards learned, was operated by Cathal Brugha personally who had declared his determination to fire on anybody entering the lane, except for members of the fire brigade.

He finally met Fr Flanagan who told him that De Valera had gone and Homan decided that he could do no more.

This account underlines the confidence Collins now felt in how matters were developing. It also underlines the divisions on the anti-Treaty side and also their poor military knowledge. Perhaps they thought that the sight of pro-Treaty troops dying on the main street of Dublin would deter the government from attacking the buildings. But lessons had been learned from 1916. Burning the buildings was far more economical in terms of the amount of casualties inflicted on the attackers and so it proved.

With Dublin now relatively secure the army prepared to carry the fight to the provinces. 20,000 recruits were sought and on 5 July O'Duffy, O'Connell and MacEoin were appointed field commanders; as the fighting developed, other leaders such as Brennan, Dan Hogan and Emmet Dalton also came to prominence. In the initial stages these men had considerable autonomy in their areas but the lessons of the War of Independence had been noted, and centralised control under a civil authority which gradually assumed control was developed as soon as possible though, in places, not quickly enough to prevent some atrocities. The problems the army began to have with some of the individuals closest to Collins only served to emphasise the evolution of a voluntary, fragmented force based on personal loyalties to a professional, regular army loyal to the state.

The lack of any coherent military policy on the part of the anti-Treaty forces, particularly regarding offensive operations, allowed the army to consolidate. However the most important development to the success of the army, and indeed the government, was the appointment of Collins as Commander-in-Chief.

I say this for three reasons. At national level, a new state must have a focus to develop a sense of identity. If it does not develop such an identity anarchy prevails, a recent example being Afghanistan. Civil war only underlines the need for such a focus. But on whom could the new state focus? With the possible exception of Arthur Griffith, who was now gravely ill, there was no other figure who could be considered. Collins had become synonymous with the War of Independence, his part in the Treaty negotiations had brought him to the attention of the general public and these aspects, combined with his charismatic personality, made him the obvious candidate. Putting him in uniform, at the head of an army defending the existence of the new state, and with a press that was largely pro-Treaty, raised his stature to heroic proportions. His death a few weeks later only served to consolidate this new sense of identity.

The army as well as the general population required a sense of identity. Without the appointment of Collins as Commander-in-Chief, it is only too likely that it would have been beset by the local rivalries and animosities exhibited during the War of Independence and by the anti-Treaty forces during the current conflict. All armies need an identifiable leader. Such a leader exudes authority and control which cannot be too readily seen in a local commander who, up to recently, would only have been known as a neighbour. Collins must have been very aware of this as he spent so much time during his last few weeks visiting units on tours of inspection.

Finally his appointment was necessary to assure those troops who were wavering in their commitment to the new army and also to assure those many civilians whose services would be required during the Civil War. Much has been made over the years of the calibre of soldier attracted to the army at this time. Ill-discipline was a major problem in the early days but, due to the inexperience of the junior leaders, this was only to be expected. Constant criticism from civilians and from the civil authority, who quickly realised the importance of winning the hearts and minds of the people, slowly helped to overcome this problem. Disparaging references to 'mercenaries' and ex-British army soldiers seem to imply that their loyalty was in doubt especially when measured against the purely voluntary anti-Treaty soldiers. As this was the first paid, full-time army to be put in the field in Ireland, there was cause to be suspicious of its loyalty. However, in the event, the vast majority remained loyal to the state.

An interesting aside to Collins becoming Commander-in-Chief is the photograph of him taken in Portobello Barracks on the day of his appointment. He was always conscious of the camera and every photograph shows him impeccably groomed, and in most cases posing for the shot. However this photograph, on this most important of days, shows him in a uniform that is missing a button and slacks that were too short. As it was well worn, I assume that it was borrowed, as any other photograph shows him in a well fitted uniform. It just goes to underline the speed with which events were developing.

During his last few weeks, Collins, as a good commander should, showed great confidence in his subordinates. If he did not, he would never have gone away on his tours of inspection. He left most of the work to Mulcahy, his Chief-of-Staff, GHQ and the field commanders. He still had time to offer opinions and make proposals on all aspects of military organisation. What is interesting during this time is that his suggestions on tactics and strategy seem to have been generated by his contacts with local leaders rather than from an overall strategic perspective.

From a military point of view his final tour to Cork was a disaster. The idea of the Commander-in-Chief driving through the heartland of the opposing forces, no matter how strong or weak the escort, is militarily inexcusable even if politically explicable. His death in the ensuing ambush, though tragic and unnecessary, had the ultimate effect of strengthening the resolve of the army and the government and of copper-fastening the sense of identity so necessary to the new state.

MICHAEL COLLINS
THE NORTHERN QUESTION 1916–22

Éamon Phoenix

More than any other Sinn Féin leader between 1917 and 1922 Michael Collins was passionately concerned about both Irish unity and the plight of the beleaguered northern nationalist minority. Of the volatile political situation in the wake of the 1916 Rising he had written to a friend: 'anything but a divided Ireland'.[1] Yet Collins' strong views on the Ulster Question did not emerge publicly until his appointment as Chairman of the Provisional Government in 1922. For much of the period 1919–21 he was overshadowed by De Valera on the northern issue while the Dáil leadership as a whole signally failed to produce any clear-sighted strategy to avert the impending threat of partition.

During those vital years, as the northern Sinn Féiner, Louis J. Walsh put it, Sinn Féin alarmed its northern supporters by its failure 'to grapple with the Ulster Question'. Whereas for northern Catholics, 'partition was the one supreme issue', the Dáil tended to rank Irish unity as a poor second to national status in the revolutionary scheme of things.[2] Collins' northern policy can be divided into two phases: the pre-Treaty period, when his strong anti-partitionist leanings were largely concealed from the public domain and the period from January 1922 until his death when 'Ulster' became an almost constant pre-occupation.

Collins' first real experience of the north came during the South Armagh by-election of January 1918 when he campaigned on behalf of the Sinn Féin candidate, his fellow-IRB man Dr Patrick McCartan, and engaged in a major recruitment campaign for the revitalised Irish Volunteers. The decisive defeat of McCartan by the Irish Party candidate – reversing the pattern of republican by-election victories following the 1916 executions – was a warning to Collins and the Sinn Féin leadership of the different perspective of many Ulster Catholics.[3] In the north the burning issue for nationalists remained partition, then being canvassed by Carson and Craig, rather than 'Home Rule *v* Republic'. In particular, they were opposed to Sinn Féin's abstentionist tactic arguing, with much credence, that while such a policy might achieve results in the nationalist south, it was calculated to enable the unionists and their allies to establish a separate 'Orange state' in the north-east.

The emergence of Dáil Éireann as the effective government of much of nationalist Ireland and the onset of the Anglo-Irish War were accompanied in the north by intense sectarian violence and the inexorable passage at Westminster of the Government of Ireland Act, 1920, with its provision for the establishment of a separate parliament and government in the six north-eastern counties. Such an 'ethnographic' bloc, Craig convinced Prime Minister Lloyd George, would provide a more viable area for permanent unionist control than the historic nine county province. The tensions generated in Ulster by the 'Partition Bill' were further increased by the extension of IRA attacks in the province and the return of militantly anti-partitionist councils in Fermanagh, Tyrone and Derry city in the local elections of January and June 1920, the first to be held under proportional representation. A 'mini civil war' between the IRA and a revived UVF in Derry in June was followed by an eruption of bitter sectarian violence in Belfast and surrounding towns. The worst episode occurred in the city in July 1920 when the assassination of a northern-born RIC commissioner in Cork resulted in the mass expulsion of some 8,000 Catholic workers from the shipyard and other industries and the first fatalities in what was to become a shocking civilian death toll.[4]

Collins was indirectly responsible for a brutal sectarian attack on the Catholic minority in Lisburn, County Antrim in August 1920 when, in his capacity as Director of Intelligence of the IRA, he authorised the assassination of District Inspector O. R. Swanzy of the RIC. Swanzy had been implicated by a coroner's jury in the murder of the Sinn Féin Lord Mayor of Cork six months earlier. The killing was the signal for what the RIC described as a general 'crusade against all members of the Catholic faith' in the largely unionist town, in which Catholic houses and shops and the parochial house were burned by incensed loyalists.[5]

In response to the northern disturbances the Dáil, under pressure from northern nationalists, imposed the 'Belfast boycott', an emotive and counter-productive reaction which failed to achieve the reinstatement of the expelled workers and merely reinforced the gulf between Ulster unionism and the rest of Ireland. Collins' reaction to the boycott proposal identified him as a 'hawk' on the northern issue while confirming his lack of any real knowledge of the intensity of unionist opposition to a united Irish Republic. He told the Dáil in August 1920 that he favoured a boycott of Belfast banks in the south but 'protested … against the attempt by two northern deputies' (Seán MacEntee and Ernest Blythe) to inflame passions on the issue.[6] 'There was no Ulster Question', he declared cryptically, perhaps reflecting the conviction of his close IRB associate, Eoin O'Duffy, that 'force should be used against Ulster. There were sufficient Volunteers in Belfast to hold it for Ireland.' Throughout the period 1921–22, Collins' private views on the northern issue were heavily influenced by O'Duffy, the most active IRA leader in the province, later IRA liaison officer in Belfast and a man regarded by Collins as a possible successor.

Collins' uncompromising militaristic stance marked him off sharply from President de Valera who was emerging as a relative moderate on the Ulster issue, ruling out coercion and even suggesting an offer of self-determination to the Protestant counties during the Dáil secret sessions of August 1921.[7] The establishment of the Ulster Special Constabulary in October 1920 to implement partition and the eventual passage of the Government of Ireland Act at Westminster in December forced the Sinn Féin leadership to face up to the reality that a six county government and parliament would be set up, regardless of nationalist opposition.[8] In a memo to the recently-returned De Valera in January 1921, Collins urged the adoption of a positive policy to prevent partition. Sinn Féin, he argued, should contest the forthcoming elections to the Northern Ireland parliament on a basis of strict abstention and 'assembly with their colleagues in the rest of Ireland'. He stressed the centrality of two facts in combating partition, the 'vital importance of the Belfast boycott' and the need to maximise Sinn Féin's strength in the six counties at the expense of the Irish Party.[9]

Collins was unimpressed by De Valera's rather simplistic thesis that abstention would precipitate a split in unionism along class lines which Sinn Féin might exploit.[10] Instead, he felt that Sinn Féin's policy should be 'to prevent the idea and acceptance of partition entering into the minds and actions of the Irish people.' To Collins, a nationalist to the core, Belfast and its hinterland represented the modern counterpart of 'the old Pale'. He impressed on De Valera:

All that must be redeemed for Ireland, and we have to keep striving in every way until that objective is achieved. The north-east must not be allowed to settle down in the feeling that it is a thing apart from the Irish nation.[11]

As a practical means of realising this aim, Collins put forward the idea of using the existence of nationalist-controlled councils in Tyrone, Fermanagh and adjoining areas to make partition unworkable 'and to reduce the partitioned counties to four'. This suggests that as early as January 1921 Collins was beginning to formulate a northern policy which would attempt to achieve Irish unity by reducing the size of the northern state to non-viable proportions.

However, the scale of the Unionist party victory in the northern elections of May 1921, despite a Sinn Féin-Nationalist pact, came as a shattering blow to Collins. Not even his triumphant return for County Armagh, reversing the Sinn Féin humiliation of 1918, nor Sinn Féin's replacement of the Devlinites as the major anti-partitionist party, could alleviate his deep sense of gloom.[12] As the unionists moved to establish their new legislature as a barrier to Irish unity, he described them in a letter to Art O'Brien as 'a handful of people in one corner of the country, whose material interests depend on the maintenance of their foreign ascendancy'. They had no love for the Irish nation.[13]

The publication on 15 August 1921 of the British proposals for qualified Dominion Status with partition, together with De Valera's correspondence with Lloyd George, dashed the hopes of northern nationalists, fearful that the new Craig government was gradually 'digging itself in'. Many northern Sinn Féin supporters, especially in Fermanagh and Tyrone, took the rather cynical view that 'to all the other pledges collected down the years since 1912, Ulster unionists could now add another one from Dáil Éireann, guaranteeing that they would not be coerced into a united Ireland'.[14] Had they known of De Valera's private offer to concede the northern counties in exchange for a twenty-six county Republic, their anger would have been unrestrained. In response to the mounting northern nationalist unease and against a background of intense sectarian violence in Belfast, Collins paid a much-publicised visit to his constituents in Armagh on 4 September 1921. In his address to the 10,000 strong meeting, which included the entire Ulster Sinn Féin leadership, Collins coupled a markedly conciliatory tone towards the Ulster unionists with a firm stand on Irish unity. While rejecting the legitimacy of the fledgling Belfast parliament he assured unionists that if they would but 'come in on equal terms' with the rest of Ireland, they would meet with a generous response. Here Collins was signalling his preparedness to settle for 'essential unity' with a separate northern assembly operating under the overriding jurisdiction of Dáil Éireann, an idea he had already discussed with Griffith in August. Turning to the northern nationalists, Collins ruled out any coercion of nationalist counties and gave a pledge 'to those who are with us … that … no matter what the future may bring, we shall not desert them'.[15] However, neither Collins' offer nor the threat of his fellow speaker, Eoin O'Duffy, to 'use the lead' against a recalcitrant unionism, altered the Northern Ireland government's determination to cling to the 'Holy Grail' of the 1920 settlement.

The Ulster issue played a confusing part during the Treaty negotiations which opened in London in October 1921. From the outset Irish unity was, in Lord Longford's phrase, 'a strange abstract factor in tactics', obscured by the dominant issues of crown and empire. At two lengthy sessions, on 14 and 17 October, Collins and his colleagues urged the British government, as the architect of the twin crime of partition and the subjugation of two nationalist counties, to force Northern Ireland to choose between the acceptance of Sinn Féin's offer of 'essential unity' and the loss of her predominantly Catholic areas along the 1920 border. When Lloyd George responded that the arbitrary six county bloc was essentially a compromise accepted by the Redmondites in 1916, Collins declared: 'The present six counties implies coercion. South and east Down, south Armagh, Fermanagh and Tyrone will not come into Northern Ireland … We are prepared to face the problem itself – not your definition of it.'[16]

For Collins and the Sinn Féin leadership the subtraction from Northern Ireland of her large nationalist districts held two attractions. Firstly, it might secure for them not just territory, but the bulk of Sinn Féin's supporters in the north-east. Secondly, the loss of two counties, Derry city and other large tracts might make the north unviable and thus hasten Irish unity 'by contraction'. Also, the tactical possibilities of the Boundary Commission, which such an excision would entail, seemed considerable: if the unionists were to be threatened with such a drastic reduction of their juridical area by the British government, they might be made much more amenable to the 'essential unity' on federal lines visualised in Sinn Féin's 'Ulster clause'.

In the event, Griffith's' diplomatic blunder in assenting to a Boundary Commission in lieu of 'essential unity', together with Craig's predictable hostility to any connection with a Dublin parliament, closed off any further progress towards an all-Ireland

Michael Collins outside the family home at Woodfield.

Collins pictured in Portobello barracks in his uniform as Commander-in-Chief of the Free State Army.
Also in the picture is Alphonsus Culliton, first mascot of the new army.

The ruins of the Four Courts following the bombardment of June 1922.

Free State troops manning a barricade.

Collins at the burial of Arthur Griffith.

Collins inspecting Free State Troops shortly before his death.

The cortege passing along Western Road.

The coffin being carried on board ship for the sea journey to Dublin.

The Kiernan family (from left): Lily, Helen, Bridget, Maud, Catherine, Peter, Rose, Christine.

The unveiling of the commemorative cross at Beál na mBláth

The wedding of Gearóid O'Sullivan and Maud Kiernan, 19 October 1922. Note Kitty Kiernan, seated on the right and acting as bridesmaid, dressed in black.

state.[17] At the final acrimonious Dáil cabinet meeting of 3 December 1921, which foreshadowed the Treaty split, Collins angrily dismissed objections from De Valera and Brugha on the provisions for the north including the Boundary Commission: 'The sacrifice of north-east Ulster made for the sake of essential unity was justified.'[18]

Collins' final decision to endorse a Treaty enshrining Dominion Status for twenty-six counties and a Boundary Commission was sealed at a private meeting on the Ulster issue with the British Prime Minister a few hours before the agreement was signed on 5 December 1921. Alarmed at a move by the Northern Ireland government to suppress those nationalist councils which had acknowledged the Dáil, he demanded a definite reply from Craig on 'essential unity'. An astute Lloyd George, exultant at Griffith's pledge of 13 November, disarmed him by handing the Irishman his own unsupported assertion that, in the wake of a Boundary Commission, 'the north would be forced economically to come in'.[19] However, Collins had reckoned without the wiles of Lloyd George and the 'fatal ambiguity' of the final draft of the boundary clause which subjected 'the wishes of the inhabitants' in any border area to 'economic and geographic conditions'. This phraseology represented a revision of the memorandum approved by Griffith in November with its simple use of 'the wishes of the population' as the criterion of any boundary award.[20] Crucially, Collins missed an opportunity to insist on the provision of a plebiscite in article twelve, as John O'Byrne, the Irish legal adviser, had suggested to Griffith. O'Byrne thought that too much had been left to the Boundary Commission itself, a view shared by some northern nationalist spokesmen.[21] As events were to prove four years later, Collins and Griffith, in their determination to avoid a return to war, were too quick to persuade themselves that the commission would ensure an early reintegration of north and south.

For both plenipotentiaries and northern nationalists (especially those in the border counties) article twelve was the crucial clause. Without its inclusion, and his psychological commitment to the idea of boundary revision as a means of ensuring Irish unity, Collins might never have signed the Treaty.[22]

Northern nationalists were shocked and disappointed at the Treaty terms. The border nationalists – centred on Tyrone, Fermanagh and other 'homogeneous' areas – were comforted by Collins' assurance that the Boundary Commission would deliver them irretrievably from the 'alien' writ of a Belfast parliament. This view was characterised by Fr Philip O'Doherty, the parish priest of Omagh, who informed a pro-Treaty meeting in the Tyrone town that 'what was good enough for Michael Collins was good enough for him and he was sure it was good enough for all of them.'[23] Such enthusiasm for the Boundary Commission was not shared by the isolated nationalist minorities in Belfast and the unionist heartland. Their view, as reflected by the *Irish News*, was that the tendentious Irish unity, implied in the Treaty option for an all-Ireland parliament with continued unionist hegemony in the six counties, was preferable to boundary changes which might maroon them as a still smaller minority within a separate 'Ulster' state.[24]

In the face of these divisions De Valera's repudiation of the Treaty and the subsequent split in the Dáil only served to compound the confusion of northern nationalists while it prevented the formulation of a united anti-partitionist strategy. During the Treaty debates in the Dáil Collins, the only one of the signatories to make reference to partition, predicted that the Treaty 'will lead very rapidly to goodwill and the entry of the north-east under an Irish parliament' and reminded deputies of the abandonment of coercion.[25] In the eyes of many northerners, however, this policy sat uneasily with 'the concrete programme of non-recognition of the authority of the Belfast parliament' which Eoin MacNeill, the Dáil Speaker and TD for Derry, had commended to a bewildered deputation of northern nationalists on 7 December 1921. At that historic meeting, only hours before the cabinet split over the Treaty, the Mayor of Derry, H. C. O'Doherty, indirectly accused Collins and his associates of having abandoned the northern nationalists, without safeguards, to their 'hereditary enemies':

> Our representatives have given away what we have fought for over the last 750 years. It is camouflaged … We are no longer a united nation. You have nothing to give us for the sacrifice you call upon the people to make … We will be ostracised on account of our creed.[26]

Yet, whatever their criticisms of Collins, the northern nationalist leaders were even less impressed by De Valera's characteristically cryptic statement to them that 'until the northern parliament is recognised by the Irish people, it has no authority in our eyes'. This blend of principled non-recognition and *de facto* acceptance of partition found striking expression in De Valera's alternative to the Treaty, 'Document Number Two', with its uncritical replication of the Treaty's Ulster clauses.[27]

In the critical period from the ratification of the Treaty by Dáil Éireann January 1922 until his death in August 1922, Collins, already taxed by the drift towards civil war in the south, was almost continually preoccupied with the crystallising reality of partition and the parlous position of the 400,000 nationalists in northern Ireland, where the peace terms had provoked a bloody sectarian backlash against the minority. Indeed, the force of events were soon to cast the new Chairman of the Irish Provisional Government in the role of official spokesman for the northern Catholics in dealings with both the British and northern governments. Thus he expended much of his energy in raising the sectarian 'pogrom' with Lloyd George, negotiating with Craig, authorising IRA attacks in the north and attempting to promote unity amongst the divided northern nationalists themselves. Their internecine differences over strategy had been compounded by the split in Dáil Éireann and the boundary issue.

The first hint of Collins' policy towards partition and the Northern Ireland government seemed to point towards the 'non-recognition' policy outlined by MacNeill on behalf of the Dáil in December 1921. In the wake of the Treaty, both Collins and O'Duffy, the Chief-of-Staff of the (as yet undivided) IRA gave private assurances to the Divisional Commanders of the force within the six county area that

> although the six counties did not benefit as much as the rest of Ireland by it, it was the best that could possibly be got at the time, and it was the intention of the Dáil members and the ... GHQ Staff who supported it [the Treaty] to work and try to overcome the Treaty position with regard to Ulster ...[28]

Simultaneously, however, Churchill, in his capacity as British Colonial Secretary with responsibility for Irish affairs, was anxious to promote some kind of *modus vivendi* between the two Irish governments which might help stabilise the Treaty settlement. The resumption of the old pattern of sectarian violence in Belfast in January, in which sixteen people died, convinced him of the urgent need for a north-south dialogue on the whole question of the Treaty settlement and the position of the northern minority.[29] Craig, motivated partly by his desire to have the damaging southern boycott of northern goods lifted, and partly by the need to alleviate his supporters' fears that the borders of the new state would be whittled away by the Boundary Commission, reacted favourably.[30] Collins favoured a peace policy towards the north in the hope that the opening of direct negotiations with Craig might soften unionist resistance to essential unity.[31]

The two leaders met for the first time at the Colonial Office on 21 January 1922. This historic encounter between the architect of the IRA campaign of 1919–21 and the architect of partition began somewhat inauspiciously with the two leaders 'glowering magnificently', in Churchill's graphic phrase.[32] Neither could have had any foreknowledge that their meeting would result in a written agreement. They ranged over the major points at issue between the two Irish governments, including the Boundary Commission, the continuing problem of the 'expelled workers' and the larger question of Irish unity. The result was the signature of what was to become known as the first Craig-Collins Pact.[33] This agreement contained three main clauses. The first – and the one which was shortly to become the object of much bitter criticism amongst northern nationalists – enshrined Craig's suggested rationalisation of the Boundary Commission. This proposed to exclude the British-appointed Chairman, envisaged in the Treaty clause, in favour of mutual agreement between north and south. Secondly, Collins undertook to end the 'Belfast boycott' in return for a pledge by Craig 'to facilitate in every possible way the return of Catholic workmen – without tests – to the shipyards', subject to the revival of trade. The final clause stipulated that the two governments would endeavour 'to devise a more suitable system than the Council of Ireland' (provided in the 1920 Act) for 'dealing with the problems affecting all-Ireland'. This reflected the unionist leader's desire to remove the last shadowy link between the two parts of Ireland. The two leaders also agreed that a further meeting would be held shortly in Ireland to discuss the vexed question of political prisoners.[34]

The pact was immediately acclaimed by the Dublin Sinn Féin press as 'a great and decided advance towards Irish union'. The *Irish News*, reflecting the views of the Belfast Devlinite middle class, welcomed Collins' action as paving the way for a united campaign of constitutional action by northern nationalists to safeguard their political and educational rights within the northern state.[35] The joint agreement to alter the Boundary Commission, it was argued, would remove its 'most objectionable feature' from the nationalist stand-point – the appointment of a British Chairman, a point stressed by Collins.[36] The raising of the boycott and the reinstatement of the ex-pelled workers would, it was hoped, banish violence and hatred in Belfast. It soon became apparent, however, that such unbridled en-thusiasm for the agreement was not shared by the greater section of the northern nationalists on whose behalf Collins had purported to act in reaching the agreement. Two sections of nationalist opinion regarded the pact with a particular mixture of suspicion and alarm. On the one hand, the border nationalist majorities saw Collins' readiness to alter the format of the Boundary Commission as enabl-ing Craig to veto any large-scale transfers of territory.[37] Amongst the Belfast expelled workers, on the other hand, the initial hope that the agreement would ensure their reinstatement quickly turned to dis-appointment and a feeling that Collins had been out-manoeuvred by the northern prime minister in agreeing to terminate the boycott without iron-clad guarantees in return.[38]

Significantly, Craig saw the pact as a personal diplomatic tri-umph, assuring his cabinet that by signing the agreement Collins had recognised Northern Ireland and had inferentially accepted that the Treaty, and thus the Boundary Commission, 'was no longer in-violate'.[39]

In the wake of the Pact, Collins decided that the 'peace policy', foreshadowed by the agreement 'should get a fair chance'. How-ever, he was convinced that such a policy must be coupled with a strict campaign of 'non recognition' of the northern parliament by the nationalist minority; 'otherwise', he told members of the Pro-visional Government on 30 January 1922, 'they would have noth-ing to bargain with Sir James Craig.'[40] Thus for ten months from Feb-ruary 1922 – the date on which the Belfast government assumed re-sponsibility for education – the Provisional Government paid the salaries of some 800 teachers in almost 300 Catholic schools in North-ern Ireland which refused to acknowledge the Belfast authorities. The necessary finance, totalling £220,000, was obtained by Collins from the Secret Service vote which was thus greatly inflated.[41] At the same time, Collins gave surreptitious military and moral support to the two pro-Treaty IRA divisions within the six counties. It would seem that while Collins was prepared to press the Free State's claims under the Boundary Commission as an absolute last resort, he hoped that through agreements like the January Pact, economic and 'essential' political unity might evolve through time. As he told the Ulster Sinn Féiner, Louis J. Walsh, in February 1922:

> Any kind of even temporary partition is distasteful to me. We may reduce the north-east to such limits that it cannot exist without us ... But there would be much rancour in the train of this action. It would be far better to fix our minds ... on a united Ireland, for this course will not leave minorities which it would be impossible to govern.[42]

By the end of January 1922 it was certain that the Pact could not indefinitely withstand the totally irreconcilable interpretations which its two signatories were publicly placing on the meaning of the boundary clause. The breakdown occurred on 2 February when Collins revealed to the northern prime minister in Dublin that he anticipated bringing (in Craig's words) 'almost half the area of Northern Ireland' into the Free State.[43]

With the collapse of the agreement, the political situation within Northern Ireland degenerated violently and dramatically in what Churchill was to describe as a 'return to that hideous bog of reprisals', both in Belfast and along the border. The border violence was closely related to the expected execution of three IRA prisoners in Derry and the continued detention by Craig's government of the so-called 'Monaghan Footballers' (a party of IRA men captured near the border). On 8 February 1922 the condemned men were reprieved by the intervention of the viceroy, but this act of grace came too late to prevent a rash of dramatic raids and kidnappings in Fermanagh and Tyrone by parties of IRA loyal to the Provisional Government.[44] In fact, these operations were the work of a special 'Ulster Council', formed under the chairmanship of Frank Aiken, OC of the Fourth Northern Division, and were sanctioned by Collins, Mulcahy (his Minister for Defence) and O'Duffy.[45] In an effort to minimise the risks involved in such a blatant breach of the Treaty, Collins made arrangements for the exchange of weapons between pro- and anti-Treaty units, thus avoiding the identification of captured arms supplied by the British to the new National Army. The IRA subsequently announced that it was holding some seventy Specials and prominent unionists as hostages for the safe return of the Monaghan IRA men. The most serious incident on the border occurred at Clones on 11 February when a train-load of B Specials was challenged by the local IRA, resulting in five deaths and the capture of several Specials.

In Belfast, the border incidents came as a match to a powder-keg. In the three day period, 13–15 February 1922, thirty-one persons died as a result of violence in the city, whilst the final toll for the month was forty-three dead including twenty-five Catholics.[46] Bishop MacRory of Down and Connor, a trenchant critic of partition and supporter of Collins, characterised the outbreak as an expression of 'the doctrine of vicarious punishment, according to which the Catholics of Belfast are made to suffer for the sins of their brethren elsewhere.'[47]

Collins' policy towards the deteriorating situation in the north was robust. He was vehement in his protestations to the Colonial Secretary against the mobilisation of the Specials 'for action against our people in the north-east' and what he saw as a concerted 'pogrom' against the Belfast Catholics. Moreover, in his military capacity, he secretly authorised the formation of a specially-paid unit of seventy IRA men to be known as the 'Belfast City Guard' to defend the Catholic enclaves from sectarian attack.[48]

The mounting complaints from northern nationalists regarding the activities of the Specials and the arrest of IRA officers drew a markedly sympathetic response from Collins. As he told a Newry complainant: 'Put plainly, these arrests are simply a challenge to us – they are a denial of the right of our own people to live in our own country. Until this attitude is dropped by the Belfast rulers, there can be no understanding with us.' Increasingly, Collins was being cast in the mould of intermediary between the minority and the British government.[49]

During February and March 1922 Collins found his stance on the Boundary Commission seriously undermined by a series of speeches from Churchill and other British Ministers in favour of the narrow interpretation of clause twelve. The British campaign in favour of 'mere rectification' of the border moved Griffith to warn Collins on 15 February of the potentially 'disastrous' political consequences for the pro-Treaty administration: 'The Treaty must be adhered to on this point. Agreement with Craig if possible, but in the event of failure, the commission to operate as provided in the Treaty … Otherwise, disaster.'[50]

This instability engendered by the boundary question coincided with a dramatic escalation of politico-sectarian violence in the north. It was largely concern at the plight of the northern minority and the impassioned appeals of the 300 Ulster Sinn Féin delegates at the Sinn Féin Árd Fheis in late February which impelled Collins to preserve at least a semblance of unity by postponing an election on the Treaty issue. As ever Belfast remained the cockpit of sectarian passions – in Churchill's phrase, 'an underworld … with deadly passions of its own'. No less than sixty died in 'a crescendo of murder, bombing, rioting and general anarchy' in March alone.[51] The Catholic population, which continued to suffer the greatest number of fatalities, supported calls for martial law, but this was strongly resisted by Craig and the British authorities. The perception of Collins and northern Catholics in general of the unceasing sequence of outrages in Belfast as an orchestrated pogrom against the minority cannot be proven. But it was shared by disinterested sections of the British press which charged the B Specials with involvement in the murders of Catholics, while Lloyd George, struck by the much higher Catholic death-rate, could inform Churchill in June 1922 that 'our Ulster case is not a good one.'[52]

Against this background, Collins found himself under growing pressure from both the increasingly bellicose anti-Treaty element in the south and his own northern supporters to take further steps towards protecting the Catholics in Belfast. He responded by setting up a Northern Advisory Committee to advise the Provisional Government on northern affairs. At the same time he met Joe Devlin and favoured the creation of a united northern nationalist movement against partition to the chagrin of northern Sinn Féiners.[53]

In March also, the Northern Ireland government moved to assert its authority through the Civil Authorities (Special Powers) Act, which was to clothe the civil authority with 'frankly despotic powers' and an expanded Special Constabulary of some 32,000-strong, financed by the British government. During March and April also, the northern government dissolved the twenty anti-partitionist local authorities which had continued to deny its authority.[54]

Collins' characteristic reaction to these measures was to authorise a concerted offensive by the IRA against the RIC and Specials in west Ulster, in the course of which six policemen were killed. In Belfast, the pro-Treaty Third Northern Division shot dead four policemen in March. These IRA attacks were repaid in kind by loyalist elements which took reprisals against Catholic civilians.[55]

As violence increased in Belfast and a state of continuous guerrilla warfare gripped the border areas, a concerned Churchill told the British cabinet that in order to avert a serious 'collision' between north and south, it was essential that Craig should meet Collins in conference and obtain from him 'a repudiation of the revolts on the part of the IRA'.[56] At the same time Collins was actually considering re-imposing the boycott of Ulster goods. The Belfast situation was to deteriorate still more drastically, however. On 23 March, the IRA murder of two Specials was to provoke, by way of reprisal, one of the most repellent murders of the Troubles of 1920–22 – that of the McMahon family in the drawing-room of their own home. The circumstances of the event and eye-witness accounts left little doubt that the assassins were members of the much-hated Specials, a possibility not ruled out by Churchill.[57]

The main effect of the McMahon murders was to convince the Colonial Secretary that urgent action in the political field was essential and he promptly summoned Collins and a reluctant Craig to London. Meanwhile, the ferocity of the violence had prompted a group of moderate Catholic businessmen in Belfast to approach Craig and Collins with a series of detailed proposals for settling the disturbances. Their draft proposals, presented by Collins at the London conference, formed the basis of the second Craig-Collins pact, signed by representatives of the three governments on 30 March 1922.[58]

The pact was essentially a blend of the proposals of the Belfast Catholic businessmen and those of the Colonial Secretary with certain amendments. Clause one carried the dramatic headline 'Peace is today declared', whilst clause two contained a pledge by the two Irish governments to co-operate to restore peaceful conditions. The third and most important clause concerned the re-organisation of the police in Belfast. This enshrined the Belfast Catholic suggestion of a scheme of 'mixed Special police' in the city, and provided for the establishment of a Catholic police advisory committee to recommend suitable Catholic recruits. Subsequent clauses provided for non-jury courts and the formation of a joint conciliation committee to prevent outrages. In clause six Collins undertook that IRA activity would cease in the six counties. Clause seven provided that the representatives of north and south should meet before the 'Ulster month' began to run to consider the larger issues of Irish unity and the Boundary Commission. Churchill himself promised that the British government would submit to the Northern Ireland Ministry of Labour the sum of £500,000 for relief work with the proviso that one-third was to be expended for the benefit of Catholics and two-thirds for the benefit of Protestants. At the same time, the northern government agreed 'to use every effort to secure the restoration of the expelled workers', subject to economic conditions. Finally, it was arranged that in certain cases, 'political prisoners', imprisoned for offences committed before that date, might be released.[59]

It is clear, however, that the peace pact, albeit detailed and well-intentioned, took too little account of the realities of the political situation in Ireland, north and south, at this critical juncture. Collins, writing to his fiancée on 31 March, was far from optimistic about the agreement 'from any point of view'.[60] Almost immediately its promise was blighted by the activities of extremist elements, north and south. In the south, the pact coincided exactly with the final split in the IRA into pro- and anti-Treaty sections. The anti-Treaty executive, in a calculated move to embarrass Collins, reimposed the boycott.[61]

In the north, on the other hand, the pact, and in particular the proposals for the reform of the Special Constabulary, invoked the unremitting ire of the more extreme sections of unionism, whilst it was signally unpopular with Dawson Bates, the hard-line Minister of Home Affairs, who showed absolutely no urgency, imagination or generosity in implementing it. Thus, whereas Catholics and nationalists thought that Collins conceded too much in January, unionists reckoned that Craig had been outwitted in March. This factor, together with the vigorous prosecution of the anti-Treaty boycott, ensured that Craig's will to pursue the policy of conciliation was seriously weakened. As one contemporary writer observed: 'He did not actually decline to fulfil his obligations under the agreement, but when he had reason to fear opposition from his diehards, he relied upon the activities of the anti-Treatyites as a complete excuse for his failure to enforce the terms of the pact.'[62]

Nor was the pact unanimously embraced by the different sections of northern nationalism. The Devlinites were unhappy at the recognition of Collins by both the British and Belfast governments as the accredited custodian of the Catholic minority, and the prestige which this tended to confer upon Sinn Féin and the IRA in the six counties. At the same time a considerable section of Sinn Féin and the pro-Treaty IRA in Belfast was instinctively averse to the idea of nationalist involvement in the Specials, and especially to the declaration of allegiance incumbent on Catholic recruits. Such a step, the Sinn Féin critics pointed out, would commit nationalists to a *de facto* recognition of the northern government and should be rejected. The practical difficulties which would surround any attempt to create the proposed new force were prefigured by the circulation by the Belfast executive of Sinn Féin of a virulent notice expressing the hope that no nationalist would 'be influenced to act a traitor's part.'[63]

In face of all these factors – the disruptive action of the anti-Treatyites, unionist hostility and the obstructive attitude of many of Collins' northern supporters – Collins' reservations about the likely success of the agreement seemed amply justified. However, the corrosive impact of all these difficulties was compounded by the continuation of violence in Belfast. Any prospect that the agreement might still win general acceptance through a lessening of sectarian tension was finally dashed by the 'Arnon Street affair' of the night of 1–2 April 1922 when, in swift retaliation for the murder of a policeman, a reprisal party – almost certainly composed of Specials – summarily killed five Catholics. Collins was convinced that the affair had been 'contrived' to destroy the pact by extremist elements in the police force.[64]

The Arnon Street killings led to a rapid deterioration in relations between north and south. The certainty that Craig would continue to reject Collins' demands for an enquiry into the atrocity and the question of whether or not the Provisional Government should break off the pact was discussed at a full meeting of Collins' Northern Advisory Committee in Dublin on 11 April 1922.[65] At this meeting, attended by leading Sinn Féin and IRA leaders in the north, three bishops and the entire Dublin cabinet, Collins made it clear that he was prepared to terminate the agreement if Craig remained inflexible. However, the discussion showed a consensus on the part of both the Provisional Government and the greater section of the nationalist leadership in the north to give the pact a trial. This feeling was most marked amongst the Belfast representatives, including Bishop MacRory and Seamus Woods, the local IRA commander, who shared Griffith's realistic view that the agreement and, in particular, the proposed formation of Catholic Specials, was the only means of protecting the beleaguered minority in Belfast. The Belfast delegates were emphatic that the city's Catholic population, war-weary, demoralised and hopelessly outnumbered, was in no position to face the implications of a 'war policy'. Woods claimed that, although the sectarian violence had united the Catholic population behind the IRA for the first time, the military position was simply 'impossible'. MacRory warned Collins that a resumption of his campaign of destroying unionist property would provoke 'a terrible punishment' on Belfast's 25% nationalist minority. Moreover, it seemed to be generally accepted by the northerners that the logic of the Treaty position required a policy of 'reasonable co-operation', and hence 'recognition' towards the Northern Ireland government pending the outcome of the Boundary Commission. Collins' policy of funding a 'non-recognition' policy in education had already been raised by the northern Minister of Education, Lord Londonderry. In a letter to Collins, Londonderry claimed to 'have definite evidence' of Irish government involvement and added: 'If there is to be reasonable co-operation between north and south … I think you will agree that the dual system of payment of teachers in the northern area, wherever the funds come from, should cease'.[66]

Nevertheless, as violence continued to escalate in Northern Ireland during April and May 1922, and nationalist opinion began to harden, Collins seems to have decided to extract as much out of the pact as possible – 'and then let it break'.[67] As a result, his policy towards the north from April until his death presents a somewhat confused and complicated picture. This undoubtedly stemmed from his dual role as head of the Provisional Government, charged with the implementation of the Treaty, and as a leading figure on the headquarters staff of the pro-Treaty IRA who 'could not for long lose sight of old loyalties and military objectives.'[68] From April onwards, Collins employed a two-pronged policy of conciliation and coercion towards the northern government. Overtly, he continued to pressure Craig to fulfil his part of the pact, whilst paying lip-service to its terms by making appointments to the various pact committees. But covertly, and apparently without consulting his 'political' colleagues, he was sanctioning a renewal of operations by the pro-Treaty IRA divisions within northern Ireland in conjunction with anti-Treaty units in the south. The aim of this strategy seems to have been to wreak such havoc and disruption within the six counties that the northern government would be forced to consider a more radical accommodation with the rest of Ireland The theory that Collins was merely trying to deflect anti-Treaty energies away from the south overlooks his conspiratorial nature and emotional commitment to the northern nationalists. Kevin O'Shiel, the Provisional Government's Assistant Legal Adviser and a key strategist on

northern policy, later attributed responsibil
inspiration and collapse to Collins. He recall
'to come to quick decision without consulting
I was urging a policy of peaceful do-nothing
mittees, the two branches of the IRA were a
preparations to invade the north in alliance
time had one policy and the civilians anothe

The original strategy, endorsed at a meeting of the IRA's 'Ulster
Council' at Clones on 21 April, envisaged a synchronised attack on
the north 'by every division having territory inside the six counties'
in May 1922. (The northern divisions, faced with immense organisational and operational difficulties, had remained loyal to Collins
after the IRA split in March 1922.) The main IRA campaign began,
as arranged, on 18 May with a concerted campaign of arson and de-
struction by the Third Northern Division throughout its three Brigade areas of Belfast, Antrim and north Down. Attacks were mainly directed at commercial property in Belfast and at RIC barracks,
stately homes, and railways in rural areas. The fundamentally political nature of the violence was underlined by the assassination of
a unionist member of the northern parliament, W. J. Twaddell, in a
crowded city street on 22 May.[70] The co-ordinated nature of the raids
came as a severe shock to the northern government but the offensive quickly collapsed owing to the failure of the border divisions
to mobilise, the swift deployment of the USC, and the apparent can-
cellation of the orders by Collins. Its main effect was to unleash a
terrible sectarian backlash against the Catholic population in Belfast. The same weekend (20–21 May) which saw the eruption of IRA
violence witnessed an orgy of planned sectarian assassinations
which claimed the lives of twelve Catholics, as well as mob on-
slaughts on isolated nationalist pockets. Oblivious of Collins' involvement, the *Irish News* blamed these deaths on those who were
'playing these hideous pranks with the very existence' of the
minority.[71]

The northern government responded to the intensification of
violence by introducing internment on 22 May 1922 and the extension of the curfew over the entire six counties. The crisis coincided
with the British cabinet's efforts to ensure that Collins adhered
strictly to the Treaty, then challenged by his electoral pact with De
Valera, signed on 20 May. This agreement was largely the result of
strong representations to the two leaders from a northern delega-

y Frank Aiken, on the grave 'danger of permanent parti-
d national disaster' if civil war was not avoided.[72] Collins'
vation in endorsing a pact which was to cause serious political
fficulties for him both with his cabinet colleagues and the Lloyd
George coalition was his deep-rooted concern about the north. In a
scribbled note on the compromise, he wrote: 'Above all, Ulster.'[73]

The Collins-De Valera pact had an immediate impact in Northern Ireland when Craig seized upon its terms in order to repudiate
once and for all the 'odious' Boundary Commission. Griffith, for his
part, regarded the pact with 'unconcealed disgust' while Churchill
described the proposed coalition arrangement as a 'farce'.[74] The agreement underlined the glaring contradictions in Collins' northern policy. Hugh Kennedy, the Provisional Government's law officer, warned Collins that its provision for northern representation in the new
Free State parliament was incompatible with the Treaty: 'It seems to
me that there is some confusion of view in applying details of policy on the partition question.'[75] This was indeed a massive under-
statement.

In order to counter British pressure over the pact and a draft
Free State constitution which sought to placate the republicans,
Collins determined at the London discussion to take the offensive
on 'Ulster' and Craig's repudiation of article twelve. Thus, during
a stormy conference with Lloyd George and Austen Chamberlain on
30 May 1922, Collins and Griffith were 'more anxious to talk about
the north-east than anything else', repeatedly referring to 'the extermination of the Catholics' and alleging that numerous murders had
been committed by Specials in British pay. When Chamberlain challenged Collins to 'disavow the IRA' in the north and urge the minority to recognise the unionist government, the Irish leader retorted
that he would not 'hold up the hands of the northern government
when Catholics were being murdered.'[76]

Lloyd George, in particular, was seriously alarmed by the mounting sectarian violence in Belfast since it enabled Collins and his colleagues to 'manoeuvre us into a position where our case is weak.'
The first murders in the north, he reminded his cabinet, had been
of members of the Catholic minority. 'No one had been punished,
we had made no enquiry, we had armed 48,000 Protestants. It would
be a bad case.' Struck by the force of Collins' charges against the
Specials, the British prime minister was inclined to support his demand for an enquiry into the disturbances as a means of detaching

the 'Ulster' issue from the main one. By early June, however, the British had won the argument over the constitution and settled for a secret one-man investigation into the breakdown of the second Craig-Collins pact.[77]

Despite an acrimonious correspondence with Craig, Collins had allowed the three committees, set up under the March pact, to be constituted by May 1922. The conciliation committee quietly lapsed when the northern government made it clear that its powers would be limited to 'moral suasion'.[78] The Catholic policy advisory committee, consisting of Collins' nominees, including two priests, IRA representatives and Devlinite businessmen, held three meetings with Craig's officials before dissolving without having made any progress towards its objective. It seems clear that its failure was predetermined by two factors – the rooted hostility of the Sinn Féin and IRA movements in Belfast to any nationalist involvement in the police, and, secondly, the northern government's distrust of the motives of a committee which included a number of prominent IRA representatives.[79] The relief clause was destined to be the only section of the pact carried out to the satisfaction of all parties. The committee worked well, partly because it dealt with British funds, but largely due to the actions of its Chairman, the northern Minister of Labour, J. M. Andrews, whose constructive role contrasted sharply with that of anti-Catholic Bates.[80]

Churchill's decision at the beginning of June 1922 to use troops and artillery to recapture the Pettigo-Belleek triangle, a salient of northern territory, from pro-Treaty forces and to occupy a Free State village, drew a vigorous protest from Collins who contrasted the attack, in which seven pro-Treaty soldiers died, with the British government's inertia 'against savage anti-Catholic mobs' in Belfast.[81] In Collins' view, the British incursion was part of Sir Henry Wilson's policy of creating tension along the border as a means of effecting the proverbial reconquest of Ireland. Collins' statement was significant in that it prefigured the assassination on 22 June of that 'archetypal unionist' and military adviser to the northern government, almost certainly on his instructions. Collins blamed 'Wilsonian militarism' for the ongoing anti-Catholic violence in Northern Ireland and probably saw the assassination of such a high-profile anti-nationalist figure as affording a much-needed boost to the demoralised northern IRA. As the historian of the Irish Civil War, which Wilson's killing precipitated, has observed, Collins' involvement was of a piece with his entire northern policy since January 1922 and can be explained in terms of his military background and the emphasis he placed both on partition and army unity: 'He remained a conspirator, attached to his IRB colleagues rather than to his government colleagues.'[82]

The outbreak of the Civil War came as a bitter blow to the northern nationalists. 'Mr de Valera,' declared the *Irish News* on 6 July reflecting the view of most nationalists, 'has insisted on a grim sacrifice from the Irish people.'[83] The spreading conflict, marked by the cessation of IRA operations in the north, was correctly interpreted by the unionist government and armed loyalism as effectively removing the threat of a concerted assault on the northern state. The result was the descent of a fragile peace in the north, a process helped by Collins' apparent enunciation of a more conciliatory northern policy at the end of June: 'There can be no question of forcing Ulster into union … with the twenty-six counties … Union is our final goal, that is all.'[84]

It seems likely that, in reverting to a 'peace policy', Collins was reacting partly to the pressing demands of the Civil War, but also to the abundant evidence that the policy of belligerence had proved unsuccessful in protecting northern Catholics. His view was undoubtedly strengthened during July and August 1922 by reports from the pro-Treaty IRA leadership in the north. Seamus Woods could report dolefully from Belfast in mid-July that 'the spirit of the people was practically dead' while the IRA was 'daily losing ground' among the nationalist population.[85] 'The people who supported us,' he told Mulcahy, 'feel that they have been abandoned by Dáil Éireann for our position is more unbearable than … in June 1921 … the people feel that all their suffering has been in vain and cannot see any hope for the future.'[86] In Belfast the 800 IRA volunteers were 'in a state of practical starvation' and demanding to be transferred to the 'regular army' in Dublin.

Collins' evolving policy on the north was revealed at a meeting with the Ulster IRA leaders on 2 August 1922. Now Commander-in-Chief of the pro-Treaty forces, Collins laid down that the nationalist minority should maintain the 'non-recognition' policy with the IRA adopting a purely 'protective' role. He assured his northern comrades that the Irish government 'intended to deal with the Ulster situation in a very definite way in the near future'. But, Mulcahy, as Minister for Defence, noted that for this to succeed, 'a peace policy was essential.' Collins' long-term intentions are not clear but his decision to retain the northern divisions and to train northern IRA men at the Curragh in guerrilla methods strongly suggests that he had not yet buried the pike in the thatch. His network of spies at this time included a registry clerk in the office of the northern Military Adviser, Major-General Arthur Solly-Flood. When this official was forced to flee in late August 1922, he brought with him to pro-Treaty GHQ some of the RUC's most sensitive files.[87]

By July 1922 also, the British government and Churchill in particular, aware of Collins' involvement in northern IRA violence and the 'non-recognition' campaign by Catholic teachers, was anxious to secure minority recognition of the Northern Ireland government and an end to Catholic reliance on Collins. Such a practice, S. G. Tallents, a senior British official in Belfast, told the Colonial Office, merely irritated the unionist government and should be abandoned: 'the ideal course is for the Catholics ... to recognise the northern government and to deal with it direct, with as little ... British intervention as circumstances may show to be expedient.'[88]

But while Churchill and a section of Belfast nationalists wished to encourage such recognition, the decision of the northern government to abolish proportional representation for local elections in July 1922 suggested that Craig and his ministerial colleagues were totally indifferent to the vital interests of its minority.[89] The Local Government Bill provided Collins, now immersed in the struggle against the anti-Treatyites with a final opportunity to assert himself as the guardian of the northern nationalists. In a lengthy protest to Churchill on 9 August 1922, he emphasised his view that the bill was a calculated political act by the northern government, designed to 'paint the counties of Tyrone and Fermanagh with a deep Orange tint' in anticipation of the Boundary Commission. The Irish leader was adamant that Britain should use its constitutional prerogative to block the bill, especially at a time when the Provisional Government were seeking 'some working basis of union' with the north.[90] In fact, the British government, in a hint of its future policy towards Northern Ireland, was not prepared to risk a constitutional showdown with Craig on the issue, thus effectively abdicating its role as the protector of the minority population.[91]

Collins did not live to see the denouement of the proportional representation issue and, even before his untimely death at Béal na mBláth on 22 August, his colleagues in the Provisional Government were moving to distance themselves form his idiosyncratic northern policy. On 1 August 1922 the cabinet appointed a committee 'to consider the question of the policy to be adopted towards the Belfast government and with regard to the North-East Ulster Question generally'.[92] Its recommendations were foreshadowed in a key memorandum, dated 9 August, by Ernest Blythe, Acting Minister for Home Affairs, and the leading northern Protestant in the Irish revolution. Blythe rejected any continuation of an aggressive policy towards the northern state as counter-productive and strongly advocated the ending of payments to the northern Catholic teachers and the winding up of the pro-Treaty IRA divisions in northern Ireland.[93] In his view, Collins' policy of financing the teachers was indefensible on financial, educational and moral grounds.

On 19 August the Provisional Government formally adopted 'a peace policy' and negotiations were authorised with the northern government on the education question subject to 'the approval of the Commander-in-Chief.' Collins was not present and may have been unaware of the sea-change in northern policy at the time of his death.[94]

Collins' death removed the one leader on the pro-Treaty side who had consistently made partition and the position of the northern nationalists a primary consideration in determining policy. As such, it came as a shattering blow to the already dispirited minority and, in particular, to the northern IRA. They had good reason to suspect that neither his successor, W. T. Cosgrave, nor his ministerial colleagues would be inclined to commit themselves overmuch to the northern nationalists. By September 1922 Woods could complain to Mulcahy that 'the attitude of the present government towards its followers in the six counties is not that of the late General Collins'. Cahir Healy, the Fermanagh Sinn Féin leader, then an internee on board the prison ship *Argenta* in Belfast Lough, was more caustic: 'We have been abandoned to Craig's mercy.'[95] Events were to show his assessment to be essentially correct.

To the Northern Ireland government, however, Collins' unexpected death came as a further stroke of good fortune in the wake of the Civil War. The British government too, aware of the inconsistencies in his northern policy, had little reason to mourn. 'I have never thought that Collins tried to meet you squarely on the Treaty', Lionel Curtis told Churchill two years after his death.[96]

Collins stands almost alone among the revolutionary leadership of 1917–22 in his genuine and consistent concern for Irish unity and the welfare of the northern nationalists. His strong attachment to the concept of an indivisible Irish nation was obscured during the Anglo-Irish War by the military and administrative burdens of challenging British rule. But as partition loomed in January 1921 Collins was adamant that the north-east 'must be redeemed for Ireland'. His emotional commitment to unity was in sharp contrast to the view of De Valera who by 1921 had effectively acquiesced in the right of the northern unionists to secede from the Irish state. Amongst the revolutionary hierarchy, only Griffith shared Collins' concern for the north though he, too, saw unity as a long-term goal.

Yet Collins' nationalism was cast in the pragmatic mould of the IRB. At the Treaty negotiations he fought hard for 'essential unity' but was forced to settle for a Boundary Commission which he saw as a means of inducing unity by territorial contraction – a kind of 'sword of Damocles' over Ulster unionism. However his failure, with Griffith, to insist on a plebiscite is inexplicable in light of European precedent, and was to rob the Free State of every inch of her anticipated territorial gains.

It was during the final phase of his career, from January 1922 until his death in August, that Collins made the Ulster question a central priority. The position of the northern nationalists, already undermined by partition, had been further eroded by the split in the south, anti-Catholic violence and internal tensions over the Boundary Question. Collins, despite his formal acceptance of the Treaty, regarded the partition issue as unfinished business. Above all, and without reference to his pro-Treaty colleagues, he remained wedded to his old IRB and IRA conspiratorial and military interests, pledging support to the northern IRA within hours of his signing the Treaty.

As sectarian violence escalated in the first half of 1922, the Provisional Government Chairman sought to assist the isolated northern Catholics by a confusing blend of 'non-recognition', diplomacy and coercion towards the unionist government. But his policy was to prove ineffective in its dual aims of protecting the minority and pushing Craig towards a recognition of 'essential unity'. Collins' non-recognition policy in education and local government was to prove impracticable and counter-productive. At a diplomatic level his two pacts with Craig offered a more constructive approach but, as a British official noted, they failed because they 'dealt with minor issues before the major issues that governed them were decided.'[97]

Collins seemed to have seen such north-south negotiations as a means of persuading the unionist leader of the advantages of Irish unity, but in this he misinterpreted Craig's guiding principle in entering the conference room: to minimise the effects of article twelve and to remove the 1920 Council of Ireland – a concession which Collins' successors finally yielded up in 1925. Only the British government, keen to make the Treaty settlement work, had any real commitment to the Craig-Collins pacts. But the detailed March agreement is significant as representing the only serious attempt in the half-century of unionist majority rule to involve the nationalist minority in the workings of the Northern Ireland state.

The pact's inevitable collapse and, especially, Craig's obstructionism underlay Collins' decision in May 1922 to launch a major IRA offensive designed to make the north unworkable. This only compounded the difficulties of the minority by provoking loyalist reprisals while the subsequent introduction of internment virtually eliminated the northern Sinn Féin leadership. Cahir Healy, writing three years later, was critical of Collins' handling of the northern question. He accused him, along with De Valera and Griffith, of a failure 'to understand the northern situation and the northern mind' and attacked 'the rather jumpy efforts which, with Collins, passed for statecraft.'[98]

Collins' policy towards the north was complex, secretive and inconsistent. Yet there can be little doubt about his commitment to the northern issue. His heated protests to Churchill and his renewed pledges to the northern IRA during his last days suggest that a Collins-led Free State government would have forced the boundary question and the larger issue of Irish unity to the forefront of Anglo-Irish politics in the early 1920s. Ironically, the northern nationalist sense of betrayal at the Cosgrave government's endorsement of the Tripartite Agreement of December 1925 was to mark the beginnings of a rapprochement between the minority, led by Devlin and Healy, and Collins' main adversary, De Valera.

MICHAEL COLLINS

THE LEGACY AND THE INTESTACY

John Regan

Michael Collins as a historical subject represents a series of fascinating anomalies. He remains a popular icon from the period of the revolution and First World War in Ireland, and arguably is the last such politico-military figure from that era in western Europe. The attractiveness of Collins' story and indeed image has generated considerable interest from biographers and film makers as vehicle for 'explaining' the Irish revolution. Conversely, professional historians have elected, with a few notable exceptions, not to wrestle with Collins either as a historical or mythical figure. Part of the reason for the discrepancy between popular biographical interpretation of Collins – some sixteen such works – and commensurate rigorous professional historical analysis is to some extent explained by the different demands made of the evidence made by the two approaches and the burden of proof.

Collins' short revolutionary life and the secret culture he thrived in did not, quite obviously, facilitate the accumulation of documentary evidence. Nor did he bequeath a readily accessible corpus of his political ideas other than in the collective journalism, speeches and notes of *The Path to Freedom*.[1] Though these writings contain what appears to be an honest, and for that matter what we would recognise as a distinctly De Valeraesque, Gaelicism they are the utterings of the public Collins and Collins was primarily a secretive man.

Collins headed the Irish Republican Brotherhood as President of its Supreme Council from 1919. The Brotherhood was arguably the most powerful and influential institution within the revolutionary movement and Collins, as his influence spread through it, became the single most important revolutionary. But the dead hand of the Brotherhood in its clandestine operations, with one or two notable exceptions, remains, like Collins himself, a mere shadow on the lighted political scene.[2] Without access to documentary evidence relating to the secret war which Collins orchestrated nor the secret organisation over which he presided anything approaching a satisfactory analysis of Collins is impossible. The biographer it would appear is pushed toward relying on oral testimony, which in some cases bares all the distortions and polish of well-told posthumous anecdote and the hero worship which enveloped Collins even before his death.

Anecdote if it has not defined the biographical genre has coloured it even at the expense of ignoring written sources. Collins' role in the War of Independence has taken precedence over his much better documented Civil War career. Even when important documentary sources relating to crucial issues of governmental organisation and administration, for example in Ronan Fanning's 1978 work *The Irish Department of Finance 1922–58*,[3] biographers have chosen not to take cognisance of Collins' crucially important but less glamorous administrative career. Instead biographers have elected to tell what is not alone a seductive story but one which conforms to readily identifiable established literary genres and resonates deep within the Irish psyche. The bright but poor boy from Clonakilty is forced to emigrate to London only to return to rid his country of the Saxon foe. Not alone this but he wins, and with his victory he receives the keys of the kingdom. At the moment of his enthronement, when he is at the height of his powers, so he is assassinated by nothing so prosaic as his own country man but by his fellow county man in his own county. In literary terms it is a political rags to riches story which ends in tragedy. His death coincides almost to the moment with the collapse of the revolutionary ideal and imagination in the Civil War, and the disappointment of the Free State. Collins is, to borrow a title from one biography, *The Lost Leader*,[4] and increasingly seen in polemical terms as an antidote to De Valera's Ireland. The fact that there is no denying that Collins' life conforms without embellishment to this 'story' adds to its potency.

If the story of the conquering hero returned is attractive it is also grossly unanalytical. The very basic questions of Collins' contribution to the new state, its legitimacy and the foundations of its democracy have been side-stepped or suppressed in the Collins biographical genre. In this essay I wish to address Collins' political legacy with particular reference to the question of his thinking on the establishment of democratic institutions in the Free State and the separation of powers and functions.

Collins' intervention in the organisation of the new police force, the Civic Guard, in the early stages of the Civil War provides a fascinating insight into his thinking on the relationship between the pro-Treaty political organisation and the nascent administrative institutions in the new state. In late July 1922, Séamus Hughes, Secretary to the pro-Treaty party organisation, sent a memorandum to the Director of Intelligence, Major-General Joe McGrath, entitled 'Suggested Scheme of Civil Organisation for Restoration of Peace and Security'. 'The conclusion of military operations in a district', wrote Hughes,

> does not necessarily bring with it a cessation of hostilities. In Dublin up to date, there are continuous firing and attempts at guerrilla warfare. The latter is certain to develop unless checked effectively now. For this the military machine is inadequate, and the time and energy necessary to unearth the opposition cannot be spared. On the other hand almost all the information needed to make guerrilla tactics impossible is in the possession of the general public, in a scattered fashion and such operations cannot be carried out without their knowledge and connivance ... efficient civilian co-operation is the complete answer to the threat of guerrilla warfare. It is inexpensive and once successfully established, it remains as a precedent available against any repetition of the disorder.[5]

Hughes went on to suggest several names for his proposed new force: 'Citizen Guards', 'Vigilance Committee', 'Committee of Public Safety' and 'Special Constables'. Hughes added: 'Note the word "Committee" connotes the non-military notion of committee rule.' But despite this semantic nicety Hughes also suggested that the new force contain 'persons of military experience and discretion ... to be allowed to carry firearms. Volunteers to join the regular army to be sought out for this work.'

Hughes' initiative, he later claimed, had been inspired by the pro-Treaty party's General and Election Committee which had organised the 'Pact' General Election in June, but the proposal was attributed to him alone by Collins and Cosgrave. The 'Treaty Election body', he informed Arthur Griffith on 28 July,

> which was semi-military in pattern and was in touch with the protagonists of the Treaty throughout the entire country should be utilised for launching the organisation. Since then evidence has accumulated of a widespread desire on the part of our people to do their part in the present crisis and news has come from different areas of spontaneous groupings of citizens toward this end.[6]

Hughes reported that, from information received from the party organisation in the country, the anti-Treaty IRA were re-organising in areas over-run by the Free State army and prophesied a return to guerrilla fighting.

Hughes' proposal was timely. The Free State was sweeping the country and driving the IRA out of its few remaining urban strongholds. But as the new army advanced there was no civil structure to maintain law and order in its wake. The new police force had mutinied in May and had to be disbanded.[7] The military advances of July had been won on the back of IRA disorganisation and tactical ineptitude as it attempted to fight a conventional war with a guerrilla army. The IRA's abilities and experience in warfare compounded by the record of July made its return to guerrilla tactics almost certain. Collins above all others must have been aware of the fragility of the Free State's position with his former comrades about to revert to the type of warfare they had proved themselves with. With no police force functioning the only thing which stood between the Free State and collapse was a ragtail army which had been hastily mustered in the previous weeks. The battle for the countryside between the guerrillas and the garrisons seemed set to play itself out again only this time Collins found himself looking out from inside the castle.

Hughes, an able and ambitious man, identified a space and a new role for the party organisation and himself in the auxiliary police force proposal. However, the augmentation or even merger of the party with the new police force raised serious questions about the separation of functions and powers within the new state. Organisation and arming Treaty supporters into 'Vigilance Committees' or 'Special Constabularies' would have in effect made part of the government's party organisation an arm of the state's administration. For a contemporary example of this suggestion the government had only to look across the border into Northern Ireland to see the operations of the A, B and C Special Constabularies. Perhaps a more exotic proposition was the formation of an Italian style *facisti* which was in effect the sum of Hughes' proposal. The term 'Special Constabularies', drawn from within the government's party organisation, had yet to enter Treatyite political consciousness. But following Mussolini's march on Rome in late October it was embraced by some Treaty supporters. The redoubtable J. J. Walsh, Post-Master General in the government, advocated the organisation of a Treatyite *facisti* in January 1923, and deputy Margaret Collins-O'Driscoll resurrected the idea in October of the same year.[8]

At a meeting of the government on 29 July Hughes' proposal was accepted in principle and it was agreed to take action without delay. A committee was formed consisting of Arthur Griffith, Joe McGrath, Ernest Blythe, intelligence officer Captain Frank Saurin and Hughes.[9] Collins was duly informed of the decision by William Cosgrave, Acting Chairman of the Provisional Government, who sent a copy of Hughes' letter to Griffith. Reacting to the proposal Collins drafted a memorandum on the subject of the new force:

> When the military effort is ended with the defeat of hostile forces, peace can be said to have been restored. But something much more than peace is needed. Peace will have to be maintained! It is here the civilian population must do its part. Peace can only be maintained by the active co-operation of the people themselves. Harassing tactics for the purpose of holding up the economic life of the Nation can be carried on almost indefinitely by a small body of reckless men, but the people themselves – co-operating with the National Forces – can stop their tactics and prevent then [sic]. We must bring this clear responsibility to the people. The work of the soldiers and of the police forces is corrective; preventative work can be done by the co-operation of the civilian population with these forces. A small committee should be set up in each locality; such committees will promote a feeling of confidence; individuals would come more readily with information to people they knew and trusted; those civilians who knew their own localities and who know the disordered elements ... the people themselves will become actively interested in the new life of the Nation; they would realise with ever increasing clearness that it is depended [sic] upon them – upon them as a community and upon them as individuals. And their loyalty to the government would be strengthened – understand, not loyalty to a particular political government, [but] as government, [and] also civil pride and responsibility would be restored, reawakened and developed.
>
> General Commanding-in-Chief[10]

The memorandum may have been for personal reflection alone rather for circulation – Collins was in the habit of thinking aloud at his typewriter. Nevertheless it delineates his immediate response to Hughes' proposal and the government's policy. Notably, he wanted the committees to inculcate a civic spirit as well as being a platform for local recognition of the new government's legitimate authority. The logic of Hughes' argument was all the more attractive because it purported to offer a pre-emptive solution to problems of crime and disorder while at the same time consolidating the

Free State's military advances in the countryside.

Over the course of the following week Collins thought through the policing situation again. He wrote to Cosgrave on 6 August: 'With reference to your letter of 29 July and the schedule forwarded by Séamus Hughes … I think it advisable that there should be recasting to a certain extent.' This second memorandum has been cited before by Hopkinson and again by Coogan, but its relevance and importance can only be understood within the context of Hughes' initiative.[11] It is also of significance because it offers an exposition of the evolution of Collins' thought process on the question of the police auxiliary within eleven short paragraphs. He begins by calling into question the wisdom of Hughes' proposal, though initially he reiterates his positive response of 29 July. Collins then argues that the Civic Guard must control the proposed new force and suggests some improvements on the idea, but, reflecting on the problems the loosely controlled Irish Republican Police Force had caused, finally concludes that the Civic Guard's formation and distribution must take precedence over the formation of any auxiliary force.

Collins displayed a characteristic impatience with Cosgrave with regard to the distribution of the Civic Guard, writing: 'You will remember that I have repeatedly asked for a scheme of distribution of the Civic Guard to certain counties where, in our judgement, the Civic Guard could now operate'. Collins divided Hughes' proposal into its component civil and military aspects:

> The scheme outlined by Séamus Hughes falls mainly under the first heading above, and it is as an auxiliary to the Civic Guard the committees proposed by him will have value. The nucleus must be the Civic Guard organisation, and to them will rally the organisation as sketched in the memorandum. Special Constables will be an auxiliary part of the Civic Guard organisation. They might, say, wear the cap of the Civic Guard with some distinctive badge. Under this heading all such activities as road-cutting, bridge demolition, rail-wrecking, public and private robbery would be dealt with. The Civic Guard, with the help of the population, would discover the perpetrators of these deeds, and if they were not strong enough to arrest all those responsible then military help would be called in by application to the nearest commanding officer.[12]

With regard to military action – 'ambushes, sniping, hold-ups' – Collins proposed that civilian help and information would be best directed through the local military intelligence system. However, his enthusiasm for the idea of the previous week ebbed away as he continued to write:

> Generally, the matter is one on which we ought to hasten slowly. We do not want local guards that would develop into a casual police force without proper training and without the due responsibility in their work. The thing we have to keep in mind is the vital necessity of building up their foundations rather than building quickly. What we have to guard against is the setting up of any kind of organisation that might weaken governmental control although possibly helpful in the initial stage. It is not necessary for me to illustrate this by pointing to the wretched Irish Republican Police system and the awful personnel that was attracted to its ranks. The lack of construction and the lack of control in this force have been responsible for many of the outrageous things which have occurred throughout Ireland. I urge, therefore, that the first step to be taken is to distribute the Civic Guard over certain areas.[13]

The reasons for the volte-face between his initial reaction on 29 July and his position of 6 August are not clear. His experience of the Irish Republican Police, however, seems to have been instrumental in changing his mind about the advisability of establishing a police auxiliary. The Irish Republican Police had been one of the less spectacular organisations which came into being under the Dáil government during 1920–21. According to Richard Mulcahy, IRA Chief-of-Staff, GHQ had twice established a republican police force and on both occasions it had disintegrated when Austin Stack, Dáil Minister of Home Affairs, took control of it.[14] The Irish Republican Police was a constant reminder to Collins of Stack's inability as a Minister and it existed as one of many sources of antagonism between the two of them in the Dáil cabinet prior to the Treaty.

Whatever the reasons for Collins' memorandum of 6 August, it vetoed the government's decision to act on Hughes' proposal and the auxiliary force was not formed. The separation of the new police force from the Treatyite political party was of critical importance to the development of the Garda Síochána. While the new force after July 1922 was exclusively drawn from pro-Treaty supporters and could hardly under the circumstances claim to be apolitical, it was a centralised, disciplined, professional, full time police force which could become apolitical and proved itself to be worthy of that epithet with the transfer of power to the anti-Treaty forces in 1932. Unlike its counterpart in the north, the Royal Ulster Constabulary, which failed so spectacularly to win the confidence of its public, the Civic Guard did not expand to absorb 'spontaneous groupings of citizens', nor did it have its authority undermined by the partisan activities of an auxiliary.

For the decision to form a professional police force and its impact on creating the conditions for a democracy to take root in the Free State, Michael Collins deserves much credit and argues for a sympathetic reading of him as a net contributor to democratic culture in the Free State. Any such reading is however, complicated by his decision to re-organise the Irish Republican Brotherhood within the army in July 1922.[15] Collins' plans for the reconstructed pro-Treaty Brotherhood were expressed in a new draft constitution which included the establishment of eleven 'vocational' representatives from the army to augment the sixteen 'county' or divisional representatives on the Supreme Council.[16] The decision to re-organise the Brotherhood, an oath-bound secret society, within the state machine sits uneasily alongside the proposition that Collins was an unqualified democrat.

It has to be conceded that the Brotherhood under Collins' leadership brought its clauses into line with the Dáil and accepted its authority after 1919.[17] This was also true of the 1922 Constitution which declared that 'political authority is exercised through instruments legitimately established.'[18] But there was no escaping the fact that there was a bald contradiction between a secret oath-bound society dedicated to using its considerable influence toward establishing a republic existing within what aspired to be a democratic state. The Brotherhood acknowledged the legitimacy of the evolving Free State but under Collins' leadership it continued to exist outside its authority. The real significance of re-organising the Brotherhood and expanding its representation in the army was that it reinforced Collins' authority and underpinned his own position as leader. Collins' leadership was the sole *raison d'être* of the re-organised Brotherhood. So much so that when he was killed on 22 August his successors ceased to see any further purpose for the Brotherhood and wound it up within a week; it was only brought back into existence in early 1923 to prevent the anti-Treaty elements claiming it for themselves.[19]

The re-organisation of the Brotherhood was part of Collins' desire to centralise power in himself. He had taken over military power at his own request, becoming Commander-in-Chief of the army at the beginning of July.[20] At the same time he remained firmly in control of the civil government with Cosgrave acting as his deputy-cum-amanuensis in the cabinet, which, as we have already seen in the case of the police auxiliary, submitted to his veto. All sources of power within the regime led back to Collins. The Dáil courts had been suspended along with *habeas corpus* on the outbreak of the Civil War, and the Third Dáil elected in June had been suspended by the Provisional Government a fortnight later. With Griffith's death on 12 August and with no parliament to which he had to account, Collins, for better or for worse, assumed dictatorial powers within the new regime.

Collins was particularly determined not to have the Third Dáil meet. On the afternoon of 21 August while in Cork he recorded a message for Cosgrave: 'It is wise to postpone the Dáil meeting as already suggested.'[21] The casualness of the direction disarms its importance. On 12 August the Labour party sent an ultimatum resolved at its annual congress to the Provisional Government demanding that the new parliament meet by the 26 August. In the event of the parliament not being convoked the Labour party threatened to resign their seats. Such action would have deprived the new Dáil of its only opposition party and, in the event of it meeting, would have turned it into a single party assembly. On receipt of Collins' instruction Cosgrave instructed Patrick Hogan to reply in the negative to the Labour party. Hogan wrote on 22 August: 'I am again to remind you that the issue at stake is not whether parliament should meet this month ranther [sic] than next, but whether parliament is to exist in this country.'[22] The decision and the letter were in tone and outlook far more negative than Collins' last report from the south-west, where he felt conditions were good enough to receive the Civic Guard.[23] Hogan's letter was never sent to the Labour party and, in all probability, it was still on his desk where he was working when the news arrived at Government Buildings in Dublin in the early morning of 23 August that Collins had been shot in west Cork.[24] One of the first decisions of the government having elected Cosgrave as Chairman was to overturn Collins' suspension of parliament and announce the convocation of the Third Dáil on 24 August.

Whatever Collins' exact intentions were it has to be acknowledged his death speeded up the return to parliamentary accountability, with the IRB being dissolved on 31 August and the Third

Dáil finally meeting in Dublin on 9 September.[25] It must be remembered that economies, governments and all power structures tend to centralise in time of war. The Provisional Government was no exception but the conditions of July 1922 suited Collins' style of conspiratorial and centralised politics. As he placed himself at the centre of the revolutionary movement in 1919–21, controlling intelligence and the Ministry of Finance, so in July–August 1922 he gathered in the reins by controlling both civil and military powers and in both instances using the Brotherhood as a secret double indemnity.

Some of the crucial decisions he made in those final weeks of his life had profound implications on the successful development of a democratic culture in the Free State. But in Collins' design it was to be a culture and polity circumscribed by the Irish Republican Brotherhood, and very much Michael Collins' personal Brotherhood. One of his last decisions was to nominate the Secretary of the Supreme Council, Seán Ó Muirthile, as Commissioner of the Garda Síochána.[26] His decision not to convoke the Dáil in August, with the risk of alienating and inducing the resignations of the Labour party deputies, was a strategy which risked the legitimacy of any later parliament and must therefore raise questions about his long term ambitions. As the crisis worsened, with Collins' death following ten days after Griffith's, it is interesting to note that his colleagues, civil and military, reversed his policies and took a sharp turn toward establishing a parliamentary democracy which accepted in principle the unquestioned sovereignty of the people.

In political terms Michael Collins died intestate. While he bequeathed strong democratic institutions like the Garda Síochána he also left a legacy of conspiratorial politics and revolutionary institutions in what aspired to be a constitutional democracy. This anomaly between constitutional and revolutionary politics went unresolved until they collided in the Army Mutiny in March 1924, which resulted in the IRB and its offshoot, the Irish Republican Army organisation, being purged from the army and regime. Michael Collins died as he had lived, an enigma. But for all the questions about his democratic credentials – and they must be asked – it was his constitutional legacy which was triumphant at the expense of his conspiratorial intestacy.

MICHAEL COLLINS
HIS BIOGRAPHERS PIARAS BÉASLAÍ AND REX TAYLOR

Deirdre McMahon

After the Truce in July 1921 Michael Collins received a number of offers to write his memoirs. The sums were immense: £10,000 from one London agent and $20,000 from the *New York World*. In 1922 Collins gave a series of interviews to an American journalist called Hayden Talbot which appear to have been intended as the basis of a biography. The day after Collins' funeral Talbot was contacted by Colonel Joe O'Reilly, one of Collins' closest friends, and was warned off writing any biography. Two days later Collins' eldest brother Seán contacted the new Chairman of the Provisional Government, W. T. Cosgrave, and told him that he wished Piaras Béaslaí to write the biography. Béaslaí had been involved with the language movement, the IRB and the Volunteers before 1916. He had fought in the 1916 Rising and was elected TD for East Kerry during the First Dáil. During the War of Independence he was Director of Publicity for the IRA and editor of the Volunteer journal *An tÓglach*.

Cosgrave consulted two of Collins' closest colleagues, Gearóid O'Sullivan (a brother in law of Collins' fiancée, Kitty Kiernan) and Diarmuid O'Hegarty, Secretary of the Provisional Government and later to the Department of the President. O'Sullivan commented, revealingly, that 'literary generals are not always endowed with sufficient keenness and greatness of mind to appreciate the enormous vices and virtues combined in one person.' He and O'Sullivan also resented Béaslaí's claim to have been Collins' 'intimate daily associate' since 1916. Their distaste for the project considerably influenced Cosgrave's attitude. Although the Civil War was raging at the time, the subject of Collins' biography came before the Provisional Government in September and October 1922, a measure of its sensitivity.

The Provisional Government imposed stringent conditions on Béaslaí: the book would be the property of the government, although the author's name would appear on the cover; it was not to be serialised; if it made a profit royalties would be considered for the author; Béaslaí would have to submit synopses of chapters to a committee consisting of O'Sullivan, O'Hegarty and Kevin O'Sheil, who was then <u>Assistant Legal Adviser to the Provisional</u> Government. Béaslaí was furious at these terms and told Eamonn Duggan, Cosgrave's Parliamentary Secretary,

> under no circumstances will I consent to have my book when completed tampered with, altered or revised by any other person. I have given a guarantee that in all disclosure of facts and presentations of points of view I would be guided entirely by the advice of the committee named and would do nothing contrary to their wishes. If that guarantee is not sufficient then they can go to Hell ... any alteration or revision to be made must be made *by myself only* ... No self-respecting writer would ever submit to such an insulting proposal ... Let the government get a civil servant at a decent salary to compile their 'official' Blue Book and I'll write the life in my own way.

Béaslaí enlisted the support of the Collins family which was firmly behind him, particularly since he had promised them most of the royalties from serialisation and from the book. Seán Collins wrote a stinging letter to Cosgrave:

> I can only say, after full consideration, that a life of Michael Collins written and published under such conditions will never be published with my consent or the consent of any other member of his family. I consider it an insult to me and the other members of his family that without consulting us you should seek to claim the work as your property, and to impose such conditions on the man whom I selected for his literary ability, close personal friendship with and absolute knowledge of my brother. Unless I am allowed a free hand with the author in bringing out the book no member of the Collins family will give any assistance in bringing out the proposed government publication.

The government could not afford to alienate the Collins family. Cosgrave backed down and agreed that Béaslaí would be released from military duties in order to devote himself to the book, that he would be given secretarial assistance, and that he would be given access to official documents.

But it was clear that these terms were granted with considerable reluctance. Béaslaí was not released from military duties and his secretarial assistance was withdrawn in September 1923, despite his protests to Cosgrave. However, he did get access to official records and actually removed files from government buildings unknown, as it appears, to senior officials at the President's Department. Béaslaí returned files to the department in 1927 and 1929 and their condition so horrified the Assistant Secretary, Michael Mc-Dunphy, that his complaints remained on file for decades as a warning not to give access to other researchers.

The tenuous co-operation between Béaslaí and the government over the book was finally terminated after the Army Mutiny in 1924. Béaslaí was demoted in the subsequent re-organisation but the government was also distinctly more lukewarm towards the Collins book in 1924, particularly since Collins' name and legacy had been invoked by the mutineers as a stick with which to beat the government. But the Collins family remained loyal and gave considerable help, notably Collins' sister Hannie with whom he had lived when working in London before 1916.

The book provoked varying reactions. The government made no comment, happy with Béaslaí's hostile comments about De Valera but much less happy about his criticisms that the Free State had not lived up to Collins' ideals. Ministers maintained a discreet silence, conscious that they had, after all, given Béaslaí access to official documents (which were not to be seen again by other researchers for forty years). There was no reference in the book to Kitty Kiernan who had married Felix Cronin in 1925. To judge from the unflattering references to her in Béaslaí's diary, he wondered what on earth Collins had seen in her. Collins' sister Hannie hated the book and refused to co-operate with the second edition in 1937. Béaslaí also received a letter from Arthur Griffith's widow Maud who expressed her loathing of Collins, singling out his underhand treatment of Griffith at the Sinn Féin Árd Fheis in May 1922, and Béaslaí's account of the shelling of the Four Courts which, she argued strenuously, Griffith had been against. Perhaps the most notable silence came from Richard Mulcahy, former IRA Chief-of-Staff and Free State Minister of Defence, who refused to review the book in 1926 and again in 1937 when the second edition was published. Mulcahy was aware of the potential sensitivity of any review in 1926 but also believed that his criticisms were too extensive for one review. After his retirement from politics he compiled an extensive 500 page commentary on the 1937 edition. His main criticisms were that Béaslaí had not consulted him nor any other senior army officer at the time, and that he also had little knowledge of the wider army organisation or of GHQ.

Béaslaí's biography of Collins was the first shot in a hard fought historical war. In the mid 1930s, within the space of two years 1935–7, there was the publication of Frank Pakenham's *Peace By Ordeal*, Ernie O'Malley's *On Another Man's Wound*, Desmond Ryan's *Unique Dictator*, Frank O'Connor's *The Big Fellow*, Dorothy Macardle's *The Irish Republic* and the second edition of Béaslaí's book. The catalyst for the second edition was the publication of Frank Pakenham's account of the Treaty negotiations, *Peace by Ordeal*, in 1935. In the senior echelons of Fine Gael it was considered vital to counter Pakenham's criticisms of the way Collins and Griffith had handled the negotiations. Despite their reservations about the 1926 biography, the Fine Gael leadership took a more active interest in the second edition and this time Béaslaí had several interviews with W. T. Cosgrave, Desmond FitzGerald, and Michael Hayes.

They were disappointed with the results which was essentially a one volume abridgement of the 1926 edition. But the political landscape had changed by 1937. When Béaslaí originally published the biography, De Valera was a political down-and-out who had just split with Sinn Féin (confirming Béaslaí's portrait of him as the archsplitter personified) and had founded a new party, Fianna Fáil, which was refusing to take its seats in the Dáil. By 1937 De Valera was the victor of three general elections, local elections and the referendum on his new constitution. Phrases about De Valera's 'road to ruin' had a hollow ring by then. In the 1950s there were tentative plans for a third edition of the Collins biography but these failed to materialise. By the time Béaslaí died in 1965 another substantial Collins biography had appeared, that of Rex Taylor in 1958.

The history of Béaslaí's book demonstrated the perils of official biography. Rex Taylor's was an unofficial biography which raised problems which have still, apparently, to be recognised by historians. Taylor, according to the blurb of his book, was a limestone quarry labourer and a poet who was a protégé of Robert Graves. He worked on the Collins biography for nine years. The book was the subject of a long report from the Irish Embassy in London on 7 October 1958 which was passed on to the Department of the Taoiseach. The report, which was written by Frank Biggar, son-in-law to Seán MacEntee, noted that the book had been extensively reviewed 'even if the reviewers tended to give a good deal more space to their own opinions of Collins and his times than to those of the author.' The extent to which the book was noticed 'does constitute some measure of the impression which Collins made on the England of his time. Indeed it would hardly be an exaggeration to say that his is one of the two Irish names which the generality of Englishmen of that generation would automatically associate with the period; the other name is, of course, the present Taoiseach.'

The reviewers included Frank MacDermot who reviewed it for the *Sunday Times* and attacked Collins for his campaign of assassination during the War of Independence. The reviewer for the *Daily Telegraph* was Lord Birkenhead, son of the first Lord Birkenhead who had been a member of the British delegation in the Treaty negotiations and whom Collins had respected. His son praised Collins warmly in his review, an attitude Biggar thought noteworthy in view of the *Telegraph*'s usual outlook on matters Irish. Robert Kee reviewed it for *The Spectator* and found it the least readable but historically the most valuable of the biographies which had been published to date on Collins. He thought Taylor was mistaken to praise Collins so fulsomely and to condemn De Valera and the republicans for entangling themselves in verbal will-o'-the-wisps. The *New Statesman* review was written by Brendan Behan and was, in Biggar's opinion, 'a characteristically rumbunctious [sic] article'. Of Desmond Williams' review in the *Manchester Guardian* Biggar commented that Professor Williams 'virtually ignored Mr Taylor in order to give his own view of Collins' life in summary form.' Williams argued that while Collins was the first effective organiser of modern urban guerrilla warfare, De Valera had supplanted him in the wider world outside the two countries. Biggar concluded that most of the reviewers accepted Taylor's version of the Treaty negotiations and the Civil War, including the view that Collins was persuaded against his better judgement to be a member of the Irish delegation and that, in doing so, he signed his death warrant. That phrase came from Collins' correspondence with John O'Kane which Taylor quoted extensively in his chapters on the Treaty and which have been cited in nearly every book on Collins and the period since then. They have been a primary source for Collins' distrust of De Valera.

According to Taylor, John O'Kane was an Irish businessman from County Galway who lived in Hampstead at whose home 'Collins was made welcome ... Mostly, whenever he found it impossible to see O'Kane personally, he sent a note or letter and it is chiefly from these documents that the real position of Collins, and the burden he bore, are to be seen.' Taylor quotes from fifteen letters between Collins and O'Kane, the first on 17 October 1921 and the last on 14/17 July 1922. The letter of 6 December 1921, just after the signing of the Treaty, is particularly well known:

> When you have sweated, toiled, had mad dreams, hopeless night-mares, you find yourself in London's streets, cold and dank in the night air. Think – what have I got for Ireland? Something which she has wanted these past seven hundred years. Will anyone be satisfied at the bargain? Will anyone? I tell you this – early this morning I signed my death warrant.

Most of the letters cited in the book were written between 17 October and 6 December 1921. Towards the end of November, when the Treaty negotiations were reaching their most critical phase, Collins appears to have been writing to O'Kane every day.

In an appendix on his sources Taylor states that he could only divulge the name of Eithne O'Kane, niece of John O'Kane, of the four people who gave him source material. He states that 'these letters, and others not mentioned in this biography, are in matchless condition owing to the fact that they have been treated, pasted onto paper and carefully bound. Papers of various sizes, in colour white or blue, are used, and, as many of them were written when Collins was pressed for time, they are invariably headed 'Cad Gdns' [Cadogan Gardens], where Collins stayed during the time he was in London for the Treaty discussions'. Taylor stated that he was 'prepared to depose on oath that the documents have been in his possession, and that the material in this book no way distorts the originals'.

Who was John O'Kane? No one of that name is listed in London business or residential directories of the period. There is no reference to O'Kane in Collins' letters to Kitty Kiernan and other biographers and historians seem to be equally in the dark about him. In his article on Collins and the assassination of Sir Henry Wilson in *Irish Historical Studies* in 1992 Peter Hart states that he contacted Rex Taylor's widow who told him that Taylor's papers could not be located. In Tim Pat Coogan's biography of Collins the mystery of O'Kane deepens. Coogan states that he was told by Valentine Iremonger, the poet and diplomat, that he had visited Taylor when he was writing his book on Collins. 'Taylor showed him research material which included Michael Collins' diaries and day books and a collection of Moya Llewelyn Davies' letters, some of which indicated a love affair'. Rex Taylor agreed to send Iremonger 'small parcels at a time' to the Irish Embassy in London so that Iremonger could have them copied and then place copies in the National Library with a thirty year prohibition. But 'following a subsequent conversation on an open telephone line ... two men in bowler hats, acting for a firm of solicitors who represented the Llewelyn Davies, showed up with an authorisation to repossess the documents and took them away'. In note 117, chapter 7, Coogan refers to a letter quoted by Taylor as 'addressed to John O'Kane, a London-based Irish businessman. The person alluded to did exist and was close to Collins throughout the Treaty negotiations. However I have reason to suppose that O'Kane was a pseudonym.'

So O'Kane was a pseudonym. For whom? If it was a pseudonym, this also presumably applies to Eithne O'Kane whose recollections of Collins are quoted at length in the biography. Taylor was the only person who had access to this material and it has disappeared since then. The question marks over this material should, I think, make scholars of the period cautious.

Heroic biographies
IN FOLKLORE AND POPULAR CULTURE

Diarmuid Ó Gilláin

The belief that De Valera was born with the mark of the cross on his back was known in County Clare.[1] It is a tradition associated with heroic figures generally and it was widely known. In the same vein are numerous traditions of Daniel O'Connell.[2] They belong to that complex of belief known as the 'heroic biography' which has been studied by various scholars since the 1870s.

Lord Raglan, writing in 1934, was struck by the similarities in the biographies of mythological heroes and of some historical ones. He applied a pattern derived initially from the biography of Oedipus to the stories of other heroes and awarded a score, based on the number of similar elements in their biographies, the maximum being Oedipus' twenty-two. Hence Moses, for example, was awarded twenty-one, Romulus seventeen, King Arthur sixteen, Joseph twelve and Siegfried of the Nibelungenlied nine.[3] It is clear that this model has influenced the recorded lives of a number of historic figures, from Cyrus of Persia to Jesus to Theodoric. In the schema of Jan de Vries the heroic biography can be broken down into ten elements, dealing with incidents in the hero's life, from the begetting of the hero, his birth, his being endangered as a youth, and continuing on to his death.[4] Raglan thinks that they deal particularly with birth, accession to the throne and death, and correspond to the three traditional rites of passage.[5]

Ríonach Uí Ógáin compares the heroic biography with Daniel O'Connell's life in folklore and finds many of the characteristic elements represented. The hero's conception and birth are of an extraordinary nature. O'Connell's parents are a childless couple, often very old, who give a poor priest money so that he can finish building a church. The priest promises to pray for them and a child is subsequently born bearing the mark of the cross on his back, indicative of the great future in store for him.[6] We have hints of this too in Collins' biography. His sister quoted her uncle, on seeing the new-born Michael, say: 'Be careful of this child for he will be a great and mighty man when we are all forgotten.'[7] Michael's father, on his deathbed, told the family to mind the six year old because 'one day he'll be a great man. He'll do great work for Ireland.'[8] The hero often reveals his powers at a precociously young age. In one of the stories told about O'Connell he gives a wise judgement on a legal complaint at seven years of age.[9] The hero is brought up in a far-away place. In O'Connell's case he is fostered. Like the hero, O'Connell was invulnerable or, like Achilles, could only be wounded in the heel. The hero shows his prowess in victory over various kinds of enemies, with D'Esterre figuring in O'Connell's case. He also has healing and poetic powers. As for his death, the tree planted on the day he was born withers and dies.[10] The hero's charisma had an un-deniably sexual element, and this is a well-known part of O'Connell's reputation,[11] and indeed of Collins' – Neil Jordan in his diary of the making of *Michael Collins* refers to 'the popular romantic image of Collins as an Irish Don Juan among the English upper classes.'[12]

De Vries tells us that the cult of the hero was found throughout the entire Greek world. A hero could be defined as an exceptionally brave man who was worshipped. Men who died in battle received the homage due to a hero. 'The hero', as he puts it, 'is a dead man who has grown far beyond ordinary life.'[13] Despite the best efforts of the medieval Christian Church there is evidence of a cult of figures from heroic legend, such as from the Chanson de Roland and wor-ship at the grave of Charlemagne, but rationalised in the capacity of these heroes as warriors for the faith against the Muslim infidel.[14]

How does a historic figure come to be identified with the heroic model? Writing of Cyrus of Persia De Vries argues that it was not a gradual process, but rather 'at a certain moment people saw in him, as the Ostrogoths saw in Theodoric, no longer an ordinary mortal but a true hero, and then his life was at once transformed in accord with the heroic pattern.'[15] Mircea Eliade writes of what he calls 'the mould of the archaic mentality, which cannot accept what is indi-vidual and preserves only what is exemplary.'[16] Thus events are re-duced to categories and individuals to archetypes and he points out that this is done almost down to our own day.

He argues that in archaic or traditional societies an act is real 'only insofar as it imitates or repeats an archetype' and 'everything which lacks an exemplary model is "meaningless".' Every warrior's acts are significant only insofar as they imitate those prototypical acts of a god or a mythical hero which took place at the beginning of time, *in illo tempore*. In the same sense the observation of the Sabbath is significant only insofar as it is an imitation of God's rest on the seventh day after the creation of the world, an *imitatio dei*. A familiar myth Eliade discusses is the combat between the hero and a monster. He argues that great monarchs considered themselves as imitators of the primordial hero. Darius saw himself as a new Thraetona, the mythical hero who slew the monster.[17] Dieudonné de Gozon, the third grand master of the Knights of St John at Rhodes who died in 1502, is famous for slaying the dragon of Malpasso but this exploit is first recorded some two centuries after his death. He was regarded as a hero, and as such could not but have fought a monster.[18]

The nature of the heroic biography also has to do with the logistics of conserving information in an oral culture. According to Walter Ong:

> oral memory works effectively with 'heavy' characters, persons whose deeds are monumental, memorable and commonly public. Thus the noetic [of the intellect] economy of its nature generates outsize figures, that is heroic figures, not for romantic reasons or effectively didactic reasons but for much more basic reasons: to organise experience in some sort of permanently memorable form. Colourless personalities cannot survive oral mnemonics.[19]

We can add to that by stating that it was much easier for the man of action to be a hero because of the memorable stereotyped images of violence associated with the model. Ong points out that in an oral culture the arrangement of knowledge in rational abstract categories is impossible: 'Oral cultures cannot generate such categories, and so they use stories of human action to store, organise and communicate much of what they know.'[20]

The physical attributes of the hero were part of his charisma. Tom Garvin mentions Todd Andrews' disappointment on seeing the small stature of many of the political leaders of the War of Independence.[21] Writing of German working class autobiographies of the nineteenth and twentieth centuries Wolfgang Kaschuba notes:

> a conspicuously keen perception and stressing of one's own (and others') 'labour power', physical constitution, and capacity to work. It functions almost like a literary-stylistic form of narrative structuring: virtually every person who enters for the first time upon the stage of some scene recalled in memory is initially described in totally external terms, a description focused on attributes of physical prowess and capacity to perform labour. Only after that is he or she characterised in respect to social attributes and modes of behaviour.[22]

An emphasis on physical prowess is less effective unless that prowess is demonstrated, and this is done through the violent actions of the hero. Ong points out that the depiction of gross physical violence is central to genres of oral literature and residual through much early literacy. 'As literary narrative moves towards the serious novel,' he argues, 'it eventually pulls the focus of action more and more to interior crises and away from purely exterior crises.'[23] We might add that as narrative moves from folklore or medieval epic to highly elaborated literary genres it also moves away from the subaltern classes of town and country, or from the medieval and early modern aristocracies who owed their land and title to success in warfare, to the urban bourgeoisie whose status is independent of their physical prowess.

Frank O'Connor's *The Big Fellow* especially emphasises Collins' charisma and physical prowess:

> People were already growing accustomed to his ways; the warning thump of his feet on the stairs as he took them six at a time, the crash of the door and the searching look, and that magnetic power of revivifying the stalest air. People still describe the way in which one became aware of his presence, even when he was not visible, through that uncomfortable magnetism of the very air, a tingling of the nerves.[24]

Liam Neeson's towering frame in Neil Jordan's film, by exaggerating Collins' height, emphasises his heroic dimensions and in the process doubly shrinks De Valera.

Charisma was what made a hero. In Weber's sociological formulation charisma can be defined as a term 'applied to a certain quality of an individual personality by virtue of which he is set apart from ordinary men and treated as endowed with supernatural, superhuman, or at least specifically exceptional powers or qualities.'[25] The shaman, heroes, certain intellectuals, the prophet or saviour all exemplified charisma. Weber saw it as being outside the domain of the everyday and 'sharply opposed to both rational, and particularly bureaucratic, authority, and to traditional authority'. He saw it receding as new permanent institutional structures were established.[26] He was treating, of course, above all of religion, but religion always intersects with other social spheres. The Greek worship of fallen warriors is a good example of this. Great villains also have charisma. In the Irish tradition Cromwell plays a particularly significant role in this regard, and often, at a more local level, so does the landlord.[27] The landlord's charisma is exemplified in the events of an armed peasant takeover of a latifundia in a Latin American country, which Paulo Freire recounts:

> For tactical reasons, they planned to hold the landowner as a hostage. But not one peasant had the courage to guard him; his very presence was terrifying. It is also possible that the act of opposing the boss provoked guilt feelings. In truth, the boss was 'inside' them.[28]

The heroic biography covers the whole life cycle of the hero. As a young man he disappears for a long time before returning and executing great deeds. His return is eagerly awaited by a people who believe he will deliver them from oppression. This messianic theme is well known, and appears in religious traditions and in literature: the *aisling*, for example.[29] Folklorists know it as the Barbarossa legend, of the hero under enchantment waiting to be released in order to free his people. In Ireland various figures appear in the role, particularly Gearóid Iarla, one of the Earls of Desmond or Kildare, Balldearg or Aodh Rua Ó Domhnaill or Aodh Ó Néill, or even Robert Bruce or Fionn Mac Cumhaill. Often the enchanted army will be awakened by unsheathing a sword, but the nerve of the intruder who begins to do so fails him as he sees the soldiers gradually awaken so he replaces the sword and they again fall asleep. He is chided for his cowardice, as in the Cavan version, where the mysterious gentleman who brought him to the spot, ostensibly for another purpose, says: 'Why didn't you pull that sword from its scabbard? If you did so, all these soldiers would awaken out of their slumber, and they would go out to free Ireland.'[30]

This messianic tradition is particularly susceptible to political manipulation, as happened in a number of celebrated cases. The ruler had died but an impostor appeared, often years later, claiming to be he and was the cause of much popular disturbance. Perhaps the most famous case is that of the Portuguese King Sebastian, killed in battle with the Moors in 1578. Shortly after the battle rumours of his survival came back to Portugal with the few boatloads of survivors. In 1584 a hermit claimed to be Sebastian and was accepted as such by some of the peasantry. He ended up as a galley slave and his advisers were executed. Shortly afterwards another Sebastian appeared, a hermit who resembled the dead king, and was the cause of a rebellion against Portugal's recent Spanish rulers. He was executed in 1585. Ten years later a third impostor appeared, directed by a monk, both of whom were executed in the same year. In 1598 a Calabrian claimed to be Sebastian before being captured in Florence and he was punished by being made a galley slave. It seems that at the beginning of the nineteenth century a sect of *sebastianistas* appeared and was opposed by the Church. The tradition of '*o príncipe encuberto*' – 'the hidden prince' – remained and was recorded in Brazil in 1838.[31]

Ideologies of the right flirted with this messianic idea, the moment of destiny, and so forth (is this not what Operation Barbarossa meant?) and a fascination with violence and death among modernist circles, such as the 'warrior poets' of the Futurists or D'Annunzio or Mishima, showed the persistence of the heroic idea in a sort of reactionary modernism.[32] As we know the idea was also attractive to elements of Irish nationalism. The messianic legend has in the twentieth century fuelled rumours of noted or notorious deceased or notoriously deceased public figures such as Hitler, John F. Kennedy, Yuri Gagarin or Elvis Presley still being alive. A particularly interesting case of a modern cult is that around the vocalist of the band *The Doors*, Jim Morrison, who died in 1971 and whose grave in Père Lachaise graveyard in Paris is its focal point, visited every year by tens of thousands of fans. The rituals are connected to the counter-culture of the 1960s and have been the subject of an anthropological monograph.[33]

A hero needs a people. The existence of a hero with a historical basis in a people's tradition often seems to suggest that the identification of the real individual with the hero has a political dimension to it. Habermas defines the public sphere as a domain of public life in which such a thing as public opinion can be formed. He argues that before the eighteenth century no distinction was made between opinion and *public* opinion. Opinion or opinions he describes as 'things taken for granted as part of a culture, normative convictions, collective prejudices and judgements' – which seems to coincide with Gramsci's idea of common sense – whereas public opinion is formed by a public that engages in rational discussion.[34] The hero belongs to 'those things taken for granted as part of a culture' but the identification of a real individual as the hero seems to be a more complicated process.

Oral communication and tradition as well as popular literature should be considered among the media of a subaltern public sphere,[35] and indeed there has always been a substantial amount of feedback between oral tradition and the various print media, which have greatly increased their reach in the course of the last two centuries. A charismatic figure may borrow from the traditional heroic biography, but also from the propaganda of a party political press and a popular press eager to satisfy the curiosity of the public with gossip and scandal. The modern entertainment industry's creation of a star system has magnified the charisma not just of actors and singers but also of other public figures, and in many ways has blurred the distinctions between them, and between our notions of charisma on the one hand and glamour on the other.[36] Hence both Collins, the revolutionary leader, and Lady Lavery, the prominent socialite, are of equal public interest in the same way that politicians or royalty are as likely as pop stars and actors to appear in the pages of gossip magazines. Let us note relatively new connotations to the words 'personality' and 'celebrity', and their obverse, the 'nonentity'.[37]

Clearly there are different types of hero. G. S. Kirk quotes Farnell's work from 1921 which distinguishes seven types of heroes in hero-cults from Greek sources: hieratic hero-gods of cult origin; sacral heroes or heroines who are associated with a god, perhaps as priest or priestess; secular figures who eventually became fully divinised; epic heroes; fictitious eponyms and genealogical heroes; functional and cultural daemons, often anonymous and always of secondary or merely local importance; and 'finally a few real men (that is, men who certainly lived) who were made heroes after their deaths and given minor cults within the full historical period', according to Kirk. 'Popular taste does not change so much,' he adds laconically, 'they seem to have been primarily boxers and athletes.'[38] Dáithí Ó hÓgáin in his book *The Hero in Irish Folk History* finds five categories of hero: the social leader, the best example being O'Connell; the liberator, who represents the messianic tradition and is exemplified in the various interpreters of the Barbarossa legend; the outlaw; the poet; and his catch-all category, 'hero extraordinary'.[39]

Tales of heroes are artistic forms bound by the conventions of the artistic work.[40] Artistic works by their nature have a structure and a dynamic which sets them apart from real life. Part of the polemic exchanges over the Collins film were motivated by an unwillingness to accept that the artistic work creates its own reality and that its logic derives not from its relationship to a supposed objective reality but from its own inner structure. Neil Jordan recounts in his film diary how on reading an early draft of the *Michael*

Collins screenplay – 'fiercely accurate to the history' as he puts it – David Puttnam 'felt it lacked a committed sense of the central character and, more important or more disturbingly, lacked an identifiable villain.'[41] Alan Parker, director of *Evita*, the musical film about the life of Eva Perón which opened to controversy in Argentina in February 1997, was quoted in the Buenos Aires daily *La Nación* as saying:

> It is certain that at the press conference here in Buenos Aires I felt more a politician than a director. Finally I am responsible for the work and therefore I showed myself open to respond to these questions ... But there were moments when I wanted to say: 'Excuse me, this is an artistic representation.' Sometimes people forget that I am an artist who simply wanted to tell a story.[42]

The semiotician Jurij Lotman argues that the leading personae of 'numerous artistic and non-artistic texts' can be divided into two groups, 'agents, and the conditions and circumstances of the action'. The former are distinguished from the latter 'by virtue of their mobility with respect to their surroundings.'

> The active hero conducts himself differently from the other personae, and he alone possesses this right. The right to behave in a special manner (heroically, immorally, morally, insanely, unpredictably, strangely, but always free from circumstances that are obligatory for immobile personae) is demonstrated by a long line of literary figures ...[43]

Ernie O'Malley had the rare and disquieting experience of seeing himself grow into a hero whose life was at odds with his own. He tells of hearing his own name in song at the few dances he attended during the 1919–21 period:

> Many of us could hardly see ourselves for the legends built up around us. The legends helped to give others an undue sense of our ability or experience, but they hid our real selves; when I saw myself as clearly as I could in terms of myself, I resented the legend. It made me other than myself and attuned to act to standards that were not my own. That was different to the other subordination of oneself to the movement.[44]

Alan Parker's *Evita* and its reception in Argentina offer interesting parallels with *Michael Collins*. In *Evita*, too, we have the cinematic depiction of a controversial heroic figure who helped to define the parameters of twentieth century national history while at the same time epitomising the subsequent lasting political division. In the case of *Evita*, though, the film was the work of a foreign director, in a foreign language and in the less realistic form of the musical. It was possible to follow the debate on *Evita* through the Argentinian press *via* the Internet.[45] *Evita* was not a great success in the Argentinian box office, perhaps reflecting a traditional lack of interest in the genre of cinematic musical as some commentators suggested, but also a hostility towards a foreign interpretation reflected by protests at the *première* by Peronist groups with placards stating: '*Viva Evita, fuera Alan Parquer*', and indicating particular hostility towards the actress Madonna.[46] Indeed the vice president in the Peronist government, Carlos Ruckauf, proposed a boycott of the film.[47] There were isolated attacks on cinemas when the film first opened.[48]

Nevertheless the film was a major event. As *La Nación* put it:

> Who, lover or not of the seventh art, will wish to feel excluded from the major filmic event of the year? Who, Peronist or not, will let the opportunity pass to applaud or denounce this work of Parker's ...? Who ... will not feel enticed, be it by the mere curiosity to see reflected on the screen this Evita who already is part of our recent history?[49]

La Nación invited a Peronist senator, Antonio Cafiero, and a Radical deputy, Federico Storani, to see *Evita* together, and interviewed them afterwards. Both agreed that only an extremist fringe hated Evita today and that Argentinians either respected her or loved her. 'Time feeds the myth', as the Radical expressed it. 'But there is respect. And above all the valorisation of a transforming political moment'. The following is part of the exchange between the two:

> *Storani:* The first part [of the film] appeared bad to me, tiresome, a caricature. Madonna acted Madonna and not the character and therefore she has a sensuality distinct from that which Evita, who was also a sensual woman, could have ...
> *Cafiero,* interrupting: No you are wrong, excuse me ...
> *Storani:* Yes, you knew her.
> *Cafiero:* Yes, of course, and Evita was not a sensual woman.
> *Storani:* But the myth, some photos and some expressions spoke of her as a more refined sensual woman and with style ...
> *Cafiero:* I who knew Evita and had dealings with her, I do not feel an identification with the character Madonna portrays. She is trying to

sell a version of Evita which is not the real one, she interprets her as an actress who plays a role she does not feel. Evita was not an actress. When she assumed the role which touched her in life, that consumed her, that was her true essence.[50]

Surely here we have in these words the essence of the hero and the essence of the saint. Female heroes have few positive categories other than the saint. The discussion indicates the tension between possible female roles in patriarchal society, between the madonna and the whore, and the portrayal of a remarkable woman – a saint to many – by a foreign actress renowned for the projection of her own sexuality was an uncomfortable coming together of the sacred and the profane. It is easy to understand why the leader of a Peronist group should declare: 'This film is not a work of art. It is a psychological aggression against the Argentinian people.'[51]

Nor should we be surprised that Senator Cafiero suspected that the film was an English attempt at revenge since Perón's government was the first, as he put it, to break with a tradition of subjection to the British empire.[52] There were similar reactions in Britain to Jordan's film. 'The *Daily Telegraph* editorialises; Paul Johnson fulminates (the polite world) in the *Spectator*; and metropolitan talking heads achieve a fine blend of ignorance and venom on the late night talk shows', as *The Scotsman* put it before explaining the furore in blunt terms: 'What British commentators really mean is that this is an Irish account of Irish history.'[53] Nor should we be surprised at the refusal to separate the personality of the actor from the role. It could be argued that Liam Neeson's heroic Collins gains from the actor's own accumulation of charisma in previous films, first as Oskar Schindler and then as Rob Roy. Alan Parker feared this, that in his film Madonna, the icon, could interfere with the role.[54]

The Argentinian Ambassador to Brazil, Diego Ramiro Guelar, in a thoughtful article in the daily *A Folha de São Paulo*, pointed out that no analysis of the figure of Eva Perón could be complete without including the 'secret dimension' of Argentinian history, 'the prolonged and never declared civil war which, almost without interruption, characterised our political history.' 'The polemic between Eva, saint and prostitute, the revolutionary leftist and the opportunistic fascist' is the reflection of that struggle, 'creating two parallel histories.' For one half of the Argentinian people, he contends, 'Evita represented dignified work, the possibility of education, holidays, the female franchise, the protection of childhood and old age.' For the other half she represented 'a shame, resentment turned into populism, a subversive threat.' He points out that 'the great myths are much more than individual anecdotes', that 'they express profound social forces.'[55]

The artist's argument of political innocence can at times be disingenuous. Yeats asked if his play had not 'sent out the men the English shot.' The Quebec-based scholar Serge Ouaknine argues:

> One knows very clearly, from an anthropological point of view that folklores are not the productions of peoples but of individuals, artefacts or legends afterwards assimilated and recuperated by the collective. Great songs are firstly the emotional extensions of poets and it is when the intimate model has succeeded that it can give elements of identification to a community.[56]

The artistic work can be a model of reality in the same way as the scholarly work. The primary difference is an aesthetic one: events to be experienced have to be framed. The anthropologist Edwin Ardener has argued that 'structural oppositions are built into history as it happens. There are, indeed, plenty of grounds for saying that the "memory" of history begins when it is registered. It is encoded "structurally" as it occurs. The structuring, by this view, is actually part of the "registration" of events.'[57]

Thus not all events survive, only memorable or significant ones, and the process of encoding them reshapes them into familiar forms. This is what the heroic biography does. Ardener wrote about history, but the artistic encoding of historical events also shapes the perception of reality.

Eliade gives an intriguing account of a Romanian ballad of tragic love. The subject of the ballad, a man engaged to be married in a few days, was bewitched by a jealous fairy and fell from a cliff. On seeing his corpse his heartbroken fiancée sang a beautiful extempore lament, which was the content of the ballad. However, enquiry by the folklorist, collecting variants of the ballad, found that the woman was still alive and was able to give a much more prosaic and mundane account of the tragedy. Eliade's comment on this is particularly eloquent, and shall be the conclusion to this paper:

> When the folklorist drew the villagers' attention to the authentic version, they replied that the old woman had forgotten; that her great grief had almost destroyed her mind. It was the myth that told the

truth: the real story was already only a falsification. Besides, was not the myth truer by the fact that it made the real story yield a deeper and richer meaning, revealing a tragic destiny?[58]

DEV AND MICK
THE 1922 SPLIT AS SOCIAL PSYCHOLOGICAL EVENT

Tom Garvin

Myth-makers: Coogan and Jordan

With the publication of Tim Pat Coogan's biographies of Michael Collins and Eamon de Valera the reputations of the two men, each in his own way a mythic figure in Irish political culture, began to undergo a sea-change.[1] This process was considerably accelerated by the release in 1996 of Neil Jordan's film *Michael Collins*. Jordan, for dramatic purposes, heightens a contrast in personality between Collins and De Valera which indeed existed in reality. Collins is presented as the brave and resourceful man who fought the British to a standstill between 1917 and 1921, De Valera as the man who prematurely tried to convert a guerrilla campaign into one of open, conventional warfare and who expressed himself as uneasy at the 'murderous' image which the republic's cause was getting in the foreign media. By rejecting the draft Treaty sight unseen in December 1921 Dev brings the house down around himself and everyone else. The film portrays Mick as the honest man, Dev as close to being treacherous. De Valera's mythic status in Irish culture has changed for the worse because of the work of Coogan, Jordan and a flotilla of often unread historians. In an almost symmetrical way Collins' mythic status has been enhanced at De Valera's expense.

So far so good. Jordan's film is excellent, but it is a film, not a documentary, and no one can ask a film to be a documentary; its values are those of drama, not those of historical science. Personally, having, quite coincidentally, done some work on the period in the past few years, I was almost afraid that the vividness of the film's imagery would wipe out of my mind the pictures of the men and the culture of the period which I had built up from my own reading and my conversations with other researchers and with people who had lived through that extraordinary time in Irish history. This paper is in part a celebration of my belief that those pictures have not only survived my seeing Jordan's picture, but have been enhanced by it.

Almae Matres: IRB and CSSp

Let us start in a time-honoured way, with some potted comparative biography. Mick was younger than Dev by about eight years, and had a very different upbringing and subsequent life-experience.[2] De Valera was a near-orphan, Mick was the youngest son in a large and apparently very happy west Cork farming family, prosperous in a modest way. Dev lived with his uncle. His material circumstances were harsh, but he seems to have been treated kindly, although perhaps with some emotional remoteness. Rejection by his mother, Kate Coll, who went on to live a fuller life in the United States than she could ever have had in puritan Victorian Limerick, must have always hurt him, if at a buried and unadmitted level. Much of De Valera's emotional life seems to have remained buried. When Dev got to Blackrock College at age twelve, courtesy of the generosity of a rich neighbour, he was surprised on his first night to hear a lonely boy in the next bed in the dormitory crying for his mammy. Dev himself was delighted by the comparative luxury in which he found himself.[3]

Mick, on the other hand, was surrounded by loving brothers, sisters and parents. He formed in particular a close relationship with his sister Katie. Coogan relates:

> Starting with Lamb's tales [*sic*], the young Michael worked his way through Shakespeare and, in the fashion of literary minded young patriots of the day, through a combination of English classics and sentimental Irish novels and ballads. Out of this medley it emerged that his favourite work was *The Mill on the Floss*. He told Katie, who was closest to him at the time, 'We're like Tom and Maggie Tulliver.' Katie replied that he could never be cruel like Tom. After a moment's silence Collins said, 'I could be worse ...'[4]

Dev went to Dublin from Bruree; Mick went to London from Sam's Cross. Dev was taken up, almost adopted, by the Holy Ghost (CSSp) priests of Blackrock College; it was only very much later that he took up with the Gaelic League, learning Irish from his future wife. Mick was given as *alma mater* the Gaelic League and the Irish Republican Brotherhood (IRB) in their London incarnations. De Valera trained as a teacher of mathematics and seems to have found difficulty in making a satisfactory career out of it; Collins started as a post office clerk, but rapidly worked his way out of Mountpleasant post office and into stockbroking. He clearly had a good, probably brilliant, career ahead of him in business. Recent research by Meda Ryan indicates that Mick was seen early on as a promising young man by the IRB, much as Dev had been by the CSSp.[5] Sam Maguire, of GAA fame, introduced him before 1915 to some members of relatively polite society in London, in particular Sir John Lavery, a Belfast Catholic and a successful portrait painter. He also met Hazel Lavery, John's wife, at about this time. It looks very much as though Mick was being groomed long before the surprise of 1916 was sprung on everyone.

It almost looks like a product of central casting. Collins, extrovert, one of the boys, secularised by London living, good-looking, popular with women and with an unrivalled range of acquaintances, in contrast to De Valera, solitary even when among his boyhood pals, aloof from men and women alike, around priests during his adolescence and young manhood, ascetic, scholarly in a narrow 'academic' way, his social experience confined to Ireland: the Jolly Jock versus the Solemn Swot, the businessman versus the teacher, or even the nineteenth versus the twentieth century.

This would be (obviously!) to caricature the two men; Collins had a well-read, practical intelligence combined with a marked administrative talent, and De Valera's strange mixture of the philosophical, the impractical and the cunning have become familiar to millions. Both were conventionally religious, but Dev was pious in a way that Collins was not. Dev was trusted by priests as one of their products; Mick was trusted by lay men, women and children. Collins, having left school at sixteen, was a self-confessed auto-didact, and a gifted one, whereas De Valera received further education of a narrow, if rigorous kind, and was, perhaps, not as innately gifted. My guess is that Collins was brighter, and De Valera knew this and feared for his career in the face of Collins' meteoric rise after 1916.

Subcultures: Moralism and Pragmatism

I have argued in my *1922: The Birth of Irish Democracy* that the opposition between Dev and Mick has come to be seen as reflecting a deep and old division in Irish political culture.[6] Personal distrusts and antagonisms existed between the two men, but their contrasting personality types also reflected Irish political subcultures of the time and later: Republican Moralism (Dev) versus Nationalist Pragmatism (Mick). All this is far too tidy, as one reviewer correctly remarked, but I believe it is a useful heuristic device.

Republican Moralism is closely connected with the austere and puritan Catholicism that grew up in Ireland in Victorian times, echoing the intensification of Puritanism in Britain at that time; the Irish evolved a sort of Papal Calvinism in imitation of the growth of what E. P. Thompson has described as Methodist religious terrorism in England. Religious and millenarian hysteria, fomented by extravagant visions of a literally hellish afterlife for the 'unspiritual', affected all popular political cultures in the British Isles. Quoting Karl Mannheim, Thompson comments:

> Chiliasm has always accompanied revolutionary outbursts and given them their spirit. When this spirit ebbs and deserts these movements, there remains behind in the world a naked mass-frenzy and a despiritualised fury.[7]

Republican Moralism was new in Ireland, and resonated well with the conformist, hard-working and puritan culture which owner-occupier free-farmer societies seem to create wherever they form a dominant sociological group in society, as in eighteenth-century New England, nineteenth-century New Zealand, nineteenth-century Scandinavia, or nineteenth-century Ontario and Quebec. Because of the doctrinally monolithic character of Catholicism, emotional extremism could not express itself through religious millenarian cults. Instead it expressed itself through what was nominally a secular cause but was actually an emotionally charged political and quasi-millenarian nationalism. The cult of the Republic stands in for the Kingdom of Christ.

Nationalist Pragmatism is rooted in Irish versions of political ideas derived ultimately from the English and French Enlightenments and their Scottish and American offshoots. The creators of the Free State constitution looked specifically to American and mainland European secular constitutional systems as exemplars to be imitated. The constitution they came up with, once one controls for the quasi-monarchic constraints put upon them by Westminster, was secular, democratic and a child of the French and American revolutions.[8] Moralism of political style is associated with what I have termed 'communalism', which is an attitude which sees each human being as being of equal worth and to be rewarded equally, regardless of the effort made by the individual and regardless of his or her special gifts or abilities; as Dev famously remarked, no man is worth more than £1,000 a year.

Pragmatism is associated more with individualism or the acceptance of the proposition that human beings have different abilities and energy and that inequality is therefore inevitable and is morally defensible. The moralist's political community is local, is supervised as a shepherd might supervise his flock, is caring, values personal contact and is profoundly distrustful of change or of individual thought. It is the political system of a successful peasantry becoming near-subsistence free farmers and of poor people anywhere. In contrast, the pragmatist's political system is an impersonal, unloved and unloving machine that processes demands from citizens impersonally and in a rule-bound way. It is the political culture of the citizen, the bourgeois, the literate and the well-off.

Francis Hackett, an acute contemporary observer and one who had extensive American and mainland European intellectual connections, wrote to Desmond FitzGerald in 1924 portraying the difference between the two sides as one between what he described as the romantic and scientific spirits, in terms quite similar to those I have suggested:

> Our people, mine and yours, are separated, not by Document One and Document Two, but by Scientific Spirit – liberty, curiosity and doubt – and Romantic Spirit – which is altitude, certitude and platitude. They start off with a castle in the air, and end up minus two damn fine public buildings.[9]

Mary MacSwiney, in a mid-1922 letter to Richard Mulcahy, put her finger on the same contrast, seen from the other side of the fence, and, significantly enough, using religious rather than philosophical terminology. For her what I have characterised as moralism was spirituality, and what I have labelled pragmatism was to her materialism. Supporters of the Treaty possessed a weaker version of the Catholic religion than did those who opposed it. The Free State was all about jobs for the boys, but Ireland would eventually recall its unique historical destiny and become a beacon of holiness in an unspiritual world. It is interesting to note that Dev was often later lampooned, half-seriously, as being not so much anti-clerical, as more Catholic than even the bishops or the pope. In a way, he was.

Actors: Dev and Mick, with a Cast of Tens

Mick revered Dev, and was very fond of Dev's wife Sinéad (Jenny Flanagan). Jenny was four years older than Dev, and about twelve years older than Mick, an aeon in the minds of the young people they all were at that time. During the Tan War when Dev was in America, Mick would cycle out to her Dublin suburban house to make sure that everybody was being looked after. He was very popular with the De Valera children, as with women and children everywhere.

The key to the division between Dev and Mick was twofold. First of all, Dev was President of the Republic during the Tan War, whereas Collins, as head of the Supreme Council of the IRB, was, in IRB theory, President of the Irish Republic of 1867, 'now virtually established.' In the back of many people's minds he was the Young Pretender to a semi-imaginary throne; *regnum appetit*. Secondly, Dev spent most of the Tan War in America, with Harry Boland, Collins' best friend and his rival in love, as his chief fixer. When Dev and Harry got back, it seemed as though Mick and his lieutenants had got overly powerful, and Dev repeatedly tried to wrest power back from Mick. In January 1922 Harry accused Mick of being tired of fighting and wanting to relax and 'have a good time; the trouble with you Mick, is that you're demoralised.' Coming from someone who had spent the Tan War rather comfortably in America, this must have seemed a bit rich.[10]

Collins had trod on a lot of local toes as well. Stack hated him, and Mick was notoriously contemptuous of Stack's administrative abilities. Stack had been responsible for a famous cock-up in Kerry in 1916, one of many such that happened during that less than well-regulated rising. Furthermore, there was widespread suspicion that Stack's father, a Fenian veteran, had been a 'stag' (informer). Brugha, Minister of Defence in the Dáil government, of part-English descent and older than Mick, had been by-passed by the younger, more energetic and more able man; his hatred of Collins was obvious. He also had a history of intra-organisational quarrels. Collins, like all good administrative politicians, had by-passed the formal hierarchy, such as it was, and had his own extensive networks. Collins was also seen as a 'desk man' by the IRA in the field, a man who had done little real fighting himself. He also attracted the odium that all Ministers of Finance attract anywhere; he had said 'no' to the requests of too many people. His cheerful lack of deference to the Catholic Church was offensive to some; to them, to have spent time in London was to have been contaminated with materialism, cosmopolitanism, atheism and, worse, Protestantism.

Pragmatists could not understand Dev's mixture of moralism and mathematics; Collins was genuinely bewildered by Dev's fine distinction between the Treaty and his own Documents Two and Three. These were the documents in which Dev tried to walk the fine line between the Free State and the Republic, between Dominion Status and complete, isolated independence, that was the doctrine of 'External Association' with the British Commonwealth and empire. Dev seems to have put forward some such proposal to Mick in mid-1921. During the Treaty debates, Collins, at lunch with Michael Hayes, said emphatically about his chief:

> How could one argue with a man who was always drawing lines and circles to explain the position; who, one day, drew a diagram (here Michael illustrated with pen and paper) saying 'take a point A, draw a straight line to point B, now three-fourths of the way up the line take a point C. The straight line AB is the road to the Republic; C is where we have got to along the road, we cannot move any further along the straight road to our goal B; take a point out there, D [off the line AB]. Now if we bend the line a bit from C to D then we can bend it a little further, to another point E and if we can bend it to CE that will get us around Cathal Brugha which is what we want!' How could you talk to a man like that?[11]

Others disliked Collins and De Valera impartially; O'Higgins reportedly remarked to Blythe in late 1921: 'That crooked Spanish bastard will get the better of that pasty-faced blasphemous fucker from Cork.'[12]

De Valera was the hero of 1916, and was held in immense deference by everybody before the split. One fan of his was Batt O'Connor of Donnybrook. O'Connor was well-known in the movement and was intimate with De Valera, Collins, and the Donnybrook IRA and Sinn Féin set. A Kerryman, he had spent five years in the United States and returned to Ireland, setting himself up as a building contractor in Donnybrook. He built Brendan Road, naming it after his county's patron saint and omitting the 'saint' from the road's title so that Protestant customers wouldn't be put off. He also built 36 Ailesbury Road, of Ernie O'Malley fame. O'Connor knew Dev well, and knew before the Treaty was brought home that Dev would reject it. O'Connor went pro-Treaty, despite his unreserved admiration for Dev. He evidently assumed that Dev's rejection of the Treaty would mean his retirement from political life, at least temporarily. It did nor occur to him at that time that Dev might declare the Treaty illegal and attempt to set up a new legality of his own, which is, of course, what he did.

Dev seems to have been heavily influenced by the 'Men of the South', who were anti-Treaty and seem to have been spoiling for a return to fighting. He also was persuaded by Stack and Lynch that such a fight might be successful. Dev seems also to have been very much under the emotional influence of the 'Republican Women'. His ancestral anglophobe paranoia was exacerbated by the advice he was being given by Erskine Childers on the inadequacy of the Treaty provisions. He was also persuaded that his own prestige would outweigh loyalties to Collins and Griffith. He miscalculated. Griffith became President of the Republic soon after the ratification of the Treaty by the Dáil, by a mere two votes. Dev's surprise and chagrin is evident, and it is significant that Griffith, President from January to July 1922, between De Valera and Cosgrave, is not on the wall in Leinster House along with all other Irish prime ministers. He was never forgiven for having pinched Dev's clothes. Dev was the only one who was permitted to perform that particular sartorial trick.

The split between moralism and pragmatism became rapidly irreversible. As late as September 1922 Mulcahy got to see Dev in a priest's house in Dublin. Collins and Griffith were now both dead, and the IRA under Lynch was now out of any political control. Mulcahy, very reasonably, put it to Dev that the IRA had mutinied against the Dáil on 26 March 1922 and that the civil government had to control the military arm. The Dáil had to control the IRA – a classic pragmatic and legal-rational argument. Dev answered: 'Some men are led by faith, others are led by reason, but as long as there are men of faith like Rory O'Connor taking the stand that he was taking, he (Dev) was a humble soldier following after.'[13]

The Irish Civil War was fought between those who believed that the morally superior should rule, regardless of majority preferences, and those who believed that those chosen by the majority should rule. Rousseau's famous distinction between the 'general will' and the 'will of all' was, then, the issue over which the Civil War was fought. The general will was the collective will as expressed by people of republican virtue, whereas the will of all was merely the arithmetical result of the rather contemptible counting of heads of all adult inhabitants, regardless of virtue or dependence on others for their political opinion. Rousseau's problem is one of the central philosophical contradictions at the heart of modern democratic political thought and one to which there is no clear solution. It is strange, and perhaps fitting, that it was the Irish, one of the most politically adept of peoples, who should fight a civil war over such a profound political issue.

Envoi

Dev was later to develop an extraordinary ability to speak both the moralistic and pragmatic languages of Irish politics. He hadn't yet quite learned that art in 1922, to the cost of all of us. Dev later realised, and said in private, that the Treaty was far better than he had made it out to be in 1922, but he never fully admitted it in public. This particular lie of silence has cost us even more in damage to our political tradition.

On 16 June 1922, the year of publication of Joyce's *Ulysses* and therefore the first Bloomsday, a new set of actors intervened and a million voters displaced the tens of the political leadership. The electorate approved of the Treaty by a landslide. As Joyce might have put it, Here Came Everybody.

'THE FREEDOM TO ACHIEVE FREEDOM'?

THE POLITICAL IDEAS OF COLLINS AND DE VALERA

Martin Mansergh

Anyone who has to grapple with the present, especially Northern Ireland, has to grapple with history. It is beneficial to study history to see exactly how problems that still confront us were actually tackled in the past. The peace process has involved revisiting the 1920–21 settlement. But anniversaries also provide an opportunity to focus on the foundation of our own state and the circumstances and people who brought it about, and to put in greater perspective both their achievement and subsequent tragic differences about it, which had external as well as internal causes. We ought to try to understand those differences, but also to transcend them, and to balance both our admiration and our critique as objectively as we can, without being too influenced by our tradition, identification or affiliation to political successor organisations on either side.

'A glorious record for four years'

In the course of the Treaty debate W. T. Cosgrave claimed that the Treaty represented work that had been done in five years, 'greater than was accomplished by Emmet, O'Connell, Mitchel, Davis, Smith O'Brien, and Parnell, down even to Mr Redmond with a united country behind him.' He went on to say that 'the two men who typified the best type of Irishmen I have ever known are the President and the Minister for Finance', Eamon de Valera and Michael Collins.[1] Arthur Griffith was added by some as a third. Pervading the debates, even amongst many opposed to the Treaty, was a sense of pride and achievement. After the conclusion of the vote, which he lost, De Valera said:

> I would like my last word here to be this: we have had a glorious record for four years; it has been four years of magnificent discipline in our nation. The world is looking at us now.[2]

Despite deep emerging differences and ominous clashes with and involving others the principals at this stage still expressed great mutual respect and confidence.

In the struggle for independence there was a large *dramatis personae*, who are still remembered both nationally and locally. A tremendous national effort had brought Ireland far beyond the point that even the most advanced nationalists pre-1914 had expected to see in their lifetime. A debt was owed to many, but it was the partnership of De Valera, Collins and Griffith in particular that brought Ireland to the threshold of independence in 1921. That is more important to us today than their subsequent differences. The quarrels over status are now long behind us.

Griffith's Sinn Féin provided the political vehicle for a united movement, including the tactic of abstention from Westminster and formation of the Dáil in Dublin, as well as much of the ideology. When something like dual monarchy prevailed, Griffith resumed the Presidency that he had ceded to De Valera.

Collins was the organising genius of the military struggle and much of the political resistance as well. He recognised early on, as one of the lessons of 1916, the futility of open warfare against a superior opponent, and had no time for the tradition of noble and chivalrous defeat. His terse speech over Thomas Ashe's grave was in stark contrast to Pearse's over O'Donovan Rossa's. He was quite ruthless, and to a disturbing degree a law unto himself. He was both boisterous and abrasive. He made enemies but he also inspired immense loyalty. He recruited remarkable collaboration from within opposing ranks, but there is no evidence that the British, from whom he had several narrow escapes, did not want to capture him. He more than anyone succeeded in disrupting their nerve centre. In May 1922 Lloyd George told Collins that if he had been caught he would have been shot.

One aspect of IRA discipline may be mentioned. Michael Collins was absolutely opposed to punishment beatings or floggings 'for any offence, under any circumstances, even as a reprisal', writing on 3 July 1921: 'It has a more degrading effect upon the person or the authority administering it than the person to whom it is administered'.[3]

Joseph Connolly, Fianna Fáil Minister in the 1930s, wrote in his memoirs:

> I am, by nature, little disposed to anything in the way of hero worship, but I have always been convinced that during the fateful years from 1919 to 1921 the one man, who more than any other carried the Herculean load of Ireland's fight, was Collins. It would scarcely be neces-

sary to say so, but for the events that followed the Treaty and which to many obscured the real qualities and genius that made Collins what he was.[4]

To Dev and many Sinn Féin TDs in 1924 he was still Mick.[5] Today, like Lemass, his contribution is acknowledged and admired across the political divide.

What distinguished the struggle was its political cutting edge. Griffith's biographer, the writer Pádraic Colum, acknowledged in 1959 that, having reconciled the Volunteers, especially Eoin MacNeill with whom he shared a platform in Clare,

> Eamon de Valera brought, and only Eamon de Valera could have brought, Sinn Féin and the Volunteers together, giving resurgent Ireland a single forceful organisation, the institution and the consensus that Griffith had looked forward to.[6]

There was a clear and persuasive political objective. The new international environment towards the end of the First World War was brilliantly exploited by the Irish. The right of national self-determination declared by President Wilson as the foundation of a new world order broke up old European empires, but even the victorious ones were much weakened. Eamon de Valera spent much time in the United States publicising the cause. Dr David Fitzpatrick wrote in the *Irish Times* on 9 November 1996 that 'in fact it was a multifaceted revolution, in which Dev's propaganda campaign was more important than the armed campaign.' It was certainly equally important. On his return he provided a sophisticated political leadership and an intellectual depth well able to fence with Lloyd George, both face to face and by correspondence, which makes it all the more of a pity that he held himself in reserve throughout the negotiations proper.

It is an observable phenomenon for at least two centuries that when the Irish people, or at least those who see themselves as such, are united, the most spectacular advances can be made: legislative independence in 1782; Catholic Emancipation; the 'New Departure' of 1878; the struggle for independence; more recently, the spectacular economic performance following the adoption since 1987 of social partnership and consensus as well as the initial élan of the peace process in 1993 and 1994. Conversely, splits and divisions have caused disastrous setbacks, such as those which pitted the Orange-

157

men and Maynooth against the United Irishmen; the disintegration of O'Connell's movement following the split with Young Ireland and his death; the unionist-nationalist split of 1886 and then the Parnell split, from which the Home Rule Party never fully recovered; and on top of partition the Treaty split which had echoes of the Parnell split.

The power factors in 1921–2

Politics is about principle, persuasion and power. Persuasion is the central factor. Principle can persuade. Power can persuade. Collins and De Valera exemplify two types of leader. There are, first, those who in any struggle put forward the political and moral principles at stake; and, secondly, those whose political positions are heavily influenced at the margins by consciousness of the power factors involved, what Collins regarded as 'the duress of facts'. For De Valera, the Republic was real, a living thing. For Collins, the 1916 leaders declared a Republic 'but not as a fact', more as a wonderful gesture. All the same, in 1920, Collins had believed that 'the same effort that would get us Dominion Home Rule would get us a Republic'.[7] De Valera and Gladstone are obvious examples of the more ideological political leader, though they may in fact have been very adept also at using power. Parnell once scorned Gladstone as a 'masquerading knight errant'. Some of De Valera's critics, past and present, have regarded him in somewhat the same light. Michael Collins was a more overtly practical politician, which did not prevent him from holding strong convictions. But he was very conscious of the limits of what could be achieved in any given circumstances, and he felt that national demands could be adjusted up or down accordingly.

Lloyd George and Churchill were also very power-conscious. Their problem was to try and find a way of deflecting a national demand based on principle, which they believed would break up the coalition and undermine the empire. Lloyd George replied to Arthur Griffith on Ulster in a revealing way: 'It is no use ignoring facts however unpleasant they may be. The politician who thinks he can deal out abstract justice without reference to forces around him cannot govern.'[8] Undoubtedly, the most successful political leaders are those, like Charles de Gaulle or George Washington or Abraham Lincoln, who are able to turn principle, persuasion and power into a seamless web. Irish leaders in 1921 came tantalisingly close to achieving this, but fell at the last fence.

The struggle for independence, and all those involved, have their critics. It is alleged that Home Rule, put onto the statute book in 1914, could have achieved in time everything achieved by the struggle for independence without the bloodshed and without the potent example to inspire a subsequent generation of northern republicans, and not just republicans. A senior loyalist veteran told me two years ago that the figure he most admired in Irish history was Michael Collins. De Valera himself expressed some private reservations about the guerrilla struggle, and undoubtedly he would have preferred a mainly political one. As a man of 1916 he hankered after open as opposed to covert warfare. Griffith abhorred armed conflict altogether.

The cost of most revolutions is high. The example and the deterrent effect on the imperial power can save conflict and bloodshed elsewhere. The benefits can be disappointing or slow in materialising. But from today's perspective there are few regrets about the achievement of independence, and no convincing demonstration that it could have been won post-1914 by purely constitutional action.

What was the difference between Home Rule as understood in 1914, and what some called Dominion Home Rule achieved as a result of the Treaty? Apart from the much more limited powers there were two critical defects in the 1914 and the 1920 legislation. A Home Rule parliament established by Act of Parliament under the absolute sovereignty of Westminster could be suppressed again at any time, as Stephen Dorrell tactlessly reminded the Scots recently. This was exactly what did happen to Stormont in 1972. The factor on which Collins placed most weight, the British army in Ireland, would have remained to enforce ultimate British sovereignty, if it were to be challenged at any time. More far-reaching Home Rule legislation for the whole of Ireland, originally contemplated in 1886 and after, while Parnell remained leader, might have evolved along with the Dominions, especially as Canada and the British North America Act of 1867 was a model for both Gladstone and Parnell. Parnell, like Griffith, was also interested in Hungary. But by 1914 the Dominions had moved on, and, with the Ulster rift apparently irreparable, the British government was determined that it would hold the rest of Ireland strictly within Home Rule limits, by force if need be.

The Truce in July 1921 represented a crossroads for both Britain and Ireland. Britain's reputation was damaged by the Auxiliaries and the Black and Tans. Lloyd George thought he was fighting another American Civil War to prevent secession, but he lacked the moral cause which assisted Lincoln's victory. Churchill, whose thinking embodied the notion of 'selfish strategic interest' and who was obsessed with the notion that an independent Ireland might start building submarines, wrote in *The World Crisis: The Aftermath*:

> The relations of Britain and Ireland were established during centuries when the independence of a hostile Ireland menaced the life of Britain. Every policy, every shift, every oppression used by the stronger island arose from this primordial fact.

Churchill claimed Ireland had done two supreme services to Britain: accession to the Allied cause in 1914, and Magyar-style secession from the House of Commons in 1919, removing the element that distorted the balance between the parties at Westminster that drove Pitt from office, dragged down Gladstone and drew Britain almost to the verge of civil war. He asked: 'Whence does this mysterious power of Ireland come? It is a small, poor, sparsely populated island, lapped about by British sea power, accessible on every side, without iron or coal'. His answer was that Ireland was a parent nation, intermingled with the whole life of the empire, wherever English was spoken, and where 'the Irish canker has been at work'. In the summer of 1921, if the rebellion were to be suppressed, military saturation and a Bolshevik-type ruthlessness would have been required. More than ever was conceded to Ireland to end what Churchill called 'a period of brutal and melancholy violence'.⁹ The 1920 Government of Ireland Act made the position of Ulster unassailable, leaving the British government freer to deal with the rest.

The Irish side coming up to the Truce was also under considerable pressure, with doubts in some places as to how much longer an effective campaign could be sustained. Collins' argument in the Treaty debate was that 'we, as negotiators, were not in the position of conquerors dictating terms of peace to a vanquished enemy. We had not beaten the enemy out of our country by force of arms.' His argument was that military force held this country over the centuries, not any particular form of government:

> Now, starting from that, I maintain that the disappearance of that mil-

itary strength gives us the chief proof that our national liberties are established … it is not a definition of any status that would secure us that status, it is the power to hold and to make secure and to increase what we have gained.

This was the basis of his famous stepping stone claim for the Treaty, that 'in my opinion, it gives us freedom, not the ultimate freedom that all nations desire and develop to, but the freedom to achieve it.'[10] No Governor General would substitute for the absence of the British army. At one point in May 1922 Tom Jones, Lloyd George's Private Secretary, anticipating the tactical possibilities, wrote: 'Collins may appoint a charwoman as Lord Lieutenant, to which I see no objection if she's a good one, but others may take a different view'.[11] Collins made it clear that he was not moved by Lloyd George's threat of immediate and terrible war in coming to a decision to back the Treaty, though others may have been. Nor do I believe that the drawing-rooms of London, Lady Lavery's included, still less the red on the map of the world in Downing Street, were major factors for someone for whom politics was a man's business, and who showed not the slightest susceptibility to imperialism. The strong *prima facie* evidence, which suggests, for example, that Parnell signed the Kilmainham Treaty in part at least so as to be able to rejoin Mrs O'Shea, is absent in Collins' case.

Both his allies and his opponents distrusted how he might intend to go about achieving ultimate freedom. The answer was soon clear, both from his pact with De Valera in April-May 1922 on a *de facto* republican constitution, which he was only forced off by intense British pressure, and his encouragement of military action to back up the Treaty provisions on the north. Collins remained a republican at heart, though not a doctrinaire one. The leaders of the Army Mutiny, Charlie Dalton and Liam Tobin, writing to Cosgrave in 1924 quoted Collins as saying: 'I have taken an oath of allegiance to the Irish Republic and that oath I will keep, Treaty or no Treaty'. Unionists attributed the remark to him the day of the Treaty, that once the Treaty Act was passed by the House of Commons and the evacuation of British troops completed, then 'the demand for full republican rights must be conceded by Great Britain.' He had no enthusiasm for dual monarchy like Griffith and Kevin O'Higgins, or for empire or commonwealth, although he did not display the anti-imperialist zeal of Mellows and some other republicans, who were more conscious of Ireland's catalytic role in the dismantling and subsequent disappearance of the British empire. The relics of feudalism in the Treaty were simply disagreeable temporary necessities that provided the British with a fig-leaf to hide their political and military withdrawal, and which would allow Ireland to start exercising its freedom positively. In 1922 the British were highly suspicious that Collins might effectively abandon the Treaty and reunite with the republican side. Lionel Curtis' view – Curtis was the drafter of the Treaty on the British side – was that Collins' death saved the Treaty. Many on the anti-Treaty side thought it dishonourable to subscribe to a Treaty that one did not intend to keep. In the 1930s De Valera in good conscience set about dismantling a Treaty republicans had never accepted. Collins was quite happy, given half a chance, to start dismantling straightaway a Treaty that he *had* accepted. A hostile critic, Mellows' right hand man, Richard Barrett, disparagingly described Collins as 'a Fenian Home Ruler', and claimed that like a dealer 'swapping donkeys at a fair, he was suspicious of what he was getting, but contented himself that what he was giving was not an honest beast.'[12]

De Valera and the anti-Treaty side did not accept the reality of Lloyd George's threat, which they called a bluff, first tried on De Valera in July 1921 without success. Collins agreed it probably was bluff. Through the summer and autumn of 1921 the threat of a return to war was always present. De Valera did not believe the British would renew war for the difference between Dominion Home Rule and External Association with the Commonwealth. Republicans were willing to fight on to achieve the Republic. Few admitted frankly like the pro-Treaty Eoin O'Duffy that 'the chief pleasure he felt in freedom was fighting for it.'[13]

Churchill admitted that after the Truce the die was cast: 'Impossible thereafter to resume the same kind of war. Impossible to refuel or heat up again those cauldrons of hatred and contempt on which such quarrels are fed!' If either the negotiations or the Treaty itself had broken down, military occupation of ports and cities, especially Dublin, defence of Ulster and blockade of trade and communications between Sinn Féin Ireland and the rest of the world would most likely have followed. Churchill wrote: 'But from the moment of the Truce, the attempt to govern southern Ireland upon the authority of the imperial parliament had come to an end'.[14] Once the split had taken place the British were in a better position to exploit their military advantage, and to pit one side against the other.

In fact, they had achieved a double coup, adding to the north-south divide a split which would further weaken those they had been fighting.

Even in the 1930s the freedom to achieve freedom, in the sense of the dismantling of the Treaty, only came about following the Economic War. The retaliation in 1921–2 would have been worse with a direct military element. But the complete reconquest of Ireland urged by some southern unionists in exile up to the mid-1920s was no longer on the agenda.[15] The last thing the high tories in 1924 really wanted was Irish MPs back at Westminster. There *was* an element of bluff involved on the British side, but it should not be exaggerated. Renewed conflict, the mixture of military, political and economic sanctions, would have been unpleasant, though not necessarily more calamitous than the Civil War which actually did follow.

The inverse relationship between the Republic and unity: the constitutional models of the Treaty negotiations

Three constitutional models existed from the Irish point of view in 1921: the isolated Republic, with no formal relationship with Britain or the Commonwealth – the ideal, but unattainable; Dominion Status involving some form of allegiance to the crown and membership of the British Commonwealth of Nations; or De Valera's compromise of External Association, which involved retention of a republican form of government associated with the Commonwealth, recognising the king as head of the association.

Alfred Cope, the brightest of the civil servants sent to Dublin Castle, captured the essence of the Irish dilemma between the Republic on one hand and Irish unity on the other, in a telegram to Tom Jones on 3 September 1921:

> It is entirely a question of symbols, and people in that revolutionary condition can't give up both their symbols. If you give them independence, they may give up unity; if you give them unity, they may give up independence, but they must have one or the other.

Cope favoured the British giving the Irish one or the other, either by telling

> the north-east they must cave in or lose Fermanagh and Tyrone and do it publicly. Then the south will give up independence for the sake

of the hope of Ulster's caving in, or the Dáil may set down in concrete
what they are prepared to accept if they may call themselves a Republic; and once the English people see that they can get more out of
Ireland if she is called a Republic, we can't fight over it.

Cope was a civil servant, not a politician, but it shows that the
options were not quite so circumscribed and predetermined as is
sometimes claimed.[16]

From the beginning of the century Irish nationalists might have
been prepared to accept perhaps even something as modest as the
Councils Bill or administrative devolution, if there had been any
guarantee that the Ulster unionists would have accepted it in the
national spirit of the Magheramorne Manifesto of the Independent
Orange Order in 1905. A united country would have found it much
easier to progress beyond that stage. On the other hand, Home Rule
was challenged, and the Nationalist party destroyed, once they
seemed to accept the principle of partition. Even as late as 1917-8
they could perhaps have salvaged their position, if they could have
reached an agreement on devolution in the Irish Convention with
the Ulster unionists. Their refusal to accept any compromise, and
the unwillingness of the British government to force their hand, removed any reason for holding back from going bald-headedly for
the Republic. Childers observed with some surprise De Valera's
admission that unity would have been the one circumstance that
might have made him reconsider Dominion Status.[17] In De Valera's
own mind External Association with the Commonwealth, even after
1949, was a door ajar that he was prepared to concede for unity. But
one of the main complaints about the Treaty was that negotiators
had come back neither with the Republic, even in the form of External Association, nor with any real form of Irish unity.

Collins had no great time for the subtleties of External Association or the mathematical formulae that De Valera used to explain
it. Cathal Brugha and Mary MacSwiney were reluctantly prepared
to accept it. But it meant little to republican officers outside the Dáil,
for whom it was all or nothing for the republic. The British, with the
precedent of the Boer republics that had accepted Dominion Status,
did not understand how difficult, indeed impossible, it was for so
many to abandon, even temporarily, the declared Republic. It was
as if the United States after the Declaration of Independence in 1776
had been forced to resubmit nominally to allegiance to King George
III. It was a limitation republicans were not prepared to accept

without a fight, even if it meant, as De Valera ill-advisedly pointed out in March 1922, in remarks that were badly misinterpreted, that the British had placed republicans in the position that they now had to wade through the blood of their former comrades to achieve freedom. This was not strictly true, as all they had to do was to be a constitutional republican opposition until they could win an election. But they believed that that would not be a free expression of opinion, given British threats, and also that obligation to the Treaty closed off the constitutional path. The underlying problem was the absence of a mechanism, such as a weighted majority or referendum, to establish constitutional legitimacy, a defect rectified in 1937. The British made it worse in the revised Free State constitution of June by ramming the king down people's throats, describing him as the source of executive power in the Free State.

There has been much discussion of why De Valera, after his initial visit to London, was not part of the negotiating team. It has been suggested that he knew that compromise was inevitable, but that he in effect set Collins up. I do not subscribe to that theory. Collins' own attitude was a bit contradictory. He wanted to go with Dev to London in July. He did not want to go in September. A pivotal figure in the delegation, by the following spring and summer Collins had become responsible for critical negotiations with the British. It was his misfortune to be confronted three times with *force majeure* – over the Treaty, over the draft constitution and finally the ultimatum after Sir Henry Wilson's assassination.

In 1982 former Government Secretary Maurice Moynihan published a memorandum, written by De Valera in 1963, justifying why he remained at home during the Treaty negotiations.[18] In essence he was following the well-established diplomatic maxim that principals should not engage in negotiations, but remain in reserve as the ultimate arbiters. Where that broke down in this case was that Lloyd George was fully engaged in the negotiations, and De Valera's absence undoubtedly meant the Irish delegation was at a disadvantage. There were other motives. By staying away he hoped to protect his status as president of the Irish Republic, and thus the Republic itself, rather than be involved in invidious negotiations about it, where he might be accused of a conflict of interest. It is nonsense to suggest De Valera was not prepared for compromise. He was prepared to give Britain expansive assurances that Ireland would never allow itself be used as a base for attack, which caused him enormous problems with some of his Irish-American allies. He spoke warmly, and I believe sincerely, about friendship with Britain on a basis of mutual respect for each other's independence. His rhetoric was, if anything, less anti-British than Collins' or most of his contemporaries. He conceded that Ulster should not be coerced by fellow Irishmen, a move upon which Lloyd George gratefully seized. He also prepared to compromise on the Republic to the extent of External Association. The result was that he had made so many compromises that many people did not see the residual difference between External Association and Dominion Status, 'that little sentimental thing' as De Valera described it, as worth fighting for. But in that case, why would it be worth Britain's while to fight for it?

De Valera's other concern, a very natural one for any political leader, was to preserve the unity of the movement. He thought he could keep the more republican wing on board by staying at home. He may have contemplated joining the delegation at the very end, but, if so, he left it too late. He was clear that the Treaty would not bring peace, even though this was portrayed as its principal benefit.

There is no doubt that Arthur Griffith, in particular, was outmanoeuvred by Lloyd George, who succeeded in dividing the delegation and in shifting the breaking point from the north, where he felt vulnerable to international opinion, to status where he felt unassailable. During the Civil War, Erskine Childers explained to Bob Brennan:

> The British can sign and find a way to repudiate their signatures ... You need not go back to the Treaty of Limerick. They always found high moral reasons for such repudiation. They are opportunists. Griffith, however, having given his word, would stick to it whatever the consequences, even though it meant the disaster of a civil war. They knew that.

In other words, Arthur Griffith was put on his honour by Lloyd George, who scarcely knew what the word meant. His threat of immediate and terrible war made a deep impression on Gavan Duffy and Barton. But the question was what of substance did they fail to gain, when one leaves aside an element of tactical shadow boxing over the north. De Valera and Childers believed they had exhausted what was on offer in relation to the north. But Collins, in particular, and Griffith both over-estimated what the delegation had obtained on Ulster. If Collins had been less sure that the north could not survive economically without the rest of the country (as he was encouraged to believe by Lloyd George) or less sure that the Boundary Commission would award Fermanagh and Tyrone to the Irish Free State (as Tim Healy may have been promised informally and socially by Birkenhead, Churchill and Lloyd George)[19] would he have been so ready to support the Treaty? The anti-Treaty side had less illusions about the north, even though they were by and large ready to accept the same clauses on the Treaty. By 3 August Collins was writing to Cosgrave: 'I am forced to the conclusion that we may yet to have fight the British in the north-east.' When calling off hostilities temporarily the previous day, he told northern officers of the IRA he would 'use the political arm against Craig so long as it is of use. If that fails, the Treaty can go to hell and we will all start again.'[20] It is unfortunately wishful thinking to present Collins as someone who had definitely decided that force *vis-à-vis* the north had had its day. Perhaps he was moving in that direction.

What view should we take of the balance achieved between status and unity? The argument about status was not only about the desirability of some form of Republic, but also as to whether Dominion Status had in fact been achieved. With the development of the Commonwealth in 1926 and 1931, aided by the Free State, Ireland's Dominion Status did constitute just sufficient freedom to achieve freedom. But Childers was also right in detecting a British intention to freeze Ireland's status under the Treaty, independent of future developments in Commonwealth status, and that was the *causus belli* of the 1930s, as to whether the Commonwealth took precedence over the Treaty or vice versa.

In relation to the north the Treaty was neither a stepping stone nor the freedom to achieve freedom it appeared to be. What was left of the essential unity of Ireland was a paper unity, in which the reality of partition was thinly disguised by a variety of devices, the nominal unity that could be instantly negated by the opt-out, the Boundary Commission and the Council of Ireland. The best that could be said for it was that it left open the possibility of Irish unity by consent in the future, with an official British bias in that direction until 1949, when it was replaced by the more negative British guarantee. In theory, from 1920 to 1949, the British government was willing to be a persuader for unity. The couple of times it tried hard

– in November 1921 and in 1940 – the unionist rebuff was adamant. Historically there is little to suggest conclusively that the British government would have been an effective persuader for unity, short of withdrawal, and probably not even then.

A weaker form of openness to future unity by agreement was renewed in article one of the Anglo-Irish Agreement and paragraph four of the Downing Street Declaration. A united Irish Dominion fighting with the empire remained, until the early 1940s, the impossible dream of some British politicians and senior civil servants.

What is tantalising to speculate about is whether a more realistic appreciation of the essentially cosmetic concessions on unity would have helped the Irish delegation to have achieved more of its objectives on status. There is no evidence, however, that a softer position on status, the entire gamut of possibilities having been gone through since 1907, would have enabled the delegation to achieve more on unity. More rigorous prioritising of objectives, with the compromise on status of External Association and county/district council opt-out taking precedence over more cosmetic appearances of unity, might have concentrated minds, and levered a better overall result on one or the other at least, as Lloyd George was not willing to renew war over Fermanagh and Tyrone.

The principle of consent

There is a notion that the principle of consent was something new adopted by forward-looking public figures at the beginning of the recent Troubles, and incorporated into Sunningdale, the Anglo-Irish Agreement, the Downing Street Declaration and the draft Report of the Forum for Peace and Reconciliation. In reality the principle of consent played a central role in De Valera's political strategy approaching the Treaty negotiations. The principle of government by consent goes back at least to John Locke's *Second Treatise of Government*. President Wilson defined self-determination as government by the consent of the governed, as opposed to imperial or autocratic government. The core Irish demand was for national self-determination. If this were conceded, there could be no argument about Ireland's unfettered right to choose its own form of government.

Lloyd George, in his reply to De Valera of 7 September 1921, stated:

> The principle of government by consent of the governed is the foundation of British constitutional development, but we cannot accept as

a basis of practical conference an interpretation of that principle which would commit us to any demands which you might present – even to the extent of setting up a Republic and repudiating the crown.[21]

It was not until December 1993 that the British government, albeit in a way qualified by the concurrent consent of the two parts, finally recognised the principle of the self-determination of the people of Ireland, north and south, in the Downing Street Declaration, a catching-up on one of the omissions of the Treaty.

The Achilles heel of the Irish case was north-east Ulster. De Valera argued, in the private sessions of the Dáil, it was essential to apply *de facto* the principle of consent to north-east Ulster. By conceding it, he hoped to advance the case for the principle to be granted *vis-à-vis* the rest of the country. He only conceded the principle *de facto* because, as codified by subsequent international law, disruption of national unity and territorial integrity is frowned upon and because, as Professor Eide informed the Forum for Peace and Reconciliation: 'Numerous territorial arrangements made in earlier times would, if they had been effected today, be seen as a violation of present day international law'.[22] That stricture undoubtedly applied to the partition of Ireland.

De Valera argued on 22 August 1921:

> They had not the power, and some of them had not the inclination, to use force with Ulster. He did not think that policy would be successful. They would be making the same mistake with that section as England had made with Ireland. He would not be responsible for such a policy ... Ulster would say she was as devotedly attached to the empire as they were to their independence and that she would fight for one as much as they would do for the other. In case of coercion she would get sympathy and help from her friends all over the world.[23]

In his letter of 10 August to Lloyd George, De Valera, having asserted the *de jure* position on Irish unity, said:

> We do not contemplate the use of force ... We agree with you 'that no common action can be secured by force'. Our regret is that this wise and true principle which your government prescribes to us for the settlement of our local problem it seems unwilling to apply consistently to the fundamental problem of the relations between our island and yours. The principle we rely on in the one case we are ready to apply in the other ...

Lloyd George in his reply of 13 August gratefully seized on the concession: 'We are profoundly glad to have your agreement that Northern Ireland cannot be coerced',[24] but rejected the logic of the rest of De Valera's argument. It is to the credit and honour of Irish nationalists that they were prepared at that critical time to apply similar logic to their own cause and to the unionist one. The importance of this was obscured subsequently by the fact that the concession was a *de facto* one not a *de jure* one. Document Number Two contained a saving clause: 'whilst refusing to admit the right of any part of Ireland to be excluded from the supreme authority of the parliament of Ireland ... nevertheless, in sincere regard for internal peace, and in order to make manifest our desire not to bring force or coercion to bear upon any substantial part of the province of Ulster, whose inhabitants may now be unwilling to accept the national authority',[25] De Valera was prepared to grant the privileges and safeguards granted in the Treaty. This formulation of 'the essential unity of Ireland', a principle originally formulated by the British cabinet in 1919, was the forerunner of articles two and three of the 1937 Constitution.

Historians are apt to play down the northern dimension of the Treaty debate. But in fact twenty deputies referred to the north. The disappointment about status was so deep partly because so little had been achieved on unity. Collins argued that once De Valera had said we would not coerce the north-east, 'what was the use of talking big phrases about not agreeing to the partition of our country?' He also argued that a split would give unionists every excuse for not caving in, as if they needed any excuse except their determination and their numbers. Seán T. Ó Ceallaigh in response said: 'we have not got Irish unity in return for this action.' J. J. Walsh said 'the alternative for a Republic for three-fourths of Ireland was the unity of all Ireland', as a Republic would definitely alienate north-east Ulster. Richard Mulcahy admitted he saw 'no solution of the Ulster difficulty' at the present moment. Seán MacEntee made the strongest attack, saying he 'never saw such guileless trust in any English statesman.' He prophesied that 'as England has found it profitable to subsidise the Emir of Afghanistan, she will find it much more profitable to subsidise Northern Ireland to remain and weaken the Free State.' While some were voting for the Treaty because it was not a final settlement, 'Sir, I am voting against it, because I believe it will be a final settlement, and it is the terrible finality of that settlement that appals me.' He foresaw a fortress 'as impregnable as Gibraltar'.[26]

A pro-Treaty deputy, Alex MacCabe of Sligo, complimenting President de Valera on his statesmanlike solution of the difficulty, made the sensible observation: 'Minorities have been forcibly brought inside the boundaries of a number of nations liberated in the recent war, with results that should give to us pause before we launch on a coercion campaign against the corner countries'.[27] (Lloyd George also warned Craig of the dangers of Balkanisation).[28] Dr Ferran, representing the same constituency as MacCabe, predicted accurately:

> You believe that under the Articles of Agreement you are to get a fair delimitation of boundary. I hold that England is going to trick you in that article, that Sir James Craig will be left with an equivalent of six counties, and there is not a single guarantee that would not be so.[29]

The device of the Boundary Commission had indeed enabled the British government to play for time on Fermanagh and Tyrone, the most vulnerable part of their case.

Michael Collins, who believed that the Treaty in effect promised Fermanagh and Tyrone at the least, was determined not to be tricked. In response to unionist attempts both physically and politically to secure their territory, by murder, intimidation and gerrymandering, he authorised and partly organised a covert IRA campaign against the north, as well as maintaining other forms of pressure which essentially backfired. Collins did produce his own initiative for peace from January to March 1922, the short-lived Craig-Collins Pact. The Pact tried to halt the violence and end the Belfast Boycott; it envisaged a mixed police force; agreement to see 'whether means can be devised to secure the unity of Ireland', or, failing that, to reach agreement on the border without recourse to the Boundary Commission; the reinstatement of the Catholic shipyard workers or, failing that, employment on relief works; and finally a reciprocal release of political prisoners. Joseph Connolly considered the Pact naive.[30] At a subsequent meeting with the northern bishops, at which Collins was present, Mulcahy stated: 'I take it that under the terms of the Treaty we recognise that parliament in order to destroy it'.[31]

Collins felt very strongly about the plight of northern nationalists. His aim was that the north should be unviable one way or the other, or at the very least make the unionist government respect nationalist rights. This remained his aim, even though he paid lip service to the principle of non-coercion. Of all the major leaders of the independence movement Collins had the politically most active and militarily most aggressive approach to the north. The culmination of this was the fateful assassination on a London street of Field Marshal Sir Henry Wilson, as one of the persons most responsible for the obnoxious treatment of northern nationalists – an act of recklessness which led to a British ultimatum and was a catalyst for civil war. It meant that republican defiance could no longer be treated as if it were a prolonged and very serious industrial relations dispute, but had to be now treated as a threat to the political survival of the state. Collins argued that if no National Government was allowed to function the English would be drawn back in and, worse, be even welcomed back.[32] After Collins' death the tougher approach to the north, which he had been easing off and might in any case have been unable to continue, was swiftly abandoned by his successors, which led to some dissension amongst his followers and the Army Mutiny in 1924. The Civil War compounded the disaster for northern nationalists, and meant that the northern government could safely ignore the south, and dismantle or neutralise the multiple safeguards for the minority in the Government of Ireland Act and the Treaty. These were the Boundary Commission, the Council of Ireland, proportional representation and a comprehensive non-discrimination clause.

On many occasions Collins protested strongly to London, with some limited effect, about the treatment of northern nationalists in a way that was not seen again systematically until the early 1970s and the 1980s, and indeed even made an agreement with Craig (admittedly repudiated by unionists) about the treatment of Catholics in the internal affairs of Northern Ireland. Unionists had the same dislike as today of northern nationalist complaints being routed via the Irish government to the British government.

Collins, like most of his contemporaries, had little empathy with Ulster unionists. This was his argument: 'Pampered for so long, they had learnt to dictate to and to bully the nation to which they professed to be loyal.' The north-east was used in bargaining by the British, making it clear that they would never go beyond Dominion Status. If the north-east had gained wealth it had not percolated through to the workers, and capitalism exploited sectarian division. Without British interference 'the planters would have been absorbed in the old Irish way.' Belfast was an inferior Lancashire, neither English nor Irish:

> We have the task before us to impregnate our northern countrymen with the national outlook. We have a million Protestant Irishmen to convert to our small population of four and a half millions … Had we been able to establish a Republic at once … we would have had to use our resources to coerce north-east Ulster into submission.[33]

De Valera's view then and subsequently was to give the north-east the maximum autonomy (with or without county opt-out) as it enjoyed under the 1920 Act with sovereignty transferred to Ireland, subject only to non-discrimination. Collins would not have disagreed. But De Valera's inclination was more to keep the north at arms length within an all-Ireland polity, whereas Collins used words, which would have unfortunate resonances today, such as convert, impregnate, even coerce.

The north was of course the biggest failure of the 1920–21 settlement, and neither Free State nor Republic was able to provide safeguards or protection for the abandoned nationalist minority in the north. The political tactics that suited the interests of twenty-six county Ireland on the road to independence, such as abstention from Westminster, did nothing to protect the interests of northern nationalists. The nationalist MP Cahir Healy complained in 1925 that neither Griffith, Collins nor De Valera really understood the north. Neither Griffith with his belief that the problem lay in London, nor De Valera's policy of non-recognition, 'nor the rather jumpy efforts which with Collins passed for statecraft' brought them one day nearer peace. Nor were northern nationalists with their failure to agree on any one policy blameless for their own situation. In fact a vigorous policy of non-recognition, though one which did not preclude direct political negotiation, was an important component of Collins' policy up to his death.[34]

The rest of Ireland tried in turn something approximating to each of the models discussed in the Treaty debate: Dominion Status in the 1920s, *de facto* External Association from 1937 to 1949, with an internal but not an external Republic, and finally something like the isolated Republic post-1949 in the 1950s, with the common travel area with Britain remaining and the Republic not to be treated or regarded in law as a foreign country. This is a point of constitutional law that unionists ignore when they talk about the interference of a 'foreign (as opposed to a separate) government'. The decade of isolation in the 1950s, before the approach to Europe, was one of the least satisfactory in our history, when we lost most economic ground comparatively. In 1949 the Inter Party government under-valued the goodwill and valuable support of other commonwealth partners, simply because they would not join in a crude anti-parti-tion campaign.

Attitudes towards minorities and women

Attitudes towards minorities and women were different from what they would be today. During the War of Independence the historical model at a policy level for the treatment of loyalists was that associated with Valley Forge, the winter camp in 1777–8 of Washington's forces, which was visited by Austin Stack in 1922. When the British evacuated Philadelphia, Pennsylvania loyalists, learning that the protection on which they had relied was to be with-drawn, asked what was to become of them, their families and their property. They were told that they must make their peace as best they could with the Patriots – or they must depart with the British forces.[35]

In the Treaty debate Seán Moylan predicted that, if a war of extermination was waged on them, no loyalist in north Cork would see it finish. In correspondence with De Valera on 27 June 1921 Collins quoted a Proclamation of 1778, and also a letter of Charles Thomson, the Irish Secretary to Congress, recommending that 'when the enemy began to burn or destroy any town, to burn and destroy the houses and properties of all Tories and enemies to the freedom and independence of America … always taking care not to treat them or their families with any wanton cruelties'. De Valera re-ferred to this in the private Dáil sessions of August 1921.[36]

Southern unionists played some role in brokering the Truce. Toleration and non-discrimination were promised in the Treaty. In the Treaty debate Griffith described them as 'my countrymen' and argued for 'fair play for all sections'. He went on, 'the person who thinks that you can make an Irish nation, and make it successfully function, with 800,000 of our countrymen in the north up against us, and 400,000 of our countrymen here in the south opposed to us, is living in a fool's paradise.' Griffith negotiated the basis of Senate representation for them.

Of course, Dominion Status and common citizenship meant that the minority were not deprived of their allegiance to the crown or their British citizenship. W. T. Cosgrave, with his contacts with Dublin businessmen, positively enthused over their conversion:

'Now, Sir, if there is one thing more than another which this movement has done it is that it has captured the imagination and support
of southern unionists as they have been known.' They were to form
a significant part of his political support base, and, as in most
newly-independent countries, he thought it unwise economically
to drive out or burn out the wealthy class with a consequent loss in
the revenue of the country and in some cases important cultural
artefacts.[37] It was for that same reason and for his valuable business
contacts that De Valera appointed Robert Barton to his 'Republican
Government' or shadow cabinet in 1924, despite the fact that he
had signed the Treaty. Ruttledge in 1924 was even to urge Sinn Féin
recruitment among younger ex-unionists.[38] The maintenance of pri-
vilege was to sit uneasily with the strong republican egalitarian
instinct. Lemass, for example, strongly attacked the Senate as running counter to the efforts of half a century 'to shake off the grip
maintained by the descendants of the plantation soldiery of Cromwell', and to put into the hands of the Irish people the economic
resources of the country.[39]

In the spring of 1922 some terrible sectarian murders took place
in County Cork. These were condemned by Dáil Éireann, which
declared: 'The Irish nation consists of no one class or creed but com-
bines all', a statement echoed by Collins. Since some of De Valera's
speeches of the spring of 1922 have attracted such criticism it is
worth citing one that does him honour. On 30 April, he said at
Mullingar:

> The German Palatines, the French Huguenots, the English Protestants
> flying from the fires of Smithfield, later the Wesleyans and the Jews,
> who were persecuted in every land, in this land of ours always found
> safe asylum. That glorious record must not be tarnished by acts
> against a helpless minority.[40]

As a person of mixed background, De Valera was generally more
sensitive to the minority than most of his contemporaries. Shortly
afterwards, on a journey to Canossa, Archbishop Gregg led a deputation to Griffith and Collins to ask if Protestants were to be
allowed to live in the Free State or if it was desired they should
leave the country. While they received some reassurance, Collins
drew their attention to the revolting murders of Catholics in the
north. He spoke publicly of the new state putting down sectarian
and agrarian crime. Later that month he told Sir Henry Robinson,

a civil servant who had been raided and threatened by republicans in Foxrock, that the Provisional Government was in no position to protect anybody, and Robinson and his family 'had much better clear out, and come back later when things had settled down a bit.'[41] They never did. In the Civil War republican attacks on and requisitions of the property of Protestants and unionists, often automatically classed as prominent Free State supporters, were resumed.

As Archbishop Walton Empey summed it up pithily in his May 1996 eve of Synod address: 'Life was not always easy down here. To put it bluntly, most of our people found themselves on the losing side in a revolution.' The British authorities, by their policy of reprisals in the Tan War which caused general disgust, and by their repeated refusal backed by military threat to compromise even half way with Republican sentiment, made the life of Protestants, most of whom regarded themselves as both British and Irish, difficult and in some cases impossible. Nevertheless, the majority managed to come through relatively unscathed and the community itself survived. One could take the view, considering all the historical factors, that, as revolutions go, the Protestant community and the former ruling élite escaped relatively lightly. Terminology drawn from other, in aggregate far more horrible, subsequent situations such as 'genocide' or 'ethnic cleansing' is not justified.

Cosgrave was typically the only deputy to begin his contribution to the Treaty debate with a theological point. A doctor of divinity had explained to him that in an oath one can be faithful to an equal without any necessary connotation of being a subject. As we know, Cosgrave at one point passed on to De Valera a proposal he had received to establish a theological senate, though to be fair to De Valera he did not at all favour the idea and it went no further. Collins reputedly once swore in exasperation at the clerical susceptibility of Cosgrave's personality. That raises the question: would the tone of the young Free State have been as confessional and deferential in matters affecting Church and State if Griffith or Collins rather than Cosgrave had been in charge in the early years?[42]

In the Treaty debate some of the principal Free State speakers countered suggestions that they had betrayed the Republic by implying subtly or not so subtly that they were more Irish than opponents like De Valera, Childers, Brugha and Markievicz. Béaslaí, born in Liverpool incidentally, argued skilfully that the Republic itself was un-Irish, that Gaelic Ireland, whether of the seventeenth or eighteenth centuries, had been monarchist with Stuart and Jacobite leanings. Collins spoke of the terror his forebears had been subjected to:

> Our grandfathers have suffered from war, and our fathers or some of our ancestors have died of famine. I don't want a lecture from anybody as to what my principles are to be now. I am just a representative of plain Irish stock whose principles have been burned into them ...[43]

This perhaps provoked De Valera's famous reply that he was reared in a labourer's cottage, that he had not lived solely among the intellectuals, and that 'whenever I wanted to know what the Irish people wanted I had only to examine my own heart.' When Dev led his followers out of the Dáil on 19 January on the election as President of the Republic of Arthur Griffith, who was bound by the Treaty to subvert it, Collins shouted after them: 'Foreigners – Americans – English.' Griffith's animus against Erskine Childers, as the supposed brains behind the Republic who had been introduced to its service by Collins, displayed a streak of intolerance and xenophobia which was to contribute to Childers being shot twelve months later. It was a hard fate for someone who had, as Cathal Brugha pointed out in his defence in the Dáil on 8 June 1922, run into Howth the guns which had facilitated the 1916 Rising and thus the whole struggle for independence. Cosgrave's rant against intellectuals on that occasion would be one source for the anti-intellectualism that became a marked feature of public life, as indeed was Kevin O'Higgins' earlier attack on 'a clique of neurotics, a clique of psuedo-intellectuals', who, he alleged, were trying to rule by the revolver in place of the people.[44]

One of the welcome features of the 1916 Proclamation was its appeal to Irishmen and Irishwomen, which seemed to presage an equal role for women. Constance Markievicz was appointed Minister for Labour, a post for which she was well qualified as Connolly's political companion. De Valera wanted to appoint Mary MacSwiney to the delegation to the Treaty negotiations, but did not do so, he claimed, because of Collins' and Griffith's strong views against women in politics.[45] A further issue arose, when the republican side pushed, no doubt partly for tactical reasons, a proposal to lower the voting age for women from thirty years to twenty-one in the spring of 1922, a reform which was implemented only after the general election later that year. Piaras Béaslaí had a curious passage in his life of Collins, where he disputed that Collins had ever used women as messengers or for other dangerous missions. The Attorney General Hugh Kennedy told Lionel Curtis 'I shan't worry as long as women speak ill of us', a reference to Hannah Sheehy-Skeffington. Cosgrave boasted in the Dáil they had the courage to arrest thousands of prisoners, and 'no three or four mad women coming in here to talk to us are going to make us release these prisoners', as long as the safety of the state was in danger.[46]

The women almost without exception opposed the Treaty. Was it that women, as at the time of the Ladies' Land League, had more attachment to principle and were less inclined to accept pragmatic compromise, or was it more that, being excluded from real power, they were driven back to the bedrock of principle? De Valera, who broke with Mary MacSwiney in leaving Sinn Féin, was subsequently to have difficulties over the constitution with some of his female supporters, including Dorothy Macardle. In Tipperary in 1923, when the Civil War was over, W. T. Cosgrave told some republican women who objected to his criticisms of Mary MacSwiney that they 'should have rosaries in their hands or be at home with knitting needles.'[47]

Tom Garvin has speculated why in the long term the Free State side won the battle but lost the war. The obvious reason is that people never especially liked the Treaty, but accepted it because they liked renewed fighting even less. They had little difficulty with a political strategy for dismantling the Treaty by constitutional methods, by either Collins or De Valera. The Labour opposition in the Dáil in the autumn of 1922 also tried to remove the king from the constitution. I do not subscribe to the notion that the Treaty won a *de facto* Republic but only the anti-Treatyites and the Tories failed to recognise it, a notion that Kevin O'Higgins poured scorn on when put forward by Gavan Duffy. In general, the Free State side tended to argue that the Republic had always belonged to the realm of fantasy. Without entering into debate as to whether constitutional monarchy in contrast to absolute monarchy is itself arguably a form of *de facto* Republic, the fact is that the British and specifically J. H. Thomas, a National Labour Minister, fought the Economic War to try to prevent the dismantling of Dominion Status and the establishment of a *de facto* Republic from 1937. The first Governor General, Tim Healy, was put on look-out for any legislation contrary to the Treaty, to alert the British, if not, in the last resort, to exercise the right of veto. O'Higgins before his death nurtured the hope that a dual monarchy Dominion of Ireland might bring about Irish unity.[45]

The second reason why the Free State side lost out in the long term was the extra-judicial executions, carried out by the government of the Free State after Collins' death in the autumn of 1922, which horrified independent opinion. Gavan Duffy, Tom Johnson and John Dillon, for instance, were all absolutely appalled. Piaras Béaslaí, in writing his biography, was clearly relieved that Collins' reputation was spared association with such deeds. Paradoxically, while the suspension of the Third Dáil in July-August 1922 and his continued leadership of the IRB in this transitional period has raised some question marks about Collins' commitment to democracy, his successors were accountable to the Dáil for far worse breaches of the rule of law. No party acted with perfect democratic propriety in 1922, but, despite the dangerous deviations, I believe all sides, with very few exceptions, wanted an independent Ireland to become a functioning constitutional democracy.

Later, the outcome of the Boundary Commission dispelled all remaining illusions about the Treaty, and the 1925 Agreement represented an ignominious abandonment of northern nationalists in exchange for financial concessions to the Free State.

The truth is that in 1922 both Collins and De Valera, Free Staters and republicans, were blown drastically off course in a tragic manner, though unfortunately in the twentieth century nothing has been more common in newly liberated states than a power struggle culminating in civil war. Many questionable, even disastrous, decisions were taken. But equally great efforts were made by both sides to avert the Civil War, and even after it had started to stop it. However, by August 1922, Collins, then his successors, were going for victory not political accommodation, nor was one ever reached, unfortunately. The surrender of arms was the unacceptable demand that almost invariably prolonged rather than shortened conflict over centuries of Irish history. In May 1922 Collins' attitude was that neither the Treaty nor the Republic was worth a civil war.

De Valera had at first been confident that the nation knew how to conduct itself, and that the army would remain subordinate. His failure to criticise Rory O'Connor's repudiation of the Dáil in March, which he bitterly regretted later, showed the weakness of the position of someone trying to preserve anti-Treaty unity at all costs. There was no exact mechanism for determining the constitutional legitimacy of the disestablishment of the Republic, and a section of the IRA was in revolt. But an army not under proper civilian control was scarcely an appropriate constitutional check or balance in a fledging democracy. A general election held under British duress was not considered adequate. The only method, reverted to after 1923, was to oppose the Free State and its legitimacy politically, accepting, according to a proclamation issued by the Republican Government and Army Council under De Valera, that subject to the sovereignty of the people,

> judgement being by majority vote should be submitted to, and resistance by violence excluded not because the decision is necessarily right or just or permanent, but because acceptance of this rule makes for peace, order and unity in national action, and is the democratic alternative to arbitrament by force.[49]

It was a tragedy that that position could not have prevailed earlier, even if that was more the responsibility of the republican army leaders than of their politicians, because, following the Treaty split in January 1922, what was intended to be a constitutional parliamentary opposition under De Valera's leadership had been established. What exactly was constitutional in the circumstances was itself bristling with difficulties and hotly disputed. Was it the Treaty accord with the British, or was it the declared Republic that was the constitutional norm?

One can be equally critical of the pendulum swings of Collins in relation to the Pact with De Valera. Having told the Sinn Féin Árd Fheis in May that 'unity at home was more important than any Treaty with the foreigner,[50] Collins abandoned the Pact on the eve of the election, even though the British-amended constitution was more unacceptable than ever. Many felt that De Valera had been double-crossed. The late Seán MacBride was convinced that the draft constitution was the key to averting the Civil War. Perhaps a united stand should have been made on that, ignoring but without directly reversing the Treaty. British sanctions could hardly have been much worse than the subsequent combined effects of the Civil and Economic Wars. The opposition of the republicans on the one side and the refusal of compromise by the British on the other, who were determined to exclude De Valera from power, left the Provisional Government in a weak and exposed position. Unless they asserted their authority, power was going to be taken away from them.

While great stress is laid as a historical fig-leaf on the kidnapping of a Free State General rather than the British ultimatum following Wilson's assassination as the trigger of the Civil War, the choice as far as Collins was concerned, when he rejected Liam Lynch's overtures in August 1922, was between the return of the British and the anti-Treatyites sending in their arms. When the Third Dáil met in September Kevin O'Higgins took the same line when he said: 'We had very good reason to believe that we anticipated by a couple of hours the creation of conditions under which this parliament would never have met, conditions that would have brought back the British power.' Mulcahy admitted the decision to attack the Four Courts to prevent them attacking the British had practically been taken before General O'Connell was kidnapped.[51]

But rather than castigate either free staters or republicans for what turned out to be tragic errors, mostly committed out of patriotic motives, we should never lose sight of the fact that the root, indeed sole, cause of the Civil War, and why so many attempts to avert it failed, was the adamant but ultimately futile efforts of Britain, which continued well into the 1930s, to deny twenty-six county Ireland the full attributes of sovereign independence, even though Churchill, as early as 1924 in 'absolutely secret' correspondence, conceded that the Free State could, in a worst case scenario, be let go republican while Britain held on to Ulster.[52] Aided and abetted by the pedantry of Curtis' intellectual crusade to reform the empire, Churchill's involvement in Ireland belongs along with the Dardanelles, the Gold Standard and India to the litany of disasters on the debit side of a great statesman's public record. Later in the century it would be accepted that to create civil war in the context of decolonisation reflected badly on the withdrawing imperial power. The mess created in Ireland was undoubtedly a deserved factor in the collapse of the Lloyd George coalition in October 1922. If more magnanimity had been shown on the question of status Anglo-Irish relations would have been very different, and thus the problem of Northern Ireland much more manageable.

The unionist historian of *The Revolution in Ireland*, Alison Phillips, while he approved the later efforts of Collins and Griffith to restore order and admired their 'capacity' and 'statesmanlike moderation, which had done something to reconcile conservative opinion to the new order', though feeling the still tougher approach of the autumn of 1922 was necessary, wrote in 1926, regarding the revised Document Number Two submitted by De Valera in January 1922:

> It is possible to regret that the British government having once made up its mind to surrender did not frankly recognise the Irish Republic on some such terms as those. To have done so would not have exposed the crown to any greater humiliation than it has suffered, nor Great Britain to any dangers from which the actual Treaty preserves her, while Ireland might have been spared the ruin, desolation and bloodshed of another year of fratricidal strife.

Presented to British public opinion as an end to 700 years of conflict and as an opportunity for Anglo-Irish reconciliation, British rigidity prevented it from being any of those things. To that extent, there was indeed a failure of statesmanship.

Like Cope's advice, like Churchill's private admission in 1924, Phillips' verdict shows that the British government could have chosen to act differently, remembering also that it did not survive the Treaty by more than 10 months. It points up the fact that De Valera was not the intransigent person he is portrayed as, but that he had thought up the most statesmanlike solution which would have spared a lot of grief, and which was the only solution would have preserved a high degree of national unity as well as far better Anglo-Irish relations for the future. From 1947 it became the model for India as opposed to Ireland.

Cosgrave's tactics, which were praised in 1994 by Albert Reynolds, forced De Valera and Fianna Fáil back into the Dáil, as a 'slightly constitutional' opposition. By the time of the handover in 1932 the state was working well and the economy was soundly functioning, although the government were very orthodox in their economic policy. As Kevin O'Higgins once said, they were the most conservative of revolutionaries. Further ground was lost by the Free State party after the peaceful change-over, both with the Blueshirt fiasco and also an equivocal stance during the Economic War, which Cosgrave and the British hoped would discredit De Valera for good.[53]

Collins' vision

Collins shared much in common with both the outlook of both De Valera and Lemass. On the one hand, Collins saw Irish history as a vast *kulturkampf*, in which England had set out to suppress Irish nationality, culture, language, religion and industry in any way that could compete with Britain. His ideal was unambiguously to build 'a free, prosperous self-governing Gaelic Ireland', once English power had been expelled. He was contemptuous of O'Connell, whom he saw as wanting simply to have the Irish people as 'a free Catholic community', preferring the vision of Davis, who 'sought to unite the whole people', fought against sectarianism, and who saw, according to Collins, that 'unless we were Gaels we were not a nation.' Cultural nationalism was not sectarian, but it was not pluralist either. True, Collins had quite a wide concept of what being Gaelic involved, as he observed that at the time of Grattan's Parliament the garrison was becoming Gaelic. He claimed:

> We are now free in name. The extent to which we become free in fact and secure our freedom will be the extent to which we become Gaels again … We can fill our minds with Gaelic ideas, and our lives with Gaelic customs until there is no room for any other … The most completely anglicised person in Ireland will look to Britain in vain.

He attacked the towns and villages as 'hideous medleys of contemptible dwellings and means shops and squalid public houses', and asserted that it was only in the remote corners of Ireland such as Achill that 'any trace of the old civilisation is found now', providing 'a glimpse of what Ireland may become again' when 'the beauty will be the outward sign of a prosperous and happy Gaelic life'. There is very little in all of that which diverges much from De Valera's 1943 vision of 'the Ireland that we dreamed of' with its simple, frugal comforts. Collins argued: 'The chance that materialism will take possession of the Irish people is no more likely in a free Ireland under the Free State than it would be in a free Ireland under a Republican or any other form of government.'[54]

But there was another, more developmental side to Collins. He was even more concerned about the effects of English economic penetration than he was about the military:

> Every day our banks become incorporated or allied to British interests, every day our Steamship Companies go into English hands, every day some other business concern in this city is taken over by an English concern and becomes a little oasis of English customs and manners.[55]

His aim was to have in the new island 'such material welfare as will give the Irish spirit that freedom' to reach out to the higher things, not crushed by destitution. He did not want the country covered with smoking chimneys and factories, or a great national balance sheet or 'a people producing wealth with the self-obliteration of a hive of bees.' The aim was to enable our people to provide themselves with the ordinary requirements of decent living, giving children bodily and mental health, and enable people to secure themselves against sickness and old age. He wanted to see agriculture improved, existing industries developed, means of transport extended and made cheap, hydro-power used, and mineral resources tapped. He wanted a housing programme, scientific farming, industry developed on a co-operative basis, as 'state socialism has nothing to recommend it, in a country like Ireland, and in any case, is a monopoly of another kind.' He had little time for the Democratic Programme of the First Dáil because of its socialist character. A large part of imported goods could be produced at home. The bogs should be developed. The docklands at the mouth of the Liffey were splendidly situated for commercial purposes. He was dissatisfied with the state of development of the fishing industry. Ireland should become 'a great exchange market between Europe and America'. Irish money should be invested in Irish industry rather than abroad. 'We shall hope to see in Ireland industrial conciliation and arbitration taking the place of strikes, and the workers sharing the ownership and management of business.' Many of these items sketched out would have a later resonance. His bottom line was that 'a prosperous Ireland will mean a united Ireland.'[56] Less eloquent and cerebral than De Valera, he had the practical qualities of Lemass and shared with him a good financial head and brilliant administrative ability. For the record, in August 1921, as Minister for Finance, he brought in a book of estimates totalling £145,000.[57]

We should avoid continually stereotyping De Valera, for example with the notion that he had no real interest in economic issues. In 1924, he told Sinn Féin deputies: 'We should throw all our strength on the economic side. Our principal efforts should be directed towards trying to devise means of helping our people economically.'[58] He wanted to bring back industries by some process of protection, and he said if there had been a proper settlement with the British a large loan could have been got at home and from America for social purposes such as housing. Todd Andrews, an eminently practical man who helped build up the state sector, believed De Valera was 'the greatest political figure in our history.' He claimed: 'As a political thinker he was the superior of Davis or Pearse. As a popular leader he was comparable to Parnell. He was as close to the common man as O'Connell or Collins.' Andrews valued above all his imperviousness to British pressure. Andrews linked the 1943 Saint Patrick's Day speech to standards of integrity in public life that were beginning to deteriorate.[59] De Valera articulated the vision of a generation, of the Gaelic League and Irish-Ireland, but he did so, by and large, with intelligence, sensitivity and moderation.

I leave my last word on Collins with my late father Nicholas Mansergh:

> In his lifetime he was acclaimed as the man who won the war. As a negotiator he won high regard from Churchill and Birkenhead, though he had his share of impetuosity in judgement. Beyond question he had the courage and ruthlessness that make for achievement in revolutionary times. Nor was there any very obvious limitation to his powers; he had all manner of qualities and with experience was deemed likely to acquire the great ones. Yet of him at the last it has to be written 'He died young'. A man may not be judged by the great things he might have done.[60]

That indeed was the tragedy. But what he had already achieved by his death had helped set the course of Ireland's future history as a nation.

'Sorrow but no despair – the road is marked'

The politics of funerals in post-1916 Ireland

Gabriel Doherty and Professor Dermot Keogh[1]

Introduction

The many funerals of nationalist activists and leaders in post-1916 Ireland were, of course, occasions to grieve and bury the fallen. But they were also an opportunity to celebrate the lives and the deeds of great men and women who had died in the cause of advancing the independence of Ireland, often at times when more explicit forms of celebration were, for whatever reason, not feasible. In times of emergency legislation and extreme political censorship, the funeral was often the only public occasion on which dissident and 'subversive' views could be put forward without fear of instantaneous arrest; that usually followed the moment the orator set foot outside the cemetery.

In this essay we will examine the place of the funeral in the politics of protest and celebration of a life given for the cause of Irish independence.

The national mourning of Parnell

In the nineteenth century, there were many memorable political funerals but none to rival that of Charles Stewart Parnell who died in Brighton on 6 October 1891. A rain-soaked Dublin received his body as tens of thousands lined the streets and thirty-three brass bands marched, joined by contingents of people representing different organisations, including over a thousand Gaelic Athletic Association members who carried hurley sticks with green and black ribbons and acted as stewards.[2]

The cortege stopped a number of times en route and the historical significance of those halts was not lost on the huge crowds. The intention was to identify the 'fallen leader', Parnell, with the great events and the great figures in Ireland's nationalist past. The first stop was at the Bank of Ireland in College Green, the home of the Irish parliament in the late eighteenth century. Then to St Michan's church, the resting place of the brothers Sheares, executed for their part in the activities of the United Irishmen. The procession made its way to City Hall where the remains lay 'in state', thousands filing past the catafalque in a few hours.[3]

When the funeral set off for Glasnevin it made two further stops, both associated with the abortive rising of 1803: firstly at the spot where Robert Emmet had been executed, and then at the house of another revolutionary, Lord Edward Fitzgerald. The cortege made its way slowly through the rain-soaked streets to Glasnevin cemetery where 'the Chief' was buried near the tomb of the other great constitutional nationalist of the nineteenth century, Daniel O'Connell. The *Freeman's Journal* reported: 'No greater upheaval of emotion had ever been witnessed in Ireland'.[4]

'The fools, the fools, the fools' – At the graveside of O'Donovan Rossa
The twentieth century was to witness other moving scenes as masses of people came out onto the streets of the capital or the other cities of the country to pay their last respects to those who had died for their country. One of the first and most important was the occasion of the burial of the Fenian Jeremiah O'Donovan Rossa, whose body was taken back to Ireland from New York and interred in Glasnevin on 1 August 1915. Patrick Pearse, dressed in the uniform of an Irish Volunteer, gave the funeral oration and finished his address with lines which were to become burned into the collective nationalist memory: 'The fools, the fools, the fools – they have left us our Fenian dead, and while Ireland holds these graves, Ireland unfree shall never be at peace'. The whole operation was, in the words of one of Pearse's biographers, 'a gigantic propaganda exercise', which involved extensive prior organisation and enlisted, in addition to Pearse, the efforts of the advanced nationalist cadre.[5]

Between 3 and 12 May 1916, fifteen of the leaders of the Easter Rising were executed. They received no public funerals.[6] Neither did Sir Roger Casement, who was hanged in London for the role he played in the preparations for the Rising.[7] In a conciliatory gesture some fifty years later the British government released his remains for reburial in Dublin. His body was exhumed from Pentonville Prison and returned to Ireland for formal reburial alongside Pearse, Connolly, Clarke, *et. al.*, in 1965. The occasion was both solemn and deeply moving in itself but was given added poignancy by the sight of De Valera, by now almost incapacitated with age, standing respectfully at the graveside notwithstanding the unseasonably inclement weather which marked the ceremony.[8]

Thomas Ashe, who had been interned for his part in leading a company of Volunteers in Ashbourne, County Meath, during the Rising, was re-arrested in August 1917 following his earlier release, and charged with incitement. Together with a number of other republican prisoners in Mountjoy gaol he participated in a campaign designed to achieve prisoner of war status. When it was clear that such a concession was not about to be granted he, together with a number of his fellow prisoners, began a hunger strike. On 25 September, five days after his protest began, he died while being forcibly fed. His funeral in Glasnevin on 31 September 1917 was destined to remembered, in the words of a prominent republican chronicler, as 'a pageant of the nation'.[9]

Public funerals during the War of Independence

Between 1917 and the Truce on 22 June 1921, graveyards frequently became the centres of protest on the occasion of burials of nationalist activists in the War of Independence. Graveside orations were occasions for the use of inflammatory rhetoric which might otherwise have placed the speakers in jail. When censorship prevailed, the graveyard became an even more important forum for the preaching of sedition and revolution.[10] Tomás MacCurtain, the Lord Mayor of Cork in 1920, was murdered at his home on 20 March 1920. He was given a hero's funeral.[11] Terence MacSwiney, who succeeded MacCurtain as Lord Mayor, died after 74 days on hunger strike in 1920. His body was accompanied through the streets of London by a guard of honour wearing outlawed uniforms. He was buried with full military honours in his native Cork.[12] There were many other funerals of IRA Volunteers and of civilians during the War of Independence. Such occasions were turned into rallies to mobilise support for a revolutionary cause.

The death of Cathal Brugha

Following the outbreak of Civil War in 1922, both sides of the Treaty divide were to have their own respective martyrologies. The death on 7 July 1922 of Cathal Brugha, for example, showed how funerals continued to be used to conduct war by other means. Brugha's wife had been called to his bedside on Friday morning, 7 July. They conversed in Irish for a time. Mrs Lalor, the wife of his employer, was also present. He received communion (the day being the first Friday of the month) from Fr Young, a hospital chaplain.[13] The last rites were administered by Fr Francis Ryan, OP. His remains rested in the mortuary chapel in the Mater Hospital where people filed past the coffin on Saturday and Sunday, 8 and 9 July. The *Freeman's Journal* reported on 8 July:

> Large numbers visited the mortuary chapel attached to the hospital where the remains were laid out yesterday evening. The body was covered with the Tricolour and three members of the Cumann na mBan, in uniform, were posted near the bier. For a considerable time a continuous procession of mourners passed reverently around the remains.

His coffin was taken to St Joseph's church, Berkeley Road, on the evening of the ninth. He was buried after a requiem high mass at 10 o'clock on Monday 10 July in the Republican plot in Glasnevin. The *Irish Times*, which was implacably opposed to Brugha's political ideas, wrote on 8 July:

> The death of Cathal Brugha in the Mater Hospital removes a remarkable personality from Irish life. Of all Ireland's many extremists he was the most extreme. The manner of his death was typical of his life. Cathal Brugha died, as he lived, in the last ditch. No other modern country save Ireland produces such types. They belong in point of time to the Middle Ages, when men would face the stake for an idea, whether it was right or wrong. Of such stuff was Cathal Brugha made. All his life he hated England with an intensity of feeling which is rarely found even in this country of painful memories. Whenever there was talk of a rebellion he was at the head of the insurgent movement. Whenever there was talk of a surrender he was found fighting to the last.[14]

The anonymous author of an appreciation in the *Irish Times* described him as 'brave as a lion, for he was a man of one idea'. He was viewed as sincere and single-minded 'for he hated more fiercely than he loved.' The writer had never heard a quibble or an evasion from his lips; at the same time 'I never heard him utter a constructive thought'. He added:

> And how bitter were the reproaches which he hurled at his former colleagues! Who will forget that eventful day at Earlsfort Terrace when he wound up the long debate against the Treaty? Cathal Brugha was as unforgiving as he was unflinching in his purpose; but he was bro-

ken by the forces against which he fought with all the strength of his fragile body and all the wild zeal of an untameable spirit … Yet he was a fond husband and a devoted father. On such human contrasts Ireland's sorrows have been built.

The tribute ended:

The stormy petrel of Ireland's tempestuous times has perished in the teeth of the gale. That final scene behind the Granville Hotel was a magnificent gesture of tragic defiance. A little pale-faced man, haggard and begrimed with smoke and powder, a peremptory call to surrender, answered by a challenging 'No!' With a hoarse cry Cathal Brugha rushed his country's soldiers with a drawn revolver. And then he fell, mortally wounded by an Irish bullet; for the man who defied the might of England sought to challenge the will of the people whom he loved.[15]

Free State troops honour Harry Boland

Harry Boland, another prominent anti-Treatyite, was shot dead by Free State troops in the Grand Hotel, Skerries, County Dublin, on 1 August 1922. According to the official report, he

made an unsuccessful attempt to seize a gun from one of the troops and then rushed out to the corridor. After firing two shots at random and calling on Mr Boland to halt, it was found necessary to fire a third shot to prevent escape.[16]

Boland died on 2 August in St Vincent's hospital, Dublin. Michael Collins, divided from his close personal friend by civil war, wrote to his fiancée, Kitty Kiernan, on 2 August: 'I passed Vincent's hospital and saw a small crowd outside. My mind went into him [Boland] lying dead there and I thought o f the times together … I'd send a wreath but I suppose they'd return it torn up'.[17]

Boland's remains were taken from the hospital on 3 August 1922 to the Carmelite church, Whitefriar Street. A very large procession, led by an advance guard of Cumann na mBan, walked behind the coffin. A large body of clergy walked behind the hearse. The male relatives of the deceased occupied the first carriage, and after the other carriages of mourners came the Citizen Army pipe band, the main body of Cumann na mBan, the Clann na Gael Girl Scouts, the women's section of the Citizen Army, the Irish National Foresters Brass and Reed Band, anti-Treaty members of Dáil Éireann, members of the GAA, the Fianna, representatives of labour, trade unions and the public.[18] The body was received by four priests.

Professor Michael Browne of Maynooth, who was later to become bishop of Galway, was the main celebrant at high mass the following day. Over a dozen priests were in the choir. Among the TDs and ex-TDs present were Larry Ginnell, John O'Mahony, T. O'Rourke, J. J. O'Kelly (Sceilg) and his fellow TD for South Roscommon, Frank Fahy. At the end of the ceremony the cortege moved along Aungier Street where the traffic was regulated by Cumann na mBan. The general public came out in large numbers to pay their last respects along the route to Glasnevin. A guard of honour walked beside the bier which was preceded by about 30 priests on foot, the chief mourners, companies of Cumann na mBan, the TDs and ex-TDs and other friends.

The journalist for the *Freeman's Journal* reported on a 'touching incident' in O'Connell Street:

> The funeral was met by a Lancia car containing National troops. The vehicle was pulled up, and the occupants, having laid down their arms, removed their caps, and stood to attention until the hearse had passed.[19]

Among those present at the graveside were the Lord Mayor of Dublin, the Lord Mayor of Cork, Mrs de Valera, Mrs Cathal Brugha, Count and Countess Plunkett. Countess Markievicz, speaking in Irish, said that there was no more loyal or faithful comrade than Harry Boland. She probably said much more, but the journalist's report was mercifully laconic. Three volleys were fired and the Last Post was sounded. The remains were buried in the republican plot.

From the press reports of the funeral, it would be hard to believe that there was a civil war going on in the countryside. The government had allowed the funeral to take place without interruption. The display of gallantry by the government troops in O'Connell Street may, it is possible to speculate, have been the only manner in which Collins could pay his last respects to his great friend. It was a noble act in a war which quickly became characterised by ignoble actions.

Mourning Michael Collins

If the anti-Treatyites could turn funerals into occasions for the mobilisation of support and the utterance of defiance, the government side had three occasions on which they mourned dead leaders and sought to strengthen the popular legitimacy of the state. The deaths in question were of Arthur Griffith (12 August 1922), Michael Collins (22 August 1922) and Kevin O'Higgins (10 July 1927). On each occasion, the funerals came to demonstrate the individuals' historical associations with past generations of patriots; their contribution to the formation of the Irish state; the difficulty of finding adequate replacements; and the will to struggle on, inspired by the life, ideals and work of the fallen.

People must have found it impossible to believe the terse reports of the death of Michael Collins in the national press on 23 August 1922. They were in a state of 'stunned despair' to quote an editorial in the *Freeman's Journal* which was bordered (as was the newspaper custom of the time) in black. Citizens of the fledgling state would have read:

> The terrible news we announce today will move Ireland as nothing has moved her in living memory. Michael Collins has fallen by the hands of his own countrymen. He had dared death so often in the struggle with England that men felt he could run all risks and emerge unharmed. That he should be killed by an Irish bullet is a tragedy too deep for tears.[20]

The loss was great, all the more so because only a week before, as we have seen, the head of the Provisional Government, Arthur Griffith had been buried. But to the tens of thousand who lined the streets of Dublin on that occasion, the writer in the *Freeman's Journal* said:

> The gleam of hope on the gloom was the sight of Michael Collins marching at the head of the army. He has now been taken from us … It is difficult not to despair. Yet to do so would be treason to Griffith and Collins alike. Great men may pass but the nation remains. Michael Collins is dead for Ireland. It is for us, who believe in the cause for which he gave his life, to see that the new Ireland shall be worthy of the sacrifice.

His death had taken place amid a civil war the outcome of which was far from assured; now it was to be a fight without Collins, the hero of the War of Independence, in the van. The chief of the general staff, Richard Mulcahy, sought to steady the men of the army thus:

stand calmly by your posts. Bend bravely and undaunted to your work. Let no cruel act of reprisal blemish your bright honour. Every dark hour that Michael Collins met since 1916 seemed but to steel that bright strength of his and temper his gay bravery. You are left, each inheritors of that strength and of that bravery. To each of you falls his unfinished work ... Ireland! The army serves – strength by its sorrow.

An editorial in the *Freeman's Journal* on 24 August – entitled 'Greatest and Bravest' – repeated part of Mulcahy's message, noting that 'General Collins died as a soldier would have wished to die', falling 'in the hour of victory cheering on his troops, and inspiring them, as he never failed to inspire his countrymen, by his gallant example and radiant confidence'. At the moment of his death, he bore no rancour, according to the paper: 'Forgive them', were the last words on his lips.[21] This theme of forgiveness was taken up by Frances McHugh in a surprisingly conciliatory piece in the pro-government paper, *The Free State*:

> His last words were 'Forgive them'; a beautiful and sentimental exit from this life? I cannot interpret these words so. No; he meant, this man who saw clearly and spoke his thoughts, 'Do not assassinate any one of my enemies' leaders to avenge me. For Ireland's sake do not start an era of assassinatory politics.' Such last words must make his death new life to Ireland.[22]

'Ireland's Via Dolorosa' was the heading on a drawing showing a woman with her arms around a broken column amid the ruins of an ancient temple. On the day of the funeral, the *Freeman's Journal* carried another drawing showing a woman in widow's black laying a garland on the broken column bearing the name of Collins.[23] The political complexion of the paper's editorial stance was indicated by the choice of the names adorning other columns in this Irish pantheon: Owen Roe O'Neill, O'Connell, Parnell and, perhaps most revealingly, Redmond.

Meanwhile, some 50,000 people lined the streets of Dublin as the remains were taken on a gun carriage to City Hall for the lying in state. Four bishops and over sixty priests took part in the procession. The headline of the following day summed up the scene: REMARKABLE SCENES OF POPULAR SORROW AND SYMPATHY AT CITY HALL – VAST THRONGS IN ENDLESS QUEUE, PAY TRIBUTE TO HEROIC DEAD.

On the evening of 27 August, the coffin was sealed. For some time before that moment William T. Cosgrave (who had taken over as Chairman of the Provisional Government from Collins) had personally stood before the remains. There were further moving displays of public grief when the body was taken from City Hall to the pro-Cathedral. Over a hundred priests, headed by Bishop Michael Fogarty of Killaloe, walked in the procession. The *Freeman's Journal* wrote:

> The sad strains of pipers' bands in the still evening air added to the solemnity of the occasion, as the gun-carriage upon which rested the coffin draped in the Irish flag, moved slowly through the streets.

The Collins family re-assembled for the occasion. A sister of Michael Collins, who was a nun in England, travelled over for the funeral.

There may have been those in the crowds who thronged the streets of Dublin to pay their last respects on 28 August who may have been present just thirty years before when Charles Stewart Parnell was buried in Glasnevin amid unprecedented scenes of public grief. The death of Collins evoked the same strong feelings in ordinary people of Dublin as Daniel O'Connell and Parnell, or so it would appear from the coverage of the funeral in the press.

The historian, Alice Stopford Green, who was present at the graveside in Glasnevin wrote of her experience:

> I was standing by a young soldier as the vast procession filed in for their last farewell of the dead – 'You are broken with fatigue and sorrow', I said. He turned away his head with a choking gasp, 'I can't bear it'.[24]

There was a great public display of grief as the Commander-in-Chief of the army, General Richard Mulcahy gave the oration. He began with a nationalist martyrology:

> Tom Ashe, Tomás MacCurtain, Traolach MacSuibhne [Terence Mac-Swiney], Dick McKee, Micheal Ó Coileain, and all you who lie buried here, disciples our great Chief, those of us you leave behind are all, too, grain from the same handful, scattered by the hand of the Great Sower over the fruitful soil of Ireland. We, too, will bring forth our own fruit. Men and women of Ireland, we are all mariners on the deep, bound for a port still seen only through storm and spray, sailing still on a sea full 'of dangers and hardships, and bitter toil.' But the Great Sleeper lies smiling with the spirit which will walk bravely upon the waters.

He continued:

> We bend today over the grave of a man not more than thirty years of age, who took to himself the gospel of toil for Ireland, and of sacrifice for their good, and who has made himself a hero and a legend that will stand in the pages of our history with any bright page that was ever written there. Pages have been written by him in the hearts of our people that will never find a place in print. But we lived, some of us, with these intimate pages; and those pages that will reach history, meagre though they be, will do good to our country and will inspire us through many a dark hour. Our weaknesses cry out to us, 'Michael Collins was too brave'. Michael Collins was not too brave. Every day and every hour he lived he lived it to the full extent of that bravery which God gave to him, and it is for us to be brave as he was – brave before danger, brave before those who lie, brave even to that very great bravery that our weakness complained of in him.

He described Collins as an energetic, Promethean figure who rose at five or six in the morning – notwithstanding whether he might have a cold or flu – and rouse others in the barracks by pulling the blankets off them or by pounding on the doors of the dormitories. He even went so far as to compare Collins to St Peter, the rock, and continued:

> And surely 'our great rock' was our prophet and our prophecy, a light held aloft along the road of 'danger or hardship or bitter toil'. And if our light is gone out it is only as the paling of a candle in the dawn of its own prophecy. The act of his, the word of his, the look of his, day by day a prophecy to us that loose lying in us lay capabilities for toil, for bravery, for regularity, for joy in life; and in slowness and in hesitancy and in weariness half yielded to, his prophecies came true in us.

He spoke of that prophecy now residing in the army:

> Our army has been the people, is the people, and will be the people. Our green uniform does not make us less the people. It is a cloak of service, a curtailer of our weaknesses, an amplifier of our strength.

The guard of honour fired volleys of shots over the grave and then the mourners dispersed.[25]

In the same edition a fellow Cabinet Minister, Eoin MacNeill wrote:

Michael Collins was, is, and is destined to be a national hero. By instinct, a sure and wise instinct, the nation hailed him its leader and champion ... No enthusiasm about chief and leaders is likely to confuse my estimate at this day. I want to give testimony, the testimony of an older man, and my testimony is that Michael Collins was and is the greatest Irishman of our time.

Mary Frances McHugh wrote under the heading 'THE DEAD LEADER – with the Heroes of all Time':

He was not afflicted by the damning taint of cynicism which threatened to afflict man ... He believed and hoped and ardently loved his hope and belief. He was selfless and he had a nobility of mind. A simplicity of aim and a genius for method, allied with whole-hearted and indeed joyous enthusiasm, were the distinguishing qualities of the dead Commander-in-Chief; a brilliant quality of thought and action translated, through an emotional capacity partly into achievement. He loved Ireland not in theory but in practice. He was a man of the people and for the people, yet a born governor and wise leader of men. That divine authority to guidance was his. Such a man must be set up in the lawgiver's seat, and the veriest fools, 'though they had knees of brass, would kneel down and worship.' Not foolishly or weakly, but with the instincts of a race, which are the fount of all order, to choose their leader. He was chosen as a leader living, he is buried as a dead leader. God rest him.

Alice Stopford Green wrote about his death:

All men wondered as he took up his Herculean task. We know the bitter schism. But Collins was never embittered. He knew a good man, and to the end he kept his esteem and affection for those of his opponents whose honour he trusted. He himself had his cruel detractors – men with no eyes for the great facts of his genius. Their tales spread where they could do harm, among the ignorant ... Whatever lesser men might say of him, in his great heart there was to the last no trace of bitterness. No leader before him in Ireland has borne away so immense a love and eternal devotion as has been given to him. Their grief will know no consolation ... All alike now strive together to carry on the work from which he was torn so piteously.

The manner of his manner of death inspired instant verse from minor poets all on the heroic theme. Shane Leslie wrote after he had seen Sir John Lavery's painting of the dead Michael Collins:

They left his blossom white and slender
Beneath Glasnevin's shaking sod;
His spirit passed like sunset splendour
Unto the dead Fiannas' God
Good luck be with you, Michael Collins,
Or stay or go you far away;
Or stay you with the folk of fairy,
Or come with ghosts another day.

The Minister for Home Affairs Kevin O'Higgins, who was to share
the same fate as Collins, wrote about how he could not take in the
brief telephone message he received telling him of the death:

'Commander-in–chief shot dead in ambush, Bealnablath, near
Bandon'. This, thought I, is some fantastic devilish lie, for bullet could
not still that great heart of his, still less bullet sped by an Irish hand,
and even as I conveyed the brief staccato message from Cork to his
colleagues – his fellow-toilers for eight crowded years – Dick Mulcahy,
Gearóid Ó Suilleabháin, Sean MacMahon and Tom Cullen, my stunned
brain kept drumming out its refusal to accept. 'This is not true! This is
not true!'

But it was true. Higgins wrote of how he had

looked upon the calm face of my friend and chief, have touched his
pale hands, have borne his coffin on my shoulder, and in common
with my countrymen I face the fact that Michael Collins, the greatest
man that ever served this Nation's cause, lies cold in death – slain by
a fellow countryman in his native Cork ... Michael Collins is dead.
The tragic waste of it; the infinite pathos of it. That brain, with all its
wonderful potentialities, dashed out by fratricidal bullet. That great
heart stilled; that great frame, every nerve and sinew of which was
bent unsparingly in loving service of his people, rigid in untimely and
unnatural death. Mourn, people of Ireland, for there is gone from
among you a great hearted man who loved you well and strove for
you mightily. Mourn, for while ye mourn, read through your tears the
lessons of his life – and of his death.

O'Higgins quoted Collins as saying to him that he regarded the
fight as a fight for the foundations of the state. A start could not be
made until there was recognition of majority rule. He addressed the
anti-Treatyites thus:

They have silenced the tongue that could tear to shreds their meta-
physical fallacies that preached a sound, wholesome doctrine of

nationalism which shamed the neurotic mouthings used as a cloak for crime. But the slaying they have given victory – to him and to the Nation that he loved. Michael Collins died. He died to establish the mastery of the Irish people in Ireland. He died to ensure that the newly won right of 'government of the people by the people' shall not perish from the land. He died to establish the foundations of a State, to vindicate the first principle of democratic government. He died that the Irish Nation might live – and grow.

He concluded:

Michael Collins toiled through dark days. He never lost faith in the Irish people nor hope in their future. It was his boundless confidence that rallied the nation when it reeled before the first shock of the terror. It was his great heart and buoyant temperament that supported it in the days when executions were almost routine in their grim monotony. His faith sowed the harvest. It will be our inspiration in the task of garnering. Sorrow – therefore, but no despair. The road is marked by Michael Collins. His dauntless spirit will be with us on the way.[26]

The Civil War was over by the spring of 1923 and an unarmed garda force was soon operating in every part of the country. The government writ ran throughout the state.

Kevin O'Higgins – death of a Minister

Eamon de Valera, jailed in August 1923, was released in July 1924. He broke with the anti-Treatyite Sinn Féin and formed Fianna Fáil in 1926. After a general election in June 1927, De Valera led his party into Dáil Éireann where they took the oath of allegiance and their seats. The deadly echoes of civil war, however, were soon to be heard again. The anti-Treatyite Irish Republican Army (IRA) sought to continue their armed resistance against the state. Kevin O'Higgins became one of their victims when he was shot dead by gunmen as he went to mass in Booterstown church on 10 July 1927. Before he died, O'Higgins was reported to have said to those who had come to his assistance: 'I am going to join my old father. They murdered him, and they have made no mistake about me'. Encouraged to hold on to life, O'Higgins said: 'Yes, I'm still a bit of a die-hard'.[27] The doctors who attended him could do nothing for him. He died at his own home that evening at about a quarter to five with, in the words of Cosgrave, 'all the consolation of his religion'.

William T. Cosgrave immediately issued a statement on the day of the assassination:

In this hour of national loss and of national mourning, mindful of the steadfast and heroic figure who has been sacrificed, the Irish people will not falter. O'Higgins, in his dauntless courage and unflinching determination, has trodden the path blazed by Griffith and Collins even unto death. Another great defender of the nation has passed. The Irish people may rest assured that the assassin's bullet will not succeed in terrorising this country. There are, and will be, men, enheartened by the noble example of the late vice-president, and profiting by his labours, ready to step into his place, and to maintain his high tradition of devotion to the welfare and safety of the nation.[28]

De Valera was quick to condemn the assassination:

The assassination of Mr O'Higgins is murder and is inexcusable from any standpoint. I am confident that no republican organisation was responsible for it or would give it any countenance. It is the duty of every citizen to set his face sternly against anything of the kind. It is a crime that cuts at the root of representative government and no one who realises what the crime means can do otherwise than deplore and condemn it. Every right-minded individual will deeply sympathise with the bereaved widow in her agony.[29]

As flags flew yet again at half mast on all state buildings, the remains of O'Higgins lay in state at the Oak Room of the Mansion House. He was dressed in a brown habit and there was a crucifix in his hands. Earlier his remains had been carried from his house in Blackrock on the shoulders of William T. Cosgrave and other members of the executive council to the awaiting hearse. At the Mansion House, members of the gardaí carried the coffin into the Oak Room and then formed a guard of honour. During the day, public bodies had met to pass resolutions of condolence.

Thousands filed past throughout the afternoon. When the doors were closed in the evening the queue stretched from the Mansion House round Molesworth Street, Kildare Street, St Stephen's Green and into Dawson Street again. The crowds formed again the following day, and the line was still stretching around the Green when the coffin was removed to St Andrew's, Westland Row.

Earlier in the day, Dáil Éireann met to pass a vote of sympathy. Thomas Johnson, the leader of the Labour party, said: 'The men who did this foul deed murdered faith; they murdered hope, and charity lies bleeding'. He ended, however, on a note of hope: 'Can hatred feuds and suspicion be dispelled? Will all good citizens dedicate anew their best services to the public weal?'[30]

On 13 July Archbishop Edward Byrne of Dublin presided at requiem mass. A number of other bishops were present as a 300-strong choir of priests sang the Gregorian chant. Afterwards, men from the guard of honour of the gardaí bore the coffin from the church to the awaiting gun carriage. Mrs O'Higgins moved to follow the coffin but 'became weak, collapsed and sank to the floor'. Helped to her feet, she was able to proceed after a minute on the arm of Colonel O'Higgins.

William T. Cosgrave and members of the Executive Council followed the gun carriage on foot together with senior members of the armed forces and the gardaí. The procession went via College Green to O'Connell Street and on to Glasnevin. An *Irish Times* journalist described the funeral as the 'the most impressive that Dublin has ever seen'. It was 'over three miles in length and was representative of all that is best in the national life. All the streets along the route were thronged with spectators, who stood for hours in reverent silence'.[31] At the cemetery gate the procession halted. The firing party, according to the report, lined each side of the approach to the entrance, the soldiers with bowed heads and arms crossed on their rifle butts.

The graveside oration was given by William T. Cosgrave who quoted the dying words of O'Higgins: 'I forgive my murderers'. He added:

> Kevin O'Higgins died a noble death and a happy death. It needs no intimate association with him to describe the character of the man. Such was his own natural power that his mind made itself felt and understood throughout the land. The Irish people know that his first and highest characteristic was an inflexible desire to do his conscientious duty. If he seemed insensible at times towards the emotions of others, he was at all times merciless towards himself. His intellect was deep and keen. To his capacity as a constructive administrator no testimony is needed.[32]

He had, said Cosgrave, helped establish a 'new and stable edifice of public order and public peace'. Concluding, the President of the Executive Council said: 'His example of duty, sanity, energy and enterprise will inspire our nation till the end'.

Conclusion

The only funeral which could compare with that of O'Higgins took place in Dublin in 1975, when the body of Eamon de Valera, former

Taoiseach and President, was laid to rest in Glasnevin cemetery. Parnell, Collins, O'Higgins, De Valera – four of the giants of modern Irish history, all laid to rest in the same small plot of land in Dublin, all of whom had had to come to terms with the bitter vagaries of Irish political fortune, but all of whom were justly celebrated in death as they had been the subject of controversy in life.

MICHAEL COLLINS

AN OVERVIEW

Ronan Fanning

The central problem facing any historian seeking to present an overview of Michael Collins seventy-five years after his death may be simply stated. It is, perhaps, best put in the form of a question: why is it that the historical profession has been so reluctant to accord Michael Collins the recognition he so richly deserves as much the most accomplished and successful revolutionary in modern Irish history?

The answer lies in a larger reluctance, the remarkable reluctance to ascribe the term 'revolution' to what happened in Ireland between 1916 and 1922. If we can unravel the reasons for this larger reluctance we can, I believe, go some way towards understanding why there has never been a coherent, consensual interpretation of the Irish revolution and, more recently, why the historiography of the revolution has become hag-ridden by the rhetoric and bombast of what is grandiosely described as the revisionist debate. The arch-revisionists, in the pejorative sense in which I use the term, are driven by political rather than historical purposes, although the line is sometimes finely drawn – I am not talking about revisionism in the sense in which it simply describes the essential business of historians from generation to generation, for, in this sense, I would subscribe to Roy Foster's ringing declaration that 'we are all revisionists now'.[1]

The arch-revisionists have a venerable lineage for they were not the first to see political advantage in denying the title of revolution to what happened in Ireland in the years before 1922. Indeed, apologists for both Left and Right have traditionally seen such advantage since the foundation of the state.

The Left had a vested interest in nurturing the prospect of future revolution by denying the reality of previous revolution. Although numerically few their influence upon elements of the intellectual élite of independent Ireland, chafing against the inhibitions of an obscurantist and priest-ridden society, was never insignificant. But the orthodoxy established by Patrick Lynch in 1966 in his seminal essay 'The social revolution that never was' has too often been crudely transmuted into 'The revolution that never was' by those on the Left less intellectually rigorous but more politically motivated than Professor Lynch.[2]

Where the Left denied the designation of a revolution in the past because it hoped for revolution in the future, the Right recoiled from acknowledging the revolutionary origins of a system of government and politics with which, ever since 1922, it has – at worst – made its accommodations and which – at best – it has effectively controlled. The Right, in short, had a vested interest in disguising the fact that power changed hands in Ireland in 1922 because of a revolution, not least because the governments which entered office in 1922 and 1932 both had to overcome the challenge of armed resistance to their authority – whether from the IRA or from the Blueshirts.

The impact of the Civil War upon the historiography of the revolution, moreover, was as cataclysmic as its impact on Irish politics. It became politically imperative to invent conflicting interpretations of the history of the revolution to sustain the rival legitimacies of the Civil War combatants. The imperatives to sustain these imagined pasts were enhanced rather than diminished when the end of the war also ended the censorship which had undermined the republicans' capacity to propagate their cause. The end of the war politicised, and thereby widened, the area of conflict and nourished the temptation to bend the history of the revolution to the purposes of party propaganda. The Sinn Féin split and the foundation of Fianna Fáil compounded the Civil War's competing legitimacies.

The climate of opinion thus created stunted the growth of all revolutionary reputations. The reputation of Michael Collins, as the effective leader of the revolution in 1919–21, inevitably suffered most. In the eyes of republicans – whether in Sinn Féin, Fianna Fáil or the IRA – he had betrayed the revolution by betraying the Republic. In the eyes of his erstwhile comrades in the Irish Free State governments (especially after the departure of Mulcahy and McGrath following the 1924 Army Mutiny) he personified embarrassing aspects of their own revolutionary past.

The winners, the pro-Treaty governments of 1922–32, preferred to highlight their democratic credentials and to gloss over their revolutionary origins, which was understandable given their determination to deny the legitimacy of the post-1921 IRA trying to do to them what they had done to the British in 1919–21. Collins' celebrated stepping-stone argument – his admission that the Treaty conferred not freedom but the freedom to achieve freedom – also contributed to the corrosion of his revolutionary reputation because it offered not so much an inducement to recognise how much had already been achieved as a calculus for future progress.

The losers, who became the winners when Fianna Fáil won power in 1932, saw the republican revolution as unfinished business and were determined to deny the mantle of successful revolutionaries to their political opponents and, above all, to Michael Collins.

Events in Northern Ireland after 1969, much the most significant eruption of violence since the Civil War, not only reinforced this consensual reluctance on the part of both the pro- and anti-Treaty establishments to focus on the revolution of 1916-22 but also gave birth to political revisionism. The perverting impact of the Troubles upon Irish history and historiography since 1969 is but an example of the axiom that truth is the first casualty of war. Thus arch-revisionism at its most extreme insists that nothing must be said or written about the effective use of violence in the Irish past in case it gives comfort to those who use violence in the Irish present. Hence the seduction of so many historians, as well as would-be historians who have strayed from other disciplines, by the charms of cultural history where they can embark upon a quest for the holy grail of identity or seek the rewards of reconciling disparate mentalities while escaping the barbarisms and brutalities of revolutionary war. Some seem to have tacitly embraced as their slogan John Cleese's catch-cry in the German tourist episode of *Fawlty Towers*: 'Don't mention the war!'

Take, for example, Roy Foster's discussion of the Treaty in his magisterial *Modern Ireland 1600-1972*, where he writes: 'whether the bloody catalogue of assassinations and war from 1919–21 was necessary to negotiate thus far may be fairly questioned.'[3] Perhaps, but it is surely less than fair that he offers us no answer or analysis beyond that very loaded question.

My own answer is that there is not a shred of evidence that Lloyd George's Tory-dominated government would have moved from the 1914-style niggardliness of the Government of Ireland Act of 1920 to the larger, if imperfect generosity of the Treaty if they had not been impelled to do so by Michael Collins and his assassins. Indeed the evidence points the other way.

Ironically, although upon reflection unsurprisingly, some of the most persuasive evidence comes from the opponents of the revolution. The earliest and still the most important work in this tradition was written by W. Alison Phillips, an Englishman who held the post of Lecky Professor of History at Trinity College Dublin when his book, unequivocally entitled *The Revolution in Ireland 1906–1923*, was first published in 1923.

The opening paragraph of his introduction captures precisely that sense of revolutionary achievement missing from accounts written from such diverse revolutionary nationalist perspectives as Dorothy Macardle's *The Irish Republic* (1937), Donal O'Sullivan's *The Irish Free State and its Senate* (1940) or any of the other works haunted by the loss of Frank Gallagher's 'Four Glorious Years' and trapped instead in Seán Ó Faoláin's nightmare of the Treaty as 'the dream that went bust'.[4]

In 1904, 'when Arthur Griffith first put forward his programme for the overthrow of British rule in Ireland', wrote Alison Phillips,

> the Sinn Féin organisation, of which he was the founder and inspirer, consisted of a handful of young teachers, poets and journalists, scarce known outside their own circle and utterly without political influence; and so they remained for twelve years longer. In 1921 these same men had made themselves the *de facto* rulers of the greater part of Ireland, had worn down the resistance of the British government and people, and were in a position to dictate terms to the ministers of a power which had just been victorious in a great war. History records no more amazing overturn.[5]

Lord Londonderry, a Minister in the Northern Ireland government, reached essentially the same conclusion in a letter to Hugh Kennedy, the Provisional Government's Law Officer, in August 1922:

> Mr Collins ... achieved his position ... by being one of the leaders of a campaign which Sinn Féin called war and which I call assassination. He has maintained his position by challenging the British government and by succeeding in compelling the British government to make terms and terms of a character far exceeding the wildest hopes of Mr Collins or any of his supporters.[6]

Michael Collins was the principal architect of Alison Phillips' 'amazing overturn'. Much of the recent controversy surrounding Neil Jordan's *Michael Collins* is due to the fact that it so powerfully portrays him in that role. Jordan's film has, moreover, indelibly and accurately described why Collins' team of assassins – the 'Squad' or 'Twelve Apostles' – succeeded where so many before them had failed: by ruthlessly refining 'the tactic of selective assassination of policemen ... the pivot of the war effort'.[7]

The essence of Collins' strategy, in the words of the late Dr Tom Bowden, was his determination

> to break the police. This was sound military sense, for the RIC [and DMP] were then both the *actual and symbolic* representatives of government in society; they were the leading edge of government regulation; they were its control force – the police of the prince. A terrorist assault upon the police would have the military utility of at best immobilising or at worst weakening that control apparatus ... And, since the police were the most visible of the government's representatives in society, any attack on them would serve to weaken the government's prestige and authority by denying its ability to uphold law and order. If the government could not protect its own agents in society, how then could it protect the people? If it could not protect the people then surely it must lose its title to rule in the name of the people.[8]

The Prime Minister, David Lloyd George, seemed to concur. 'The Irish job,' he told his cabinet in June 1921, within weeks of the Truce that ended the War of Independence, 'was a policeman's job'; if it became 'a military job only' it would fail.[9]

But Lloyd George, as ever, was disingenuous. The British army's Irish GHQ had concluded that the political intelligence section of the DMP – the G Division – had 'ceased to affect the situation' as early as January 1920 with the assassination of Assistant Commissioner Redmond.[10] The 'policeman's job' – although not, of course, the British military campaign – collapsed under the sustained onslaught of Collins' Squad throughout 1920. The collapse culminated in the counter-intelligence coup on Bloody Sunday, 21 November 1920, when they assassinated the British secret service agents in Dublin; so much for Lloyd George's claim, made only twelve days before at the Lord Mayor's banquet in London, to 'have murder by the throat'. The proclamation of martial law in Cork, Kerry, Limerick and Tipperary on 10 December – and its extension to all of Munster on 4 January – testified to the emptiness of that boast and to the collapse of the 'police job'.

And here Neil Jordan has it right. For no historian who has

read the British cabinet minutes and the related correspondence from Dublin Castle to Downing Street which has survived in the papers of David Lloyd George and his ministerial colleagues or the diaries of Tom Jones and Mark Sturgis can be in any doubt that Bloody Sunday was the pivotal point in the War of Independence. Although the war dragged on until July 1921, Bloody Sunday (together with the Kilmichael ambush a week later) made nonsense of the hawkish optimism of Lloyd George's military and police advisers and shattered their predictions that the IRA could be swiftly defeated. Lloyd George began looking for olive branches, initially through the intermediacy of Archbishop Clune, later, and more successfully, through Andy Cope (in effect the Prime Minister's personal agent in Dublin Castle where he was nominally an Assistant Under Secretary). Within a month of Bloody Sunday these first gropings towards peace had led to De Valera's return from America.

By April 1921 Lloyd George was ready to admit to a golfing *confidant* what the time was not yet ripe to admit to his Tory cabinet colleagues, that the key question was:

> whether I can see Michael Collins. No doubt he is the head and front of the movement. If I could see him, a settlement might be possible. The question is whether the British people would be willing for us to negotiate with the head of a band of murderers ... I had him seen [by Cope], but nothing effective happened. I must see him myself. It is a strong order to see a man who has given orders to shoot down innocent, unoffending policemen.[11]

'Who'll give in first, Joe? Us or them?' Neil Jordan has Collins say to Joe O'Reilly in the church over the coffins of the Croke Park victims of Bloody Sunday. The answer comes in the dinner-dance scene in the hotel when O'Reilly rushes in and tells Collins that the British have agreed to a truce. 'You mean it's finished?' replies Collins. 'You mean we've won? Lloyd George has thrown in the towel? We've brought the British empire to its knees?'[12]

Dramatic licence aside, Charles Townshend, author of *The British Campaign in Ireland*, arrived at a similar conclusion:

> given time, strength and public support, the British forces could have reduced rebel operations to negligible proportions. But these quintessential conditions were missing. While the IRA survived, political pressure on the British government increased and though the balance was tantalisingly fine, the IRA held out longer than the government's nerve. That was what mattered.[13]

The resonances with the present situation in Northern Ireland are unmistakable and, for some, unbearable. Hence the recent *Sunday Times* headline 'Myth of Collins, master spyhunter' over a story prompted by Neil Jordan's film, which made much of Paul Bew's analysis of recently released British documents. Bew is quoted as saying that 'the IRA did not beat the British ... In a purely military sense, the British position was getting stronger when the Truce was being negotiated. Political realities, however, pointed in a different direction'.[14]

Political realities dictated, as Charles Townshend has pointed out, 'that, on the British side, some form of military struggle was inevitable before Irish demands would be taken seriously' and Townshend argues that Collins' oft-cited remark to Hamar Greenwood after signing the Treaty – 'You had us dead beat. We could not have lasted another three weeks' – should be taken with a pinch of salt, because 'if the rebel leaders were beginning to smell military defeat, the British government had already been forced to accept political and moral defeat. Only rapid military success could have averted [British] public pressure in favour of a settlement, and without such success the [British] government were driven to compromise.'[15]

Political realities always weigh more heavily in guerrilla wars than in regular warfare. The point has been best made by Henry Kissinger, writing of the American debacle in Vietnam:

> We fought a military war; our opponents fought a political one. We sought physical attrition; our opponents aimed for our psychological exhaustion. In the process, we lost sight of one of the cardinal maxims of guerrilla war: the guerrilla wins if he does not lose. The conventional army loses if it does not win.[16]

In Ireland, as in Vietnam, truce was tantamount to victory.

The hauling down of the Stars and Stripes as the last Americans were helicoptered out of their embassy in Saigon was the mirror image of the hauling down of the Union Jack when the British handed over Dublin Castle. Neil Jordan and his English film crew were surprised that they were strangely affected by filming that scene – it was interrupted, he tells us, by the delicious irony of President Robinson's driving 'through in mid-shot to attend a meeting of the Forum for Peace and Reconciliation. Liam [Neeson] salutes her, in uniform. I don't know if she returns the gesture.'[17]

Michael Collins, however, would not have been surprised for, as he wrote of his own emotions at that moment, he never

> expected ... to see the day when ships should sail away to England with the Auxiliaries and the Black and Tans, the RIC and the British soldiery ... Nor did we ever expect to see the Auxiliary Division marching out of Beggar's Bush Barracks ... How could I ever have expected to see Dublin Castle itself formally surrendered into my hands? ... We had red carpets laid for us on that momentous morning and I recalled my only previous visit to those grim precincts as the driver of a coal-cart, with a price upon my head! That was the time that we planned our counter-intelligence system in the Holy-of-Holies itself.[18]

What mattered to Collins was the reality of independence, not the rhetoric of republicanism. Thus, although his 1918 election address to the voters of South Cork sought 'the supreme, absolute and final control of all this country, of all the affairs of this country, external as well as internal', it nowhere mentioned the word 'Republic'. For Collins 'it (was) not the Treaty as such that (was) all-important. Rather (was) it the complete withdrawal and evacuation of the alien forces of domination and permeation ... the Treaty has brought Ireland to the last oasis beyond which there is but an easy march to go'.[19]

The moment of surrender of Dublin Castle – 'throughout the ages ... the symbol and citadel of British rule in Ireland' – was the only moment when Collins allowed himself that fleeting taste of victory which the Civil War so swiftly turned to ashes. In his resurrection of Michael Collins Neil Jordan correctly identified him as 'the man who won the war', the man who, more than anyone else, deserves the credit for the achievement of 'a government of our own'.[20]

The story of how a native Irish government achieved power in Ireland for the first time since the twelfth century, of how power changed hands on a scale not witnessed since the seventeenth century, cannot be brushed under some disinfected carpet just because it is bloody and brutal. It is not right for historians fastidiously to avert their attention from the more hideous malignancies in the body politic which is the object of their inquiry, any more than it would be right for a surgeon to ignore a patient's cancerous tumours. It remains, of course, open to all who are so minded to challenge the morality of Michael Collins' methods, but such challenges – however magnified by the prism of the contemporary crisis in Northern Ireland – cannot encompass the right to deny the magnitude of his achievement.

NOTES

THE CHALLENGE OF A COLLINS BIOGRAPHY

1   I am grateful to the President's Fund of University College Cork for supporting the research on which this paper is based, and to Gillian Nic Gabhann for research assistance.

2   The film attracted a great deal of comment, much of which offers a treasure trove to students of the mentalities of the 1990s, however little it adds to an understanding of Collins. My own observations, from a historical perspective, appeared in my *Sunday Tribune* column, 20 October 1996. For a stimulating critique, from a more wide-ranging perspective, see Hopper, Keith, '"Cat-Calls from the cheap seats": the third meaning of Neil Jordan's *Michael Collins'* in *Irish Review*, vol. 21, Autumn–Winter 1997, pp. 1–28.

3   As in Taylor, Rex, *Michael Collins*, Hutchinson, London, 1970, pp. 173–4.

4   Wall, Maureen, 'Partition: the Ulster Question (1916–1926)' in Williams, T. D. (editor), *The Irish Struggle 1916–1926*, Routledge and Kegan Paul, London, 1966, p. 87.

5   See the attention devoted to it in Middlemas, Keith (editor), *Tom Jones Whitehall Diary*, Oxford University Press, London, 1971.

6   Lee, J. J., *Ireland 1912–1985: Politics and Society*, Cambridge University Press, Cambridge, 1989, p. 7.

7   Middlemas, *Tom Jones Whitehall Diary*, p. 131.

8   Lee, *Ireland*, p. 142.

9   Lee, *Ireland*, p. 61.

10 Townshend, Charles, *The British Campaign in Ireland, 1919–1921*, Oxford University Press, Oxford, 1978, p. 193. This work, unlike so much written on this period, is a work of genuine historical scholarship.

11 This crucial decision seems to be glossed over in most biographies of Collins, which makes it all the more notable, that Frank O'Connor identified this fundamental issue in his otherwise highly uneven *The Big Fellow*, Corgi, London, 1969, p. 185 (originally published in 1937), and wrote about it in the active rather than the passive sense.

12 An obscurity and confusion reflected in the cryptic reports in the *Freeman's Journal, Irish Independent* and *Irish Times*, 16 January 1922.

13 As Tom Garvin suggests in his *1922: the Birth of Irish Democracy*, Gill & Macmillan, Dublin, 1996, p. 115.

14 Lee, *Ireland*, p. 64.

15 There are still lessons to be learned from the challenges confronted by the 'authorised' biographer of Collins probed by Deirdre McMahon, '"A Worthy Monument to a Great Man": Piaras Béaslaí's Life of Michael Collins' in *Bullán*, vol. ii, no. 2, Winter/ Spring, 1996, pp. 55–65. Stimulating reflections on the challenge of a Collins biography can be found in Regan, John, 'Looking at myth again: demilitarising Michael Collins', *History Ireland*, Autumn 1995, pp. 17–22 and Hopkinson, Michael, 'Review article: Biography of the revolutionary period Michael Collins and Kevin Barry', *Irish Historical Studies*, vol. xxviii, May 1993, pp. 310–16.

MICHAEL COLLINS, MINISTER FOR FINANCE

1   Forester, Margery, *Michael Collins – The Lost Hero*, Sidgwick & Jackson, London: 1971, p. 30f; Coogan, Tim Pat, *Michael Collins: a Biography*, Arrow, London, 1991.

2   Dáil Éireann, *Minutes of the Proceedings of the First Parliament of the Republic of Ireland*, p. 36 (hereafter *Minutes of the First Dáil*).

3   Forester, *Michael Collins*, p. 99.

4   *Minutes of the First Dáil*, pp. 37–8, 41, 47.

5   Mitchell, Arthur, *Revolutionary Government in Ireland: Dáil Éireann 1919–22*, Gill & Macmillan, Dublin, 1995, pp. 58–9.

6   *Minutes of the First Dáil*, pp. 92–5.

7   Béaslaí, Piaras, *Michael Collins and the making of a new Ireland*, Phoenix, Dublin, 1926, vol. i, pp. 353–7.

8   Béaslaí, *Michael Collins*, p. 348.

9   Finance report to the Dáil, November 1919, DE 2/7, NAI.

10   Finance report to the Dáil, November 1919, DE 2/7, NAI.
11   Béaslaí, *Michael Collins*, p. 347.
12   Finance report to the Dáil, June 1920, DE 2/7, NAI.
13   Béaslaí, *Michael Collins*, pp. 358–9.
14   Béaslaí, *Michael Collins*, pp. 344–5.
15   Mitchell, *Revolutionary Government*, pp. 59–60; Forester, *Michael Collins*, pp. 107–8.
16   Béaslaí, *Michael Collins*, pp. 341–4.
17   Mitchell, *Revolutionary Government*, p. 54.
18   Béaslaí, *Michael Collins*, pp. 351–2.
19   Mitchell, *Revolutionary Government*, p. 56.
20   M. Collins to E. de Valera, 12 April 1921, DE 2/244, NAI.
21   Forester, *Michael Collins*, pp. 109–10.
22   Finance report to the Dáil, June 1920, DE 2/7, NAI.
23   Mitchell, *Revolutionary Government*, p. 64.
24   Audit of accounts, 7 April 1921, DE 2/7, NAI.
25   Finance report to the Dáil, June 1920, DE 2/7, NAI.
26   *Minutes of the First Dáil*, p. 182; Mitchell, *Revolutionary Government*, p. 308.
27   Finance reports to the Dáil, June 1920 and August 1920, DE 2/7, NAI.
28   Finance reports to the Dáil, June 1920 and August 1920, DE 2/7, NAI.
29   *Minutes of the First Dáil*, pp. 259, 267; Statement of financial position as at 31 March 1921, DE 2/9, NAI.
30   M. Collins to A. O'Brien, 22 January 1920, Art O'Brien Papers, MS 8,430, NLI.
31   Cited in Fanning, Ronan, *The Irish Department of Finance, 1922–58*, IPA, Dublin, 1978, p. 25.
32   Mitchell, *Revolutionary Government*, p. 84f.
33   McCarthy, Andrew, 'Financial Thought and Policy in Ireland, 1918–45', Unpublished Ph.D. thesis, National University of Ireland, University College Cork, 1996, p. 53.
34   See, for example, Neeson, Eoin, *The Life and Death of Michael Collins*, Mercier, Cork, 1968, p. 42f.
35   *Minutes of the First Dáil*, p. 251.
36   Coogan, *Michael Collins*, p. 171ff.
37   *Minutes of the First Dáil*, pp. 123–4.
38   *Minutes of the First Dáil*, p. 129.
39   *Minutes of the First Dáil*, p. 181.
40   Finance report to the Dáil, August 1920, DE 2/7, NAI.
41   Ministry meeting, 9 October 1920, DE 1/3, NAI.
42   Ministry meeting, 8 March 1921, DE 1/3, NAI.
43   *Minutes of the First Dáil*, p. 162.
44   Resolution by Secretary for Finance, 27 February 1920, DE 1/2, NAI.
45   *Minutes of the First Dáil*, p. 169.
46   *Minutes of the First Dáil*, p. 180.
47   Cited in Fanning, *Department of Finance*, p. 26.
48   M. Collins to E. de Valera, 7 January 1921, DE 2/242, NAI.
49   *Minutes of the Second Dáil*, p. 65.
50   McCarthy, 'Financial Thought', pp. 126–7.
51   Mitchell, *Revolutionary Government*, pp. 301–2.
52   Ó Broin, León, *No Man's Man*, IPA, Dublin, 1982, p. 99f.
53   McCarthy, 'Financial Thought', pp. 52–3.
54   16 January 1922, G1/1, NAI.
55   McColgan, John, *British Policy and the Irish Administration 1920–22*, Allen & Unwin, London, 1983, pp. 90–91.
56   McColgan, *British Policy*, p. 110.
57   *Ibid.*, p. 90ff; 7 February 1922, G1/1, NAI.
58   10 February 1922, G1/1, NAI.
59   McColgan, *British Policy*, p. 111.
60   McCarthy, 'Financial thought', p. 12; table 1.4, p. 98.
61   15 May 1922, G1/1, NAI.
62   *Minutes of the Second Dáil*, p. 141.
63   Minutes of Dáil Éireann, 15 March 1922, DE 1/4. NAI.
64   Meetings 17, 18, 24, 26, 27 and 28 July 1922, G1/1, NAI.

65   D. O'Hegarty to Secretary of the Irish Banks' Standing Committee, 5 August 1922, Department of the Taoiseach, S1385, NAI.
66   Two telegrams from H. A. Pelly to M. Collins, 21 August 1922, Joseph Brennan Papers, MS 26,011, NLI.

COLLINS AND INTELLIGENCE
1   The myths continue to flourish, as *The Examiner* supplement 'The Big Fellow' of 26 February 1997 demonstrates. See Tim Pat Coogan's 'Routing the revisionists', where he claims that 'the fact is that Collins was virtually airbrushed out of history until my biography appeared only seven years ago.' Yet the period from 1922 to 1990, Mr Coogan's historiographic Year Zero, saw the publication and distribution of a rather greater range of biographical studies of Collins than appeared of Mr de Valera, in the interests of whose reputation the supposed airbrushing took place.
2   Garvin, Tom, *1922: the Birth of Irish Democracy*, Gill & Macmillan, Dublin, 1996, pp. 40–51, 95–6.
3   On this see Coogan, Tim Pat, *Michael Collins: a Biography*, Arrow, London, 1991, pp. 94–184.
4   Evidence of Major General Russell to the Army Inquiry, 10 May 1924, Mulcahy papers, P7/C/29, UCDA; Valiulis, Maryann Gialanella, *Portrait of a Revolutionary: General Richard Mulcahy and the Founding of the Irish Free State*, Irish Academic Press, Dublin, 1992, pp. 47–8; O'Halpin, Eunan, 'The army and the Dáil: civil/military relations within the independence movement' in Farrell, Brian (editor), *The Creation of the Dáil*, Blackwater, Dublin, 1994, pp. 115–7; Ó Broin, León, *Michael Collins*, Gill & Macmillan, Dublin, 1980, pp. 72–3. For a contrary argument, advanced from what might be termed a republican legitimist viewpoint, see Murphy, Brian P., *Patrick Pearse and the Lost Republican Ideal*, James Duffy, Dublin, 1991, p. 128.
5   Ó Broin, *Michael Collins*, p. 49.
6   O'Donoghue, Florence, *No Other Law*, Anvil, Dublin, 1954.
7   O'Donoghue, *No Other Law*, p. 120.
8   Godson, Roy, 'Counter-intelligence: an introduction' in Godson, Roy (editor), *Intelligence Requirements for the 1980s: Counter-Intelligence*, National Strategy Information Center, Washington, 1980, p. 1.
9   Andrews, C. S., *Dublin Made Me: an Autobiography*, Mercier, Dublin, 1979, p. 151.
10   Daly, Mary, 'Local government and the First Dáil' in Farrell, *The Creation of the Dáil*, pp. 123–36; Garvin, *1922*, pp. 63–91.
11   The only alleged exception to this was Emmet Dalton, whom some inveterate conspiracy theorists claimed was a British agent. See Feehan, John M., *The Shooting of Michael Collins: Murder or Accident?*, Mercier, Dublin, 1981, pp. 91–4. On this egregious claim see Coogan, *Collins*, pp. 416–8. On Cope's supposed manipulation of Collins see Murphy, *Patrick Pearse*, pp. 126–9, 189.
12   Coogan, *Collins*, p. 188; Bell's notebook is in the P[ublic] R[ecord] O[ffice] London, CO 904/188/1. The frequency with which Bell's assassination is attributed to his financial investigations begs the question of whether Collins was even aware of his other covert work.
13   Bowden, Tom, *The Breakdown of Public Security: the Case of Ireland 1916–1921 and Palestine 1936–39*, Sage, London, 1977, p. 308.
14   Sturgis diary, 7 December 1920, 30/59/1–4, PRO; O'Donoghue, *No Other Law*, p. 118. We may note that amongst those who took fearful risks by passing themselves off as Irish countrymen was the late Major General Sir Kenneth Strong, Eisenhower's highly regarded intelligence adviser, who, when a battalion Intelligence Officer in 1920 and 1921, went on largely fruitless sallies throughout Offaly on a donkey and cart. Strong, Sir Kenneth, *Intelligence at the Top*, Cassell, London, 1968, pp. 1–5.
15   Winter, Sir Ormonde, *Winter's Tale: an Autobiography*, Richards, London, 1955, p. 303.
16   'Summary of intelligence', Dan Bryan papers, P71/171, UCDA.
17   Coogan, *Collins*, p. 168.
18   Report of the committee of inquiry into the detective organisation of the Irish police force, dated 7 December 1919, French papers, 75/46/12, Imperial War Museum; Townshend, Charles, *The British Campaign in Ireland, 1919–1921: the Development of Political and Military Policies*, Oxford University Press, London, 1975, pp. 129–31, 175–7.

19 O'Donoghue, *No Other Law*, pp. 118–27.
20 Hart, Peter, 'The Protestant experience of revolution in southern Ireland' in English, Richard and Walker, Graham (editors), *Unionism in Modern Ireland*, Macmillan, London, 1996, p. 89.
21 Coogan, *Collins*, pp. 238–9.
22 Summary of intelligence, as in note 16 above.
23 Evidence of Major General Russell, 10 May 1924, as in note 4 above.
24 *Ibid.*
25 Evidence of Colonel Neligan, as in note 4 above.
26 Summary of intelligence, as in note 16 above.
27 *Ibid.*
28 Collins to Director of Intelligence, 10 August 1922, Mulcahy papers, P7/B/4, UCDA.
29 Draft circular, 17 July, and McGrath to Collins, 25 July 1922, Mulcahy papers, P/7/ B/4, UCDA; O'Malley to Lynch, 16 August 1922, O'Malley papers, P17a/176, UCDA.
30 Evidence of Major General Russell, as in note 4 above.
31 Dan Bryan transcript, n.d., 1984, in the author's possession.
32 Command Intelligence Officer to Director of Intelligence, 7 August 1922, Mulcahy papers, P7/B/4, UCDA; Andrews, *Dublin Made Me*, p. 237; interview with Col Bryan, 29 January 1983.
33 Collins to McGrath, 14 July and 1, 3 and 7 August, and to Tobin, 19 and 24 July 1922, Mulcahy papers, P7/B/4, UCDA.
34 Coogan, *Michael Collins*, p. 410.
35 Notes of meeting with disaffected officers, 7 July 1923, Mulcahy papers, P7/B/ 195, UCDA. On the evolution of Army intelligence between 1923 and 1926, see O'Halpin, Eunan, 'Army, politics and society, 1923–1945' in Fraser, T. G. and Jeffery, Keith (editors), *Men, Women and War: Historical Studies XVIII*, Lilliput, Dublin, 1993, pp. 158–74.

MICHAEL COLLINS: A MILITARY LEADER
1 *Leadership*. Text for students published by the Command and Staff School, The Curragh Military College, July 1996.
2 *An tÓglach*, 7 April 1923, pp. 14–5.
3 O'Mahony, Seán, *Frongoch: University of Revolution*, FDR, Killiney, 1987, p. 58.
4 Author's interview with Major Roger McCorley 1981. Typescript in Military Archives, ref. PC 50, Cathal Brugha Barracks.
5 Memorandum to Chief-of-Staff from OC 1 Southern Division, 4 January 1922, Mulcahy papers, P7/A/32, UCDA.
6 McCorley typescript, Military Archives, ref. PC 50, Cathal Brugha barracks.
7 Extracts are taken from a copy of J. F. Homan's diary of the period. The original diary was given to Frank Saurin in late 1922 or early 1923. Saurin handed it over to Col J. Lawless in 1950 who was then a member of the Bureau of Military History. As it did not relate to the period being then studied by the Bureau Col. Lawless lodged it in the National Library.

MICHAEL COLLINS AND THE NORTHERN QUESTION
1 Tim Pat, *Michael Collins A Biography*, Hutchinson, London, 1990, p. 333.
2 *Irish Weekly*, 12 April 1919; Phoenix, Éamon, *Northern Nationalism: Nationalist Politics, Partition and the Catholic Minority in Northern Ireland, 1890–1940*, Ulster Historical Foundation, Belfast, 1994, pp. 145–6.
3 Author's interview with the late Cardinal Tomás Ó Fiaich, 1979; Memoirs of J. McCoy (unpublished memoir, original in possession of G. McCreesh, Belfast), pp. 41–7.
4 Phoenix, *Northern Nationalism*, pp. 87–94.
5 *Ibid.*, p. 89; RIC County Inspector's Report (Antrim), August 1920, CO904/112, Public Record Office (PRO).
6 Dáil Éireann, *Minutes of the Proceedings of the First Parliament of the Republic of Ireland*, 6 August 1920, pp. 191–4.
7 Dáil Éireann, *Private Sessions of the Second Dáil*, Stationery Office, Dublin, 1972, 22 August 1921, pp. 28–9.
8 Mansergh, Nicholas, *The Unresolved Question: the Anglo-Irish Settlement and its Undoing*

   1912–72, Yale University Press, New Haven, 1991, p. 154.
9 Memo circulated by Collins, 11 January 1921, Dáil Éireann papers, DE2/266, National Archives (NA).
10 De Valera to Collins, 13 January 1921, Dáil Éireann papers, DE2/266, NA.
11 Collins to De Valera, 15 January 1921, Dáil Éireann papers, DE2/266, NA.
12 Phoenix, *Northern Nationalism*, pp. 129–30; Elliott, Sydney *Northern Ireland Parliamentary Election Results, 1921–72*, Political Reference Publications, Chichester, 1973, p. 12.
13 Cited in Mitchell, Arthur, *Revolutionary Government in Ireland: Dáil Éireann, 1919–21*, Gill & Macmillan, Dublin, 1995, p. 285.
14 Wall, Maureen, 'Partition: the Ulster Question' in Williams, Desmond (editor), *The Irish Struggle 1916–22*, London, 1966, p. 84; Phoenix, *Northern Nationalism*, pp. 147–8.
15 *Armagh Guardian*, 9 September 1921; Dáil Éireann papers, DE 2/274, NA; for Collins–Griffith correspondence, see Costello, Francis (editor), *Michael Collins: in his own words*, Gill & Macmillan, Dublin, 1997, pp. 60–62.
16 Phoenix, *Northern Nationalism*, pp. 149–53; Middlemas, Keith (editor), *Thomas Jones Whitehall Diary: vol. iii Ireland 1918–1925*, Oxford University Press, London, 1971, pp. 134–5.
17 Mansergh, *The Unresolved Question*, pp 186–9; Middlemas, *Whitehall Diary*, p 164.
18 Mitchell, *Revolutionary Government*, p. 323; Collins cited in Costello, *Michael Collins*, p. 77; Longford, The Earl of and O'Neill, Thomas P., *Eamon de Valera*, Arrow, London, 1970, pp. 161–2.
19 Forester, Margery, *Michael Collins – The Lost Leader*, Sphere, London, 1972, pp. 249–50; Pakenham, Frank, *Peace by Ordeal*, Sidgwick & Jackson, London, 1972, pp. 215–7, 236–7.
20 Pakenham, *Peace by Ordeal*, pp. 177–8; Gwynn, Denis, *The History of Partition, 1912– 1925*, Browne & Nolan, Dublin, 1950, pp. 215–7.
21 Hopkinson, Michael, *Green Against Green: a History of the Irish Civil War*, Gill & Macmillan, Dublin, 1988, pp. 78–9; Mansergh, *The Unresolved Question*, pp. 187–8; see also the view of Father O'Neill, CC, Eglinton, County Derry, *Strabane Chronicle*, 31 December 1921.
22 Mansergh, *The Unresolved Question*, p. 225; Costello, *Michael Collins*, p. 78.
23 *Ulster Herald*, 31 December 1921; Collins and Griffith reassured a Newry nationalist delegation on 2 February 1922 that, in demanding large-scale boundary changes, they were 'trying to force an open door'. *Frontier Sentinel*, 4 February 1922.
24 *Irish News*, 9, 30 December 1921; Phoenix, *Northern Nationalism*, pp. 172–3.
25 Dáil Éireann, *Official Report: Debate on the Treaty between Great Britain and Ireland, 21 December 1921*, p. 35.
26 'Minutes of Conference of Representatives of the Six County Area held in Mansion House', 7 December 1921, Cahir Healy papers, D2991/B/2, Public Record Office of Northern Ireland (PRONI).
27 *Ibid.*; Lee, J. J. and Ó Tuathaigh, Gearóid, *The Age of de Valera*, Ward River, Dublin, 1982, pp. 92–4.
28 Letter from Seamus Woods to Richard Mulcahy, 29 September 1922, S1801/A, NA.
29 Kenna, G. B., *Facts and Figures of the Belfast Pogrom*, O'Connell, Dublin, 1922, pp. 67–8, 111–2.
30 Gilbert, Martin, *Winston S. Churchill, vol. iv, 1916–22*, Heinemann, London, 1975, pp. 684–6.
31 Minutes of the Provisional Government, 19 January 1922, G1/1, NA.
32 Gilbert, *Winston Churchill*, p. 686.
33 Minutes of the Provisional Government, 23 January 1922, G1/1, NA.
34 Text of Pact, 21 January 1922, S1801/A, NA.
35 *Irish News*, 23 January 1922.
36 *Irish Independent*, 23 January 1922.
37 Bishop Mulhern (Dromore) to S. Milroy, TD, 24 January 1922; circular letter from C. Healy to Fermanagh Sinn Féin, 29 January 1922, S1801/Q, NA; *Irish Independent*, 28 January 1922.
38 Councillor F. Harkin cited in the *Irish News*, 31 January 1922.
39 Northern Ireland Cabinet Minutes, 26 January 1922, CAB 4/30/1–13, PRONI.
40 Minutes of the Provisional Government, 30 January 1922, G1/1, NA.
41 For a full account of the northern teachers' issue, see Phoenix, *Northern Nationalism*, pp. 178, 189–91, 210–11.
42 Collins to L. J. Walsh, 7 February 1922, Ms 3486, National Library of Ireland (NLI).
43 See Craig's press statement, 3 February 1922, S1801/A, NA.

44 Gilbert, *Winston Churchill*, p. 689; *Irish Independent*, 6–9 February 1922; Hezlet, Sir Arthur, *The B Specials: a History of the Ulster Special Constabulary*, Pan, London, 1973, pp. 60–61.
45 Memorandum on pro-Treaty IRA in north, 1927, Blythe papers, P24/554, University College Dublin Archives (UCDA); *Irish Independent*, 9, 10 February 1922; Hopkinson, *Irish Civil War*, p. 80.
46 Hezlet, *B Specials*, p. 103.
47 *Irish Independent*, 27 February 1922.
48 *Irish News*, 11 February 1922; *Irish Independent*, 17 February 1922; memorandum on pro-Treaty IRA in north, 1927, Blythe papers, P24/554, UCDA.
49 Collins to J.H. Collins (Newry), 19 February 1922, J. H. Collins papers, D921/3/7, PRONI.
50 Phoenix, *Northern Nationalism*, p. 186; Griffith to Collins, 15 February 1922, S1801/A, NA.
51 *Irish Independent*, 22, 23 February 1922; Hezlet, *B Specials*, pp. 77, 113–5.
52 *Hansard* (Northern Ireland), House of Commons debates, 1st series, vol. ii, 1922, col. 15; *Daily News*, March 1922, cited in *Irish Independent*, 9 March 1922; Gilbert, *Winston Churchill*, p. 729.
53 S1801/A, NA; *Freeman's Journal*, 9 March 1922; draft circular letter by Collins, 7 March 1922, Ms. 13,539, NLI.
54 Buckland, Patrick, *A History of Northern Ireland*, Gill & Macmillan, Dublin, 1981, p. 40; *Report of Ministry of Home Affairs on Administration of Local Government Services, December 1921–March 1923*, Cmd. 30, Government of Northern Ireland, p. 9.
55 Farrell, Michael, *Northern Ireland: the Orange State*, Pluto, London, 1976, p. 51; 'Position of Second Northern Division in 1922', Blythe papers, P24/554, UCDA.
56 Gilbert, *Winston Churchill*, pp. 697–8.
57 *Ibid.*; *Irish Independent*, 24–25 March 1922; S. G. Tallents, a senior British civil servant, wrote in 1922 of the Ulster Special Constabulary 'the Catholics regard it with a bitterness exceeding that which the Black and Tans inspired in the south'. Tallents to Sir J. Masterton-Smith, 4 July 1922, Tallents papers, CO 906/30, PRO.
58 Gilbert, *Winston Churchill*, p. 698; 'Proposals for a Settlement of Disturbances', 25 March 1922, Dougal papers, CO 906/26, PRONI; Phoenix, *Northern Nationalism*, pp. 196–7.
59 'Heads of Agreement', 30 March 1922, S1801/A, NA.
60 Coogan, *Michael Collins*, p. 355.
61 Good, J. W., 'Partition in Practice', *Studies*, vol. xi, 1922, pp. 275–6; *Irish Independent*, 31 March 1922.
62 Phoenix, *Northern Nationalism*, pp. 199–201; Good, 'Partition', *Studies*, p. 277.
63 T. P. O'Connor to John Dillon, 8 April 1922, Dillon papers, 6744/884, Trinity College Dublin; W. Spender to Craig, 14 June 1922, CAB 6/13, PRONI; Sinn Féin hand-bill, April 1922, Dougal papers, CO 906/26, PRONI; Minutes of Northern Advisory Committee, 11 April 1922, S1011, NA.
64 Hezlet, *B Specials*, pp. 81–2; Confidential memorandum circulated to Executive Council, 20 February 1924, Blythe papers, P24/176, UCDA.
65 Minutes of meeting of Northern Advisory Committee, 11 April 1922, S1011, NA; telegram from Collins to Craig, 4 April 1922; Craig to Collins, 5 April 1922, Tallents papers, CO 906/29, PRO.
66 Letter from Londonderry to Collins read to Northern Advisory Committee, 11 April 1922, S1011, NA.
67 *Ibid.*
68 Lyons, F. S. L., *Ireland Since the Famine*, Fontana, London, 1973, p. 457.
69 O'Shiel memorandum to each member of the Provisional Government, 6 October 1922, Mulcahy papers, P7/B/287, UCDA.
70 Seamus Woods to Richard Mulcahy, 27 July 1922, Mulcahy papers, P7/8/77, UCDA; Woods to O'Duffy, 19 May 1922; Mulcahy papers, P74/173, UCDA; Buckland, *Northern Ireland*, p. 171.
71 *Northern Whig*, 22 May 1922; *Irish News*, 22 May 1922.
72 Buckland, Patrick, *Irish Unionism Two: Ulster Unionism and the Origins of Northern Ireland*, Gill & Macmillan, Dublin, 1973, p. 172; P. Lavery and F. Aiken to Collins and De Valera, 12 May 1922, Mulcahy papers, P7A/145, UCDA; memorial presented to Collins *et al.*, 18 May 1922, Mulcahy papers, P7A/145, UCDA.
73 Hopkinson, *Irish Civil War*, p. 100.

74 Craig to Churchill, 26 May 1922, Tallents papers, CO 739/14, PRO; Lyons, *Ireland since the Famine*, p. 458; Macardle, Dorothy, *The Irish Republic*, Irish Press, London, 1968, p. 648; Gilbert, *Winston Churchill*, pp. 713–4.

75 Kennedy to Collins, 20 May 1922, Mulcahy papers, P7A/145, UCDA.

76 Minutes of the Provisional Government, 25 May 1922, cited in S1801/A; Jones, *Whitehall Diary*, p. 202; Younger, Carlton, *Ireland's Civil War*, Fontana, London, 1982, pp. 297–8.

77 Younger, *Ireland's Civil War*, pp 298–300, 307–8; Minutes of meeting at 10 Downing St. between Craig, Lloyd George, *et. al.*, 16 June 1922, Tallents papers, CO 906/26, PRO.

78 W. Govan and G. Martin to R. D. Bates, 19 April 1922, Tallents papers, CO 906/23, PRO.

79 Minutes of 'Belfast Catholic Recruiting Committee', 16, 31 May and 7 June 1922, Tallents papers, CO 906/23, PRO; note by Arthur Solly-Flood, 31 May 1922.

80 S. G. Tallents, 'Summary of Report on Agreement of March 30th 1922', Tallents papers, CO 906/23, PRO.

81 Gilbert, *Winston Churchill*, pp. 726–7; *Irish Independent*, 12 June 1922.

82 Hopkinson, *Irish Civil War*, p. 133; Coogan, *Michael Collins*, pp. 372–7.

83 *Irish News*, 6 July 1922.

84 *Belfast News Letter*, 30 June 1922 for Collins' speech; Seamus Woods to Richard Mulcahy, 27 July 1922, Mulcahy papers, P7/8/77, UCDA.

85 Seamus Woods, 'Report on No. 1 (Belfast) Brigade', 20 July 1922, Mulcahy papers, P7/B/77, UCDA.

86 Seamus Woods to Richard Mulcahy, 27 July 1922, Mulcahy papers, P7/B/77, UCDA.

87 Seamus Woods to Richard Mulcahy, 29 September 1922, S1801/A, NA; memorandum on 'Meeting of Six County Officers', 31 July 1922, Mulcahy papers, P7/B/33, UCDA; memorandum by Mulcahy, Mulcahy papers, P7/B/79, UCDA; HA/ 32/1/271, PRONI.

88 S. G. Tallents, 'Notes on situation in Northern Ireland', Tallents papers, CO 906/30, PRO.

89 Buckland, Patrick, *The Factory of Grievances: Devolved Government in Northern Ireland, 1922–39*, Gill & Macmillan, Dublin, 1979, pp. 207, 231–3; Phoenix, *Northern Nationalism*, pp. 243–5.

90 Collins to Churchill, 9 August 1922, Kennedy papers, P4/V/10, UCDA.

91 Buckland, *Factory of Grievances*, pp. 271–3; Churchill to Cosgrave, 5 September 1922, Kennedy papers, P4/V/1, UCDA.

92 Minutes of the Provisional Government, 1 August 1922, cited in S1801/A, NA.

93 Ernest Blythe, 'Policy in regard to the north-east', 9 August 1922, Blythe papers, P24/70, UCDA.

94 Minutes of the Provisional Government, 19 August 1922, cited in S1801/A, NA; 'Payment of Catholic teachers in north', 18 August 1922, S1973A, NA; Coogan, *Michael Collins*, pp. 384–5.

95 Seamus Woods to Richard Mulcahy, 29 September 1922, S1801/A, NA; Cahir Healy to Kevin O'Shiel, 30 September 1922, Mulcahy papers, P7/B/287, UCDA.

96 Curtis to Churchill, 19 August 1924, cited in Costello, *Michael Collins*, p. 113.

97 Tallents to Masterton-Smith, 4 July 1922, Tallents papers, CO 906/30, PRO.

98 Cahir Healy writing in the *Irish Statesman*, February 1925, cited in the *Ulster Herald*, 21 February 1925.

MICHAEL COLLINS: THE LEGACY AND THE INTESTACY

1 Collins, Michael, *The Path to Freedom*, Mercier, Cork, 1996.

2 According to P. S. O'Hegarty the Second Dáil's composition was controlled by the IRB's conspiracy to select radical candidates at the 1918 election who were subsequently returned unopposed at the 1921 general election. O'Hegarty, P. S., *The Victory of Sinn Féin*, Talbot, Dublin, 1924, pp. 75–6; see also Figgis, Darrell, *Recollections of the Irish War*, Benn, London, 1927, pp. 228–9.

3 Fanning, Ronan, *The Irish Department of Finance 1922–58*, IPA, Dublin, 1978.

4 Forester, Margery, *Michael Collins – The Lost Hero*, Sidgwick & Jackson, London, 1971.

5 'Suggested scheme of civil organisation for restoration of public peace and security', 22 July 1922, Mulcahy papers, P7/B/29(71–77), UCDA.

6 Séamus Hughes to Arthur Griffith 28 July 1922, Mulcahy papers, P7/B/29(69), UCDA.

7 McNiffe, Liam, *A History of the Garda Síochána*, Wolfhound, Dublin, 1997, pp. 18–25.

8 Margaret Collins-O'Driscoll wrote to every member of the Cumann na nGaedheal party circulating a letter she considered to be of 'outstanding importance' from Fr Benedict

O'Sullivan from Tallaght, County Dublin. O'Sullivan advocated that the Government 'should first of all imbue itself with the spirit of fascism which briefly means government by those naturally fit to rule … the Organisation should become a union of self-sacrificing enthusiastic workers, who by the example of their own endeavours may ultimately evoke the inherent manliness of the race.' Memorandum of Party Meeting by Richard Mulcahy 12 January 1923, Mulcahy papers, P7/B/325, UCDA; Margaret Collins-O'Driscoll to each member of the Cumann na nGaedheal party 19 October 1923, Kennedy papers, P4/1387, UCDA; Fr Benedict O'Sullivan, OP, to Margaret Collins O'Driscoll 18 October 1923, *ibid.*

9   William Cosgrave to Collins, 29 July 1922, Mulcahy papers, P7/B/29(68), UCDA.
10   Collins Memorandum, 29 July 1922, Mulcahy papers, P7/B/28, UCDA.
11   Hopkinson, Michael, *Green against Green*, Gill & Macmillan, Dublin, 1988, p. 91; Coogan, Tim Pat, *Michael Collins*, Arrow, London, 1991, p. 397; Allen, Gregory, 'Policing the new Democracy', *Irish Times*, 19 February 1997.
12   Collins to Cosgrave, 6 August 1922, Mulcahy papers, P7/B/29(66–7), UCDA.
13   *Ibid.*
14   Mitchell, Arthur, *Revolutionary Government in Ireland: Dáil Éireann 1919–22*, Gill & Macmillan, Dublin, 1995, pp. 239–40.
15   Joe MacSweeny interview with Ernie O'Malley, O'Malley notebooks, P17b/97, UCDA.
16   IRB Constitution no. 43. 1922, MacEoin papers, Franciscan Library, Killiney, County Dublin, uncatalogued.
17   O'Beirne-Ranelagh, John, 'The Irish Republican Brotherhood in the Revolutionary Period, 1879–1923' in Boyce, D. G. (editor), *The Revolution in Ireland*, Macmillan, Dublin, 1988, pp. 147–56.
18   *Ibid.*
19   Evidence of Seán Ó Muirthile at Army Inquiry, 29 April 1924, Mulcahy papers, P7/C/13, UCDA.
20   Hopkinson, *Green against Green*, p. 136.
21   I would like to record my sincere thanks to Captain Dan Harvey for giving me access to Collins' notebooks held at the Collins Barracks, Cork. Collins to Cosgrave draft in notebook, 3:30pm 21 August 1922, Museum, Collins Barracks, Cork.
22   Patrick Hogan to Labour party, 22 August 1922, FitzGerald papers, P80/694(2–3), UCDA.
23   Collins to Cosgrave 21 Aug. 1921, Mulcahy papers, P7/B/29(68), UCDA.
24   Draft article on Collins by Desmond FitzGerald August 1943, FitzGerald papers, P80/1316(1), UCDA.
25   Seán Ó Muirthile Memoir, Mulcahy papers, P7a/209(2), UCDA.
26   *Ibid.*

I would like to express my sincere gratitude to the British Academy for awarding me a personal research grant which permitted me to visit Dublin and undertake some of the research which is represented in this paper.

HEROIC BIOGRAPHIES

1   I remember hearing this from Dr Kevin Danaher, the eminent folklorist and ethnologist.
2   See Uí Ógáin, Ríonach, *An Rí gan Choróinn*, An Clóchomhar, Baile Átha Cliath, 1984.
3   Raglan, Lord , 'The Hero of Tradition' in Dundes, Alan (editor), *The Study of Folklore*, Prentice-Hall, New Jersey, 1965, pp. 144–50.
4   De Vries, Jan, *Heroic Song and Heroic Legend*, Oxford University Press, London, 1963, pp. 210–26.
5   Raglan, 'The Hero', in Dundes, *Study of Folklore*, pp. 150–56.
6   Uí Ógáin, *An Rí*, p. 287.
7   Coogan, Tim Pat, *Michael Collins: a Biography*, Arrow, London, 1991, p. 8. I am grateful to Dr Andy Bielenberg for this and the next reference.
8   *Ibid.*, p. 9.
9   Uí Ógáin, *An Rí*, p. 296.
10   *Ibid.*, pp. 296–302 *passim*.
11   *Ibid.*, p. 140 *et seq.*
12   Jordan, Neil, *Michael Collins Screenplay and Film Diary*, Vintage, London, 1996, p. 9. I am grateful to Mr Gabriel Doherty for bringing this work to my attention.

13 De Vries, *Heroic Song*, p. 235.
14 *Ibid.*, p. 239.
15 *Ibid.*, pp. 210–18.
16 Eliade, Mircea, *The Myth of the Eternal Return, or Cosmos and History*, Princeton University Press, Princeton, 1954, p. 44.
17 *Ibid.*, pp. 23–43.
18 *Ibid.*, p. 39. See also Boyle, J. A., 'Historical Dragon Slayers' in Porter, J. R. and Russell, W. M. S. (editors), *Animals in Folklore*, The Folklore Society, Cambridge, 1978, pp. 25–6.
19 Ong, Walter J., *Orality and Literacy*, Methuen, London, 1982, p. 70.
20 *Ibid.*, p. 140. It should be pointed out that Ong's work has given rise to much scholarly controversy.
21 Garvin, Tom, *1922: The Birth of Irish Democracy*, Gill and Macmillan, Dublin, 1996, pp. 41–2.
22 Kaschuba, Wolfgang, 'Popular Culture and Workers' Culture as Symbolic Others: Comments on the Debate about the History of Culture and Everyday Life' in Lüdtke, Alf (editor), *The History of Everyday Life*, Princeton University Press, Princeton, 1995, pp. 182–3.
23 Ong, *Orality*, p. 44.
24 O'Connor, *The Big Fellow*, Poolbeg, Dublin, 1979, p. 52.
25 See Morris, Brian, *Anthropological Studies of Religion: an Introduction*, Cambridge University Press, Cambridge, 1987, p. 72.
26 *Ibid.*
27 See Ó hÓgáin, Dáithí, 'Nótaí ar Chromail i mBéaloideas na hÉireann' in *Sinsear*, vol. ii, 1980, pp. 73–83; MacPhilib, Séamas, 'Ius Primae Noctis and the Sexual Image of Irish Landlords in Folk Tradition and in Contemporary Accounts' in *Béaloideas*, no. 56, 1988, pp. 97–140; MacPhilib, Séamas, 'Profile of a Landlord in Oral Tradition and Contemporary Accounts – The Third Earl of Leitrim' in *Ulster Folklife*, no. 34, 1988, pp. 26–40.
28 Freire, Paulo, *Pedagogy of the Oppressed*, Penguin, London, 1972, pp. 39–40.
29 See Ó Buachalla, Breandán, 'An Mheisiasacht agus an Aisling' in De Brún, Pádraig, Ó Coileáin, Seán and Ó Riain, Pádraig (editors), *Folia Gadelica*, Cork University Press, Cork, 1983, pp. 72–87.
30 Ó hÓgáin, Dáithí, 'An É an tAm Fós É?' in *Béaloideas*, nos. 42–4, 1974–6, pp. 213–308.
31 Caro Baroja, Julio, 'Sobre la formación y uso de arquetipos en Historia, Literatura y Folklore' in Caro Baroja, Julio, *Ensayos sobre la cultura popular española*, Editorial Dosbe, Madrid, 1979, p. 132 *et seq.* See also Alonso del Real, Carlos, *Superstición y supersticiones*, Espasa-Calpe, Madrid 1971, p. 197 *et seq.* and Thomas, Keith, *Religion and the Decline of Magic*, Penguin, London, 1973, *passim.*
32 Iesi, Furio, *Cultura di destra*, Garzanti, Milano, 1993.
33 See Söderholm, Stig, *Liskokuninkaan mytologia* ['The Mythology of the Lizard King'], Suomalaisen Kirjallisuuden Seura, Helsinki, 1990. The book has a brief abstract in English.
34 Habermas, Jürgen, 'The Public Sphere' in Mukerji, Chandra and Schudson, Michael (editors), *Rethinking Popular Culture*, University of California Press, Los Angeles, 1991, pp. 398–9. For Gramsci's notion of 'common sense' see Forgacs, David and Nowell-Smith, Geoffrey (editors), *Antonio Gramsci: Selections from Cultural Writings*, Lawrence & Wishart, London, 1985, pp. 420–21.
35 Armand Mattelart, quoting the work of Arlette Farge, speaks of a 'plebeian public sphere'. Mattelart, Armand, *The Invention of Communication*, University of Minnesota Press, Minneapolis, 1996, pp. 32–3.
36 For example see Ortoleva, Peppino, *Mass media nascita e industrializzazione*, Giunti, Firenze, 1995, pp. 116–7.
37 For 'personality' see Williams, Raymond, *Keywords*, Fontana, London, 1983, pp. 232–5.
38 Kirk, G. S., *Myth Its Meaning and Functions in Ancient and Other Cultures*, Cambridge University Press, Cambridge, 1973, pp. 175–6.
39 Ó hÓgáin, Dáithí, *The Hero in Irish Folk History*, Gill & Macmillan, Dublin, 1985.
40 Lotman, Jurij, *The Structure of the Artistic Text*, University of Michigan, Ann Arbor, 1977.
41 Jordan, *Michael Collins – Screenplay and Film Diary*, p. 4.
42 'La gente tiene derecho a opinar por sí misma', *La Nación On Line*, 20 February, 1997. This interview was presumably given in English but was published in Spanish. The translation and the other translations from South American newspapers are my own.
43 Lotman, *Artistic Text*, p. 243.

44   O'Malley, Ernie, *On Another Man's Wound*, Anvil, Dublin, 1979, p. 317.

45   I will not attempt to locate this debate in terms of Argentinian history, which is beyond my competence, but direct readers to Rock, David, *Argentina 1516–1987*, University of California Press, Los Angeles, 1987.

46   'Con protestas y poco brillo se estrenó "Evita" en Buenos Aires', *La Nación On Line* 18 February 1997; 'Compañeros de una noche para "Evita"', *ibid.*, 19 February 1997; 'Evita no es pasión de multitudes', *ibid.*, 25 February 1997.

47   '"Ruckauf es un ignorante"', *ibid.*, 18 February 1997.

48   'Incidentes menores en el estreno de Evita', *ibid.*, 21 February 1997.

49   'La visión de un espectador común', *ibid.*, 20 February 1997.

50   'Dos rivales de la política unidos por Eva Perón', *ibid.*, 22 February, 1997.

51   '"Evita" é agressão psicológica ao povo argentino", diz perónista', *A Folha de São Paulo*, 19 February 1997.

52   'Dos rivales ...', *La Nación On Line*, 22 February 1997.

53   *The Scotsman*, 15 November 1996.

54   'Alan Parker no es simpático ni quiere parecerlo', *La Nación On Line*, 9 March 1997.

55   'Personagem reflete confronto de duas Argentinas', *A Folha de São Paulo*, 28 February 1997.

56   Ouaknine, Serge, 'Les rêves menacés de la transculturalité' in Langlais, Jacques, Laplante, Pierre and Levy, Joseph (editors), *Le Québec de demain et les communautés culturelles*, Éditions du Méridien, Montréal, 1990, p. 218.

57   Ardener, Edwin, 'The Construction of History: "vestiges of creation"' in Tonkin, Elizabeth, McDonald, Maryon and Chapman, Malcolm (editors), *History and Ethnicity*, Routledge, London, 1989, p. 25.

58   Eliade, *Eternal Return*, pp. 44–6.

DEV AND MICK: THE 1922 SPLIT

1   Coogan, Tim Pat, *Michael Collins: a Biography*, Hutchinson, London, 1990; *idem, De Valera: Long Fellow, Long Shadow*, Random House, London, 1993.

2   Coogan, *Collins*, pp. 3–31.

3   Farragher, Sean P., CSSp, *Dev and His Alma Mater*, Paraclete Press, Dublin, 1984, p. 15.

4   Coogan, *Collins*, p. 9.

5   Ryan, Meda, *Michael Collins and the Women in his Life*, Mercier, Cork, 1996, pp. 22–4; Brendan Halligan, conversations, 31 December 1996.

6   Garvin, Tom, *1922: the Birth of Irish Democracy*, Gill & Macmillan, Dublin, 1996, pp. 123–55.

7   *Ibid.*, p. 147.

8   *Ibid.*, pp. 147–8.

9   *Ibid.*, p. 148.

10   Sighle Humphreys, conversations, 1980s.

11   Michael Hayes Papers, P53/299, UCDA.

12   Mathews, James, *Voices: a Life of Frank O'Connor*, Random, New York, 1981, p. 400.

13   Garvin, *1922*, p. 15.

'THE FREEDOM TO ACHIEVE FREEDOM'?

1   Dáil Éireann. *Official Report: Debate on the Treaty between Great Britain and Ireland, 21 December 1921*, pp. 105–6 (hereafter *Treaty Debate*).

2   *Ibid.*, 7 January 1922, p. 347.

3   Coogan, Tim Pat, *Michael Collins: a Biography*, Hutchinson, London, 1990, pp. 326–7. Suspicions about a price on Collins' head are expressed in Murphy, Brian P., *Patrick Pearse and the Lost Republican Ideal*, James Duffy, Dublin, 1991, pp. 121–9; Augusteijn, Joost, *From Public Defence to Guerrilla Warfare: The Experience of Ordinary Volunteers in the Irish War of Independence 1916–21*, Irish Academic Press, Dublin, 1996, p. 152.

4   Gaughan, J. Anthony (editor), *Memoirs of Senator Joseph Connolly*, Irish Academic Press, Dublin, 1996, p. 166 (hereafter *Connolly Memoirs*).

5   Minutes of Cómhairle na dTeachtaí and the Second Dáil, August 1924 in Gaughan, J. Anthony, *Austin Stack: Portrait of a Separatist*, Kingdom Books, Dublin, 1977, pp. 319–59.

6   Colum, Pádraic, *Arthur Griffith*, Browne & Nolan, Dublin, 1959, p. 343.

7   Collins, Michael, *The Path to Freedom*, Mercier, Cork, 1996, pp. 26, 53–4; Coogan, *Michael Collins*, p. 192.

8   Cited in Middlemas, Keith (editor), *Thomas Jones Whitehall Diary: vol. iii Ireland 1918– 1925*, Oxford University Press, London, 1971, pp.129–30; Conference on Ireland, Fourth Session, 14 October 1921.

9   Churchill, Winston S., *The World Crisis: The Aftermath*, Scribner, London, 1929, p. 278. Speech to the House of Commons, 15 December 1921, cited in Gilbert, Martin, *Winston S. Churchill: vol. iv 1917–1922*, Heinemann, London, 1975, pp. 680–81.

10   *Treaty Debate*, 19 December 1921, pp. 32–3.

11   Middlemas, *Tom Jones Whitehall Diary*, p. 199: Tom Jones to Sir Maurice Hankey, 5 May 1921.

12   1924 Ultimatum in De Vere White, Terence, *Kevin O'Higgins*, Methuen, London, 1948, pp. 159–60; Kennedy, Dennis, *The Widening Gulf: Northern Attitudes to the Independent Irish State 1919–1949*, Blackstaff, Belfast, 1988, p. 152; Lavin, Deborah, *From Empire to International Commonwealth: a Biography of Lionel Curtis*, Clarendon, Oxford, 1995, p. 203; Greaves, C. Desmond, *Liam Mellows and the Irish Revolution*, Lawrence & Wishart, London, 1971, p. 363.

13   *Treaty Debate*, 4 January 1922, p. 227.

14   Churchill, *The World Crisis*, p. 297.

15   Curtis, Lionel, 'The Irish Boundary Question', *The Round Table*, no. 57, December 1924, pp. 24–47.

16   Middlemas, *Tom Jones Whitehall Diary*, p. 105.

17   Bowman, John, *De Valera and the Ulster Question*, Oxford University Press, Oxford, 1982, p. 65.

18   *Sunday Independent*, 29 August 1982, p. 5; see also Moynihan, Maurice, *Speeches and Statements by Eamon de Valera*, Gill & Macmillan, Dublin, 1980, pp. 97–104 for analysis of De Valera's speeches in March and April 1922.; Brennan, Robert, *Allegiance*, Browne & Nolan, Dublin, 1950, pp. 254–5.

19   Dwyer, T. Ryle, 'Key to ending Partition that Michael Collins couldn't turn', *Sunday Independent*, 22 August 1982; Callanan, Frank, *T. M. Healy*, Cork University Press, Cork, 1996, pp. 576–82.

20   Coogan, *Michael Collins*, p. 383.

21   Cited in Macardle, Dorothy, *The Irish Republic*, Irish Press, Dublin, 1951, pp. 512–3.

22   Eide, Asbjorn, 'A Review and Analysis of Constructive Approaches to Group Accommodation and Minority Protection in Divided or Multicultural Societies', *Forum for Peace and Reconciliation Consultancy Studies*, Forum for Peace and Reconciliation, Dublin, 1996, pp. 46, 51.

23   Dáil Éireann, *Private Sessions of the Second Dáil*, Stationery Office, Dublin, 1972, 22 August 1921, p. 29.

24   Cited in Macardle, *The Irish Republic*, pp. 489–94.

25   *Ibid.*, p. 963.

26   *Treaty Debate*: Collins, 19 December 1921, p. 35; 10 January 1922, p. 392; Ó Ceallaigh, 10 January 1922, p. 65; Walsh, 20 December 1921, pp. 88–9; Mulcahy, 22 December 1921, p. 143; MacEntee, 22 December 1921, pp. 155–7.

27   *Ibid.*, pp. 219–20.

28   Lloyd George to Craig, 14 November 1921 in Trimble, David, *The Foundation of Northern Ireland*, Ulster Society Publications, Lurgan, 1991, p. 41.

29   *Treaty Debate*, 6 January 1922, p. 287.

30   *Connolly Memoirs*, p. 185.

31   Coogan, *Michael Collins*, p. 357.

32   Collins, *The Path to Freedom*, pp. 9–10, 17: Notes by General Michael Collins, August 1922.

33   *Ibid.*, pp. 75–84: 'Partition Act's Failure'.

34   Phoenix, Eamon, *Northern Nationalism. Nationalist Politics, Partition and the Catholic Minority in Northern Ireland 1890–1940*, Ulster Historical Foundation, Belfast, 1994, p. 315; O'Halloran, Clare, *Partition and the Limits of Irish Nationalism: an Ideology under Stress*, Gill & Macmillan, Dublin, 1987, pp. 97–100.

35   Alden, John R., *A History of the American Revolution: Britain and the Loss of the Thirteen Colonies*, Knopf, London, 1969, pp. 390–91.

36   *Treaty Debate*, 22 December 1921, p. 146; Béaslaí, Piaras, *Michael Collins and the Making of a New Ireland*, Phoenix, Dublin, 1926, vol. ii, pp. 237–41; Dáil Éireann, *Private Sessions of the Second Dáil*, 26 August 1921, pp. 76–7.

37 *Ibid.*, 21 December 1921, p. 106; Dáil Éireann, *Official Report*, 11 September 1922, vol. i, col. 74.

38 *Minutes of Second Dáil in Session*, 8 August 1924 in Gaughan, *Austin Stack*, p. 350; P. J. Ruttledge, 'Memorandum', ibid., p. 366.

39 O'Sullivan, Michael, *Seán Lemass: a Biography*, Blackwater, Tallaght, 1994, pp. 58–9: Speech in the Dáil, 5 July 1928.

40 Macardle, *The Irish Republic*, p. 705.

41 Colvin, Ian, *Life of Lord Carson*, Gollancz, London, 1936, vol. iii, p. 429; Buckland, Patrick, *Irish Unionism: 1 The Anglo-Irish and The New Ireland 1885–1922*, Historical Association, Dublin, 1972, pp. 278–9.

42 *Treaty Debate*, 21 December 1921, p. 102; Keogh, Dermot, *Ireland and the Vatican: the Politics and Diplomacy of Church-State Relations 1922–1960*, Cork University Press, Cork, 1995; Fanning, Ronan, *Independent Ireland*, Helicon, Dublin, 1983, pp. 54–7; Mitchell, Arthur, *Revolutionary Government in Ireland: Dáil Éireann 1919–22*, Gill & Macmillan, Dublin, 1995, p. 286.

43 *Treaty Debate*, 19 December 1921, p. 35; Gaughan, *Austin Stack*, p. 276.

44 *Treaty Debate*, 6 January 1922, p. 274; 10 January, p. 410; Dáil Éireann, *Official Report*, 28 November 1922, vol. i, cols. 2364–6; Cosgrave: 'Are we to let off the intellectual … and is there to be another law for the unfortunate dupes of these very people … We are going to see that the rule of democracy will be maintained, no matter what the cost, and no matter who the intellectuals that may fall by reason of the assertion of that right.' Kevin O'Higgins, *ibid.*, 11 September 1922, col. 98.

45 Longford, The Earl of and O'Neill, Thomas P., *Eamon de Valera*, Arrow, London, 1970, p. 149; Fallon, Charlotte H., *Soul of Fire: a Biography of Mary MacSwiney*, Mercier, Cork, 1986, p. 78.

46 Lavin, *Empire to International Commonwealth*, p. 215; Béaslaí, *Michael Collins*, vol. ii, p. 235; Dáil Éireann, *Official Report*, 21 September 1922, vol. i, col. 546.

47 Fallon, *Soul of Fire*, p. 102.

48 'De Valera and Tories failed to see reality of republic', *Irish Times*, 10 January 1997. Garvin's account of the political misogyny of the period is contained in Garvin, Tom, *1922: the Birth of Irish Democracy*, Gill & Macmillan, Dublin, 1996, pp. 96–9.

49 O'Donoghue, Florence, *No Other Law*, Irish Press, Dublin, 1954, p. 309.

50 Cited in Hopkinson, Michael, *Green against Green: the Irish Civil War*, Gill & Macmillan, Dublin, 1988, p. 98.

51 O'Donoghue, *No Other Law*, p. 285.

52 Lavin, *From Empire to International Commonwealth*, p. 224, citing correspondence between Churchill and Curtis, August-September 1924. As late as 1941 Churchill's formal position was: 'We have tolerated and acquiesced in it, but juridically, we have never recognised that southern Ireland is an independent sovereign state', cited in Canning, Paul, *British Policy towards Ireland 1921–1941*, Clarendon, Oxford, 1985, p. 306.

53 'At this distance in time, it is easier to acknowledge that credit is due to W. T. Cosgrave for quickly including the participation of the newly formed Fianna Fáil Party in democratic politics in the Dáil, but also for allowing them to put their own presentation on what that involved.' Address by the Taoiseach Albert Reynolds at the Liam Lynch Commemoration, 11 September 1994; McMahon, Deirdre, *Republicans and Imperialists: Anglo-Irish Relations in the 1930s*, Yale University Press, New Haven, 1984, pp. 52–4, 60, 70–1, 82, 113–4, 136–7.

54 Collins, *The Path to Freedom*, pp. 3, 12, 46–7, 113, 126, 131.

55 *Treaty Debate*, 19 December 1921, p. 34.

56 Collins, *The Path to Freedom*, pp. 109–22: 'Building up Ireland: Resources to be Developed'.

57 Dáil Éireann, *Private Sessions of the Second Dáil*, 25 August 1921, p. 73.

58 Minutes of Cómhairle na dTeachtaí, 7–8 August 1924 in Gaughan, *Austin Stack*, p. 333.

59 Andrews, C. S., *Man of No Property*, Mercier, Cork, 1982, p. 231.

60 Mansergh, Nicholas, *The Unresolved Question: the Anglo-Irish Settlement and its Undoing 1912–72*, Yale University Press, New Haven, 1991, p. 214.

'SORROW BUT NO DESPAIR – THE ROAD IS MARKED'

1 We are very much indebted to Pat Connolly and Teresina Flynn, Special Collections, Boole

Library, UCC, for the help they gave us in the preparation of this article.

2   This account of the funeral is taken from Kee, Robert, *The Laurel and the Ivy – The Story of Charles Stewart Parnell and Irish Nationalism*, Hamish Hamilton, London, 1993, pp. 1–12, passim.

3   *Ibid.*

4   *Freeman's Journal*, 7 October 1891.

5   Edwards, Ruth Dudley, *Patrick Pearse: the Triumph of Failure*, Faber, London, 1979, pp. 235–8. See also the comments by MacDonagh on the revolutionary import of this speech in MacDonagh, Oliver, *States of Mind: a Study of Anglo-Irish Conflict*, Allen & Unwin, London, 1983, p. 86 cited in Murphy, Brian, *Patrick Pearse and the Lost Republican Ideal*, James Duffy, Dublin, 1991, together with Murphy's own cautionary comments on the funeral's relatively limited impact.

6   For the rather scanty public coverage of the Rising and more particularly of the executions see Dudley Edwards, Owen and Pyle, Fergus (editors), *The Easter Rising*, MacGibbon & Kee, London, 1968, appendix i 'The *Irish Times* on the Rising', pp. 241–9 and appendix ii, 'Press Reaction to the Rising in General', pp. 251–71; see also Caulfield, Max, *The Easter Rebellion*, Gill & Macmillan, Dublin, 1995, pp. 283– 95 and Lee, J. J., *Ireland 1912–1985: Politics and Society*, Cambridge, Cambridge University Press, 1989, pp. 29–36.

7   For details of the burial see *The Daily Worker*, 13 March 1936.

8   Longford, The Earl of and O'Neill, Tomas P., *Eamon de Valera*, Arrow, London, 1974, pp. 456–7.

9   Macardle, Dorothy, *The Irish Republic*, Irish Press, Dublin, 1937, pp. 228–9. See also the *Freeman's Journal*, 1 October 1917.

10 For a discussion on the problems faced by the Irish newspaper industry in covering the violence arising out of the War of Independence see Oram, Hugh, *The Newspaper Book: a History of Newspapers in Ireland 1649–1983*, MO Books, Dublin, 1983, pp. 123–53.

11 O'Donoghue, Florence, *Tomás MacCurtain*, Tralee, Kerryman, 1958, pp. 197–9.

12 Chavasse, Moirin, *Terence MacSwiney*, Dublin, Clonmore and Reynolds, 1961, pp. 183– 90.

13 *Freeman's Journal*, 8 July 1922.

14 *Irish Times*, 8 July 1922

15 *Ibid.*

16 *Freeman's Journal*, 1 August 1922; Another man in the room at the time, Joseph Griffin, was taken into custody.

17 Ó Broin, León (editor), *In Great Haste: the Letters of Michael Collins and Kitty Kiernan*, Gill & Macmillan, Dublin, 1983, p. 210 cited in Keogh, Dermot, *Twentieth Century Ireland – Nation and State*, Gill and Macmillan, Dublin, 1994, p. 10.

18 *Freeman's Journal*, 4 August 1922.

19 *Ibid.*, 5 August 1922.

20 *Ibid.*, 23 August 1922.

21 *Freeman's Journal*, 24 August 1922.

22 *The Free State*, 30 August 1922.

23 *Freeman's Journal*, 28 August 1922.

24 *The Free State*, 30 August 1922.

25 *Ibid.*

26 *Ibid.*

27 *The Irish Times*, 11 July 1927.

28 *Ibid.*

29 Moynihan, Maurice (editor), *Speeches and Statements by Eamon de Valera 1917–1973*, Gill and Macmillan, Dublin, 1980, p. 148.

30 *The Irish Times*, 13 July 1927.

31 *Ibid.*, 14 July 1927.

32 *Ibid.*

MICHAEL COLLINS – AN OVERVIEW

1   Foster, Roy, 'We are all revisionists now' in *The Irish Review*, no. 1, 1986, p. 1.

2   Lynch, Patrick, 'The social revolution that never was' in Williams, Desmond (editor), *The Irish Struggle 1916–1926*, Routledge and Kegan Paul, London, 1966, pp. 41–54. The title of this volume of Thomas Davis Lectures itself testifies to the determination to avoid the

term 'Irish revolution'.

3   Foster, R. F., *Modern Ireland 1600–1972*, Allen Lane, London, 1988, p. 506.

4   Seán Ó Faoláin used this phrase in an RTE interview on *Gallery* on 24 October 1980.

5   Phillips, W. Alison, *The Revolution in Ireland 1906–1923*, Longmans, London, 1923, p. 1.

6   Garvin, Tom, *1922: the Birth of Irish Democracy*, Gill & Macmillan, Dublin, 1996, p. 159.

7   Bowden, Tom, *Beyond the Limits of the Law*, Harmondsworth, London, 1978, p. 175.

8   *Ibid.*, p. 176.

9   Middlemas, Keith (editor), *Thomas Jones Whitehall Diary: vol. iii Ireland 1918–1925*, Oxford University Press, London, 1971, p. 73.

10 Townshend, Charles, *The British Campaign in Ireland 1919–1921: the Development of Political and Military Policies*, Oxford University Press, Oxford, 1975, p. 42. See also *ibid.*, pp. 50–51 on the weakness of British intelligence.

11 Riddell, Lord, *Lord Riddell's Intimate Diary of the Peace Conference and After 1918–1923*, Gollancz, London, 1933, pp. 288–9.

12 Jordan, Neil, *Michael Collins: Screenplay and Film Diary*, Vintage, London, 1996, p. 134.

13 Townshend, *British Campaign in Ireland*, p. 186.

14 *Sunday Times*, 24 November 1996. See also Dr Brian Murphy's response (*Sunday Times*, 1 December 1996) which persuasively argues that the headline is quite unjustified by 'the so-called new information Bew has revealed'.

15 Townshend, *British Campaign in Ireland*, pp. 206, 192.

16 Kissinger, Henry A., 'The Viet Nam Negotiations' in *Foreign Affairs* , January 1969, p. 47.

17 Jordan, *Michael Collins: Screenplay and Film Diary*, p. 37.

18 Collins, Michael, 'Clearing the road – an essay in practical politics' in FitzGerald, William (editor), *The Voice of Ireland*, Virtue, Dublin, 1930, p. 42.

19 Coogan, Tim Pat, *Michael Collins: a Biography*, Hutchinson, London, 1990, pp. 92.

20 Jordan, *Michael Collins: Screenplay and Film Diary*, pp. 137, 140.